FURY

Women's Lived Experiences During the Trump Era

WITHDRAWN

Edited by Amy Roost and Alissa Hirshfeld

Published by Pact Press
An imprint of
Regal House Publishing, LLC
Raleigh, NC 27612
All rights reserved

pactpress.com

ISBN -13 (paperback): 9781646030002
ISBN -13 (epub): 9781646030279
Library of Congress Control Number: 2019949643

All efforts were made to determine the copyright holders and obtain their permissions in any circumstance where copyrighted material was used. The publisher apologizes if any errors were made during this process, or if any omissions occurred. If noted, please contact the publisher and all efforts will be made to incorporate permissions in future editions.

Interior and cover design by Lafayette & Greene
lafayetteandgreene.com
Cover image by Anonymous

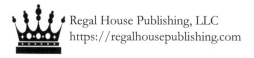

Regal House Publishing, LLC
https://regalhousepublishing.com

Printed in the United States of America

CONTENTS

PREFACE

My mother—to whom this book is dedicated—wanted a career and children. Unfortunately Mom married the wrong man during the wrong era and was forced to choose one. She chose children. Though her career ambitions were stymied, she nevertheless remained true to her principles and managed to use her voice for good. She led picket lines against segregated housing policies in our hometown of Deerfield, Illinois, during the late 1950s and was acknowledged by and had her picture taken with Eleanor Roosevelt for those efforts. To this day, that photo sits on my desk as inspiration. In 1965, against my father's wishes, she took a Greyhound bus to Selma, Alabama. Along with Martin Luther King Jr. and other prominent civil rights leaders, she marched across the Edmund Pettus Bridge and continued for five days, twelve miles a day, to Montgomery to deliver a petition demanding equal voting rights for all.

Mom had high hopes for me (many of them retreads of her own aspirations). In fact, she used to call me "Prez" because she truly believed that someday I'd be the first woman president. I did work on Capitol Hill for a U.S. senator and I studied politics, but ultimately, I chose a different career path. Like Mom, I held strong opinions but was more of an activist "lite" than a true activist. I attended some demonstrations during my college years, but I didn't find my "Selma" until Donald Trump was elected.

Like so many American women, many adverse physiological and psychological effects began to surface for me and the other contributors of this volume as the contours of a new era began to take shape. Contributor Lisa Kirchner describes her anxiety after the election as "soreness in my chest, difficulty breathing, numbness in my left arm." Lisa drove herself to the emergency room where she was diagnosed with swelling of the cartilage around her sternum, brought on by anxiety. Susan Shapiro recounts sleep deprivation and the inability to concentrate. Krystal Sital, Susan Fekete, and Katherine Morgan also lost sleep. Beth Couture became depressed. Emily Sinclair was panicky. Jennifer Silva Redmond, angry. Jessica Handler and Sarah Einstein, fearful. For me, it was a game of *Choose Your Own Adventure*: chronic neck pain one day, emotional reactivity the next. Flip a coin. Heads it was irritable bowel syndrome; tails it was a racing pulse.

Our cups, once filled to the brim with the nervous "what-ifs" of a possible Trump presidency, now spilled over with worst-case-scenario realities. Everything we stood for—agency over our bodies, the feminine ethos of caring and humane treatment of others, role modeling for our children, to name a few—suffered a direct hit in the form of the ultimate self-aggrandizing toxic male. For a while, all we could do was wade through wastewater, hearing filthy dog whistles and watching putrid executive orders float by. We covered our mouths, held our collective breath, and lifted our eyes to the sky, desperate for some indication that the sun would appear and make it all go away.

Dawn Marlan adeptly captures what began to happen instead: Trump-world corrupts our language, our culture, our planet. What choice do [women] have but to abandon our cocoons and move into the uncomfortable space in the center? Not the center of the spectrum but the center of power, the virtual polis, the place where the range of the acceptable is adjudicated.

And so on January 21, 2017, I bundled up, pulled on a pair of Wonder Woman knee highs (satin red streamers and all) and went out in the rain to join the San Diego Women's March. I was happy to discover a bustling community of angry yet purposeful women and a surprising number of erstwhile allies. We marched down Harbor Drive past the shadows of the Star of India sails. I jabbed my home-made sign at the dark clouds above. In neat neon-pink lettering, it read, "Pussy Riot, American Style" on one side and "The ACA Saved My Son's Life" on the other.

Right then and there, I realized I needed to somehow document what I was personally experiencing along with the urgency Trump's election had stoked for millions of women across the world. And so a few weeks after the march, I put out a call for submissions to private women's groups I belonged to on Facebook, asking for personal essays about what I referred to as the "Trump Effect." Based on the outpouring of responses, it was clear that I'd hit a nerve. Women gonna share, and share they did.

Fury: Women's Lived Experiences During the Trump Era is the result. It brings together a diverse community of women who reveal the impact that Donald Trump's behavior, words, and presidency have had on us, and how we have coped and evolved along the way. Reema Zaman more eloquently describes this metamorphosis: "Each blow is like that of a blacksmith's hammer pummeling iron. Each hit fortifies our metal. No group knows this better than women—we are privy to unique grief, singular hostility. Thus, forged in fire, we are all the more prepared and capable for leadership, resilience, grit."

It is fair to say this book is like a hymnal for the choir. I believe there's no such thing as too much empowerment. My co-editor, Alissa Hirshfeld, writes, "Encouraging women to speak can be healing, not only giving [women] a sense of agency regarding current politics but more generally teaching them that their voice matters."

I had two other purposes in mind while gathering these essays. First, I fervently believed this collection would help readers understand and develop empathy for what women have been going through since the election. After reading this, if you agree, I invite you to share it with your friends, colleagues, and loved ones who may have had some trouble understanding the impact of what's been going on during this time. I share Alissa's observation gleaned from counseling women during these difficult times:

"I never imagined that empathy would become a political act, but—alas!—it has. People on different sides of the political divide, as well as people of different cultural backgrounds and faiths, seem unwilling and sometimes unable to empathize with others' perspectives. But when we listen deeply to one another's stories—meaning we practice seeing things from another's perspective while silencing the voice inside us that wants to disagree or tell our own side—we learn that we all want the same basic things: a good life for ourselves and our families, good health, an adequate income to provide for our needs, and a sense of meaning and purpose."

My second purpose was to create a record for posterity. Decades from now, much will have been written and documented about Donald Trump's presidency. Just as the news media should not focus excessive attention on a deranged assailant after a mass shooting, neither should any future generation focus all its attention on the deranged person currently occupying the Oval Office. Instead, let this collection of authentic voices stand as a monument to those who suffered and coped, persevered and overcame, and marched and fought for justice during the Trump Era. If this book is ignored today but read in even one classroom a hundred years from now, it would make every sacrifice you read about in this collection worthwhile.

Amy Roost
January 2019

Amy Roost is a documentary podcaster and freelance journalist. She is an Annenberg School of Journalism 2019 California Health Journalism Fellow and recipient of numerous journalism awards for her op-ed columns appearing in *San Diego Union Tribune* publications. Her forthcoming memoir is based on a 2017 Snap Judgment podcast she wrote and produced about how she replaced a black child that her parents adopted and later returned in 1962

Subscribe and listen to *Fury*, the podcast.
https://www.criticalfrequency.org/fury

OUR BODIES

Catholic Bodies or Notes from the Kavanaugh Hearings

By Mary Catherine Ford

It happens even before you know you have a body. When you are a whirl of running, plucking earwigs from rotting tree trunks, kickball, and laughter, without knowing how you sound, how you look. Before you know you are to be an object, you are told. Before you can understand your hips, the new shape of you, an expansion beyond the body you've always known and believed to be your true body, before you understand your breasts and can come to accept them as belonging to you, you're told by boys and men what they are to the world: too small, too big. You come to know yourself through the words of those boys and men.

There is a Catholic way of talking about puberty, and, in my experience, it is this: Do not wear shorts that are too short, even at home. You have older brothers. Do not try to tame your frizzy hair with Vaseline and put your curls in a side ponytail and then try to leave the house, because your mother will say that you could be mistaken for a prostitute and raped. Given your neighborhood, this may have been a credible fear. There is a van that sits by the park with blackout windows where prostitutes work. You fear more than anything disappearing into that van. You do not know what sex is, but you instinctively know what a violation would do: erase you.

How can a mother shield her daughter? When mothers transmit these messages to their daughters it feels like an act of desperation, reflexive, a recitation of what they were told when they were young. If I had really heard what my mother told me, would I have been safe? And what of the lessons mothers neglect to teach their sons? The catechizations come at the same time your body is changing, your emotions a torrent.

Gradually, a girl's body starts changing into a woman's body. But these surging hormones can also make your mood go up and down—and sometimes it may seem as if your body is out of control.[1]

But no one told you the reason for your mood swings. You think you are falling apart, losing your mind to a darker expanded reality. You know so little about the physiology of your own body that when you are fourteen and backstage at play practice and a boy says something to you about babies and vaginas, you blurt out, "But babies come out of your butt, don't they?" He bursts out laughing. You are fourteen years old and you do not know the evolutionary function of your vagina.

It is withheld from you, the why and how of your body changing. This takes something from you. It isn't something you can necessarily recover once you understand what is happening, because while your body transforms you know only the messy shame of it. The biological explanation for what is happening to you is as unknown and mysterious as transubstantiation. Shame becomes part of the change.

You are not told the physiological reasons for your breasts and menstrual cycles and pubic hair, only the risks your new body poses to your soul and the souls of every boy and man you come into contact with, from your father to your brothers to the men and boys at Mass, at the pool, on the playground, down the block, on the bus, on the L train, at the dog show, at the Museum of Science and Industry, at Church's Chicken, at the laundromat. Your body is not an organism and its living parts. Instead, you are an unwitting trap, a parable of temptation. You learn that these changes mean your body is a thing of danger.

As you grow up, there is a war coming at you from within and from without. There is a Catholic way of talking about puberty, in my experience, and it is this: Your body is a thing you must restrain. But how can you command a body when it has morphed from something unnoticeable into something you don't recognize? And it's awkward and uncomfortable, the hairy legs and arms and armpits and, worst of all, the wiry, stubborn pubic hair that refuses to clear away even with persistent shaving. The stubble and ingrown hairs

[1] http://www.teens.webmd.com/features/puberty-changing-body#1

2

plague you and you don't want to go to the pool, but it's so hot, the Chicago summer, and so you run from the safety of your Strawberry Shortcake towel to the pool's edge in a flash. You pray all anyone saw of you before plunging into the deep blue pool was a blur. You pray to be just a blur.

There is a Catholic way of talking about puberty, in my experience, and it is this: Do not go from the pool to five o'clock Mass in shorts and a T-shirt and sit alone when you are twelve. You do not know yet that a boy might be drawn to you, let alone find you desirable. After all, what is desire to a girl who is scandalized by the book *Are You There God? It's Me, Margaret.*

Do not go to that Mass. After you stand and sing, "One bread, One Body, One Lord of All" and kneel and pray and wish peace upon your neighbors, after you take communion, a teenage boy with shaggy brown hair who is two heads taller than you will walk up to you as you are leaving your pew and say calmly, *I wanted you to know that because of your outfit I had impure thoughts and couldn't take communion.*

He will walk away, and you will stand there alone in St. Edmund's church as the late light of the afternoon pools in rich purples and greens around your bare legs. The church is your favorite because of the music and the huge stained-glass windows depicting the stories of Lazarus rising and the Wedding at Cana, because its walls are covered with tiny squares of gold leaf and if you stare at the flecks of gold and then press hard on your closed eyelids the gold covers your vision until the whole universe inside you is shining.

You will not have said a word to the boy. The lesson he has taught you is one you will hear again and again, until you finally leave the Catholic Church: your body is at fault.

That fall, after you start middle school at the Opus Dei school for girls, you begin going to the Opus Dei Center on the weekends. There, the numeraries, in their ankle-length jean skirts and pale Laura Ashley blouses, lead talks detailing the Opus Dei take on everything that might concern a young Catholic girl on the precipice of womanhood.

In the Opus Dei, female numeraries are celibate like nuns but don't wear habits and can marry if they are called. To assist in the goals of this ultra-conservative body of the Catholic Church, a numerary submits to *plena disponibilidad,* full availability.

You were at the Center because you had been invited and someone picks you and your sister up and drives you there. At twelve years old, you don't know much of the small but storied organization, not that Pope John Paul has recently favored it as the first personal prelature, not that the numeraries are rumored to whip themselves in penance.

Was it at the Opus Dei Center you told one of the numeraries about the day you tempted a boy into sin? Or was it on the long car ride to Washington D.C. for the March for Life?

In September 2018, Dr. Christine Blasey Ford comes forward and accuses Supreme Court nominee Brett Kavanaugh of sexually assaulting her in 1982. Sexual assault takes over the news, your thoughts. For some of us, it happens even before memories form. There is someone in your family, an uncle, who drinks himself to sexual violence against his sons, against his daughters. You spend some weeks at your cousins' house when you are two years old. Your mother is in the hospital and there's been a terrible fire in your house. You come back home with an infection in your vagina. The infection goes unexplained or is explained away as neglect. What did your family doctor say, the same doctor who treated all your cousins after their assaults? Did a tear in your hymen occur then? Did something happen during those two weeks to form the strip of scar tissue over the middle of your vaginal opening?

The story of the electrical fire in your house will be told again and again throughout your childhood until the flames and the subsequent escape down Mr. Freeman's housepainter's ladder becomes something like a memory. Even walking barefoot through the heavy frost in your cousins' yard, a memory your older sister relays to you will come to feel like a memory of your own. But it is not.

All through your childhood, what no one tells you is that you came home from your aunt and uncle's home with a vaginal infection. It's another silence. But when you are fifteen, your sister says you might have been sexually abused by your uncle when you were two years old. And your uncle's home, that time, becomes rebuilt in your nightmares. In those nightmares, the bedroom you and your sister shared with your cousins is too dark to see. Your spirit leaves your body as your uncle squeezes you until you can't breathe. Though you have no memory of this time, you discover what you think is a scar from then. A strip of flesh stretches over the middle of your vaginal opening and causes tampons, once expanded with your menstrual blood, to become stuck inside you. You sit on the toilet in the bathroom for what feels like hours, crying quietly, desperately, painfully trying to extract the fattened wad of cotton. The toilet tank drips and drips, you re-read the Morning Offering glued to the bathroom mirror. *Oh Jesus, I offer you my prayers, works, joys, and sufferings of this day.* That cord of tissue does not break. Not then. Not years later when you try to have sex for the first time.

You text your sister: *What did Mom tell you about when we had a fire in our house and went to stay with the cousins? I used to have this weird scar tissue over the middle of my vagina.*

She sends you a link: *14 things you never knew about the hymenal ring.*[2]

You send her back a link to Johnny Cash's song, "Ring of Fire."

The hymen has variations on the theme. The microperforate hymen completely covers the vaginal opening and an imperforate hymen has only a very small hole and the septate hymen has an extra strip in the middle that creates two vaginal openings where there should be one. "The extra tissue (of the septate hymen) can be torn during tampon insertion or sexual intercourse."[3]

Hymen, from the Greek word for thin skin, membrane. A hymen can break easily, when a girl does the splits, when she is horseback riding, speeding down her block on her pink banana seat bike, colored tassels streaming from the handlebars. These hypotheticals belong to a girl who is not you.

Along the edges of a damaged hymen a process known as re-epithelialization can take place. Epithelial cells migrate across the new tissue to form a barrier between the wound and the environment.[4]

Did your body, after it was violated, build an obstacle to protect itself from future abuse?

---

[2] http://www.feministmidwife.com/2013/01/07/14-things-you-never-knew-about-the-hymenal-ring/#.XD4NDi3MyqC

[3] http://www.texaschildrens.org/health/septate-hymen

[4] http://www.quizlet.com/225962061/medical-terminology-quiz-3-flash-cards

At sixteen, when you move away from Chicago, you tell your mother, "I won't go to Mass anymore. I am tired of how guilty Catholicism makes me feel."

"Well, what do you have to feel guilty about?" she retorts.

You have your own room in your new house, and you start to use a small mirror to look at your vagina. Think back to that age. Can you still remember what that tissue looked and felt like? It was ropy and thick. Like a vine of flesh had trailed down from your clitoris and firmly embedded itself in the inferior portion of your vagina. How could it have been anything but scar tissue?

One hundred seventy-nine thousand search results for "septate hymen." You stare and stare at the search images on Google. This is not what you remember from all those years ago. Though it is smooth and deep pink like the rest of your hymen, the flesh is too thick to have ever been broken by a tampon or sex. And it hadn't been.

When you try to have sex with a boy for the first time, he can't enter you, despite all his attempts. You go home that night and use a pair of scissors to cut the ropy flesh apart.

Here is another point of fear, another way your changed body could betray you and cast you into hell—abortion. You grew up going to Pro-Life Action League marches in Chicago in the 1980s. Come January 22, your parents would bundle up you and your siblings against the freezing cold in itchy wool and corduroy and you'd all hop on the L train to the Loop with enlarged photos of aborted babies, their limbs like tiny crushed wings, broken jaws, their tiny fingers glued to heavy-duty poster board.

All you ever understood about abortion as a young child was that it was murder. Birth control was murder also, only the baby was tinier, almost invisible, like the soul itself, seen by God but unseen by the mortal eye. You knew that abortion doctors lied to the women and then killed the babies. And the murder of their unborn children would haunt those women all their lives. While premarital sex was almost unthinkable, you knew abortion was far worse. Abortion was an unforgivable sin that cut you off from communion, from the Church, from Jesus himself. The aborted babies were killed before they could be baptized, and so they all crowd together, waiting for the Second Coming in limbo. Limbo was not hell, certainly, but was beyond the Gates of Heaven, beyond the touch of God.

As you got older and had your first kiss, a paralyzing fear gripped you. Would you become pregnant and have to choose between giving up the future you envisioned for yourself—making your way through Ireland by working on a steamer ship, becoming a poet—or killing your own baby in a secret abortion?

One New Year's Eve, you and your first boyfriend keep to one side of his basement while your best friend and her boyfriend have sex on the other side. Your boyfriend kisses you and you tell him to take you home. He breaks up with you the next day. When you hear that his next girlfriend has two abortions, all you feel is relief that it wasn't you.

Here's what a young woman who is you understood: the worst sins come from your body.

Here's what a woman, who has spent the past thirty years weeding out those lessons of shame, is trying to wrap her head around today: white Catholic women defend men and boys at the expense of girls and women.

Dr. Christine Blasey Ford's accusations against Brett Kavanaugh bring you back to the lessons from your Catholic school days. The conservative Catholics you grew up with question Dr. Ford's veracity, her timing, the motives of Democrats. Every aspect of the process is scrutinized unless it involves Brett Kavanaugh. You should have anticipated it, but you didn't, and now you are angered by the number of women who defend him and question his accuser.

The women defending Kavanaugh say:

This isn't a conversation about sexual assault that should be guided by the "Me Too" movement.

We can't believe her just because she's a woman.

With abortion at stake, it seems they will stop at nothing to preserve their unholy sacrament.

You find yourself spinning back into the orbit of the conservative Catholic world you left decades ago. How have these women stayed loyal to a way of being that had so poisoned you? In a Facebook thread with women who were also raised in the Opus Dei, you and your sister try to voice that Opus Dei Catholicism injected a toxic ideology into you and infected your understanding of female sexuality, of consent.

Your sister writes: *Girls were taught that they were responsible for boys or men having "impure thoughts" about them. We were often told a story about a girl who went to Mass in a short skirt. She went to communion as usual but when she knelt afterwards the boy/man sitting behind her tapped her on the shoulder and told her that he had not been able to receive communion because he had had impure thoughts about her, and that she had made him sin.*

Someone on the thread asks: *Who told the story?*

Your sister responds: *A numerary.*

You immediately DM your sister to tell her the story was about you. Your sister writes back: *Some people are Twitter famous. You're Opus Dei Shaming Famous.*

Your sister was a year ahead of you in your Opus Dei school. She went to Center meetings that were only for the older girls. It was there the numeraries told her about the girl who made the boy sin, a story she came to think of as a fable made up to scare her and the other girls into modesty and submission and deference to men. The numeraries knew you, they knew she was your sister, but they never told her they were recounting her own sister's story.

Everyone has their own story. Every woman has more than one.

As you grew up, a war came at you from within and from without. Here is what you learn by walking through the wider world too quickly: You learn that when you are walking home from play practice alone, after dark, in winter, and the street is empty other than you and a man, you should cross the street. You learn to cave your chest in, slump your shoulders, drop the light from your eyes. You learn to wear headphones meant to deter conversation, big bulky ones to cancel men's voices, even though they peel them off when they speak to you so you have to hear them, have to respond. Always you must respond. You cannot count how many men have catcalled and followed up your silence with the word "bitch" or the number of men who have assessed you. *I'm usually a tit man, but you have such incredible legs, you mighta changed that.*

There was the man who took a picture up your skirt on the Fifty-Seventh Street subway steps. The way he stood his ground and stared and stared into your eyes when you yelled at him stays with you. These men are in your pulse, which quickens at night when you walk alone; they are in the jerk of your head to check the back seat of your locked car. They have always haunted you, but during the week of the Kavanaugh hearing, they swarm about you like angry ghosts.

In the past, election polls felt like abstractions, but since Trump's election, you've consulted polling numbers like bones thrown by an oracle to understand how we got here, where we are going. In 2016, sixty percent of Catholics voted for Trump.[5] Above all, Trump held the promise of Supreme Court appointees who could overturn *Roe v. Wade*. In 2018, polls taken after Blasey Ford and Kavanaugh testified before the Senate revealed that seventy percent of Republican women still supported Kavanaugh's nomination.[6] It adds up to a story about the community you come from.

Days before the final confirmation vote on Brett Kavanaugh, the conservative advocacy group Catholic Vote released a video, "Moms for Kavanaugh."[7] In it, they say, "We are mothers. We give everything for our sons." In the video baby boys are cradled, bathed tenderly by their Catholic mothers. As the music swells, the boys grow into strong men, glistening with virtue, integrity, and courage. Their babies have become soldiers and doctors; they have become Judge Brett Kavanaugh. It ends with this ominous warning: "If it could happen to him, it could happen to your brother, it could happen to your husband, it could happen to your father, to you."

As you watch the video you think, for some of us, it happens even before memories form. Within a day of posting the "Moms for Kavanaugh" video on the Catholic Vote Facebook page, a stream of comments tallies the appreciation of mainly white women for supporting Judge Kavanaugh. He has been smeared, they say, victimized because he is Catholic, because he is a white man in a time

---

[5] http://www.pewresearch.org/fact-tank/2016/11/09/how-the-faithful-voted-a-preliminary-2016-analysis

[6] http://www.cbsnews.com/news/brett-kavanaugh-confirmation-christine-blasey-ford-hearing-spurs-more-division-cbs-news-poll

[7] http://www.heavy.com/news/2018/10/catholic-moms-for-kavanaugh-ad-video

when white men are under attack, and because he would take away the Left's sacrament, abortion.

For all the reasons they feel he is being demonized by the Left, these women support him. A central reason they stand by Kavanaugh is rooted in the recognition that he is one of their own. *We are mothers. We give everything for our sons.*

The same white, conservative, Catholic women who now stand with Brett Kavanaugh were once your primary instructors. They acted in chorus, teaching you to hold your tongue, to keep your knees together, to keep silent, to submit your body and your spirit to the service of God, to Jesus, to the Holy Spirit, to your husband. To trust everything but your own voice.

When you watch Dr. Christine Blasey Ford testify, you see her body as the focal point of the crowded Senate room. In this theater, ten Democrats thank her for coming forward. The eleven Republicans, all white men, sit silently, raised on a platform above her. They ask questions to punch holes in her motivations, her story, not with their own voices but through a female surrogate.

As Dr. Blasey Ford speaks, her voice shakes. Her blonde hair wraps around an arm of her glasses and you have the urge to reach through the screen and fix it for her. "I am here because I believe it is my civic duty to tell you what happened to me while Brett Kavanaugh and I were in high school."[8] As she recounts her assault, she controls her volume. She makes her tone exceedingly gentle. She does not cry. She does not yell. She does not sob or sniff loudly or jab her finger in the air. She offers to be helpful. She asks for coffee but not a break. She apologizes. Dr. Blasey Ford is picture perfect, her body cloaked in a navy suit. Perfect in her manner, in her patience and restraint. She surpasses what is required of her as a victim. She tells her truth in measured steps, and her monologue quietly sets the house aflame.

The wound she reopens before the world breaks open your own. "I believed he was going to rape me. I tried to yell for help. When I did, Brett put his hand over my mouth to stop me from screaming."

You watch Brett Kavanaugh's testimony but cannot face writing

[8]http://www.c-span.org/video/?451895-1%2Fprofessor-blasey-ford-testifies-sexual-assault-allegations-part-1

10

it. You do not need to quote him. His voice does not need to be heard again. The only way Dr. Blasey Ford can be disbelieved is to believe that her truth is not the right truth. Which is what fifty U.S. senators will say when they return to the floor eight days later to vote against her truth. What follows the hearing is eight days of turning down the radio on assault stories. It feels like eight days of running. On the eighth day, you open your laptop to the livestream of the hearing just as the last speech finishes and the vote to confirm Brett Kavanaugh to the Supreme Court commences.[9]

On the floor, the senators face Mike Pence at his elevated marble rostrum. The legislative clerk calls the roll for the vote. *Mr. Alexander. Ms. Baldwin. Mr. Barrasso. Mr. Bennet. Mr. Blumenthal. Mr. Blunt.* The women there to protest are off-camera. You picture them circling the chamber like birds. Are they close enough to beat their hands on the ceiling, as blue as a September sky? As the senators' names are called, a woman's voice breaks through from the galleries above. "I am a mother and a patriot! I do not consent!"

As you study the pomp and circumstance, the senatorial traditions and decorum, you think of the ancient Greeks and how paltry women's rights had been in the ancient Greek world compared to those of their male counterparts. You wonder how the women made themselves heard.

Barred from participating in the exclusively male public political scene, (ancient Greek) women...developed another mode of expressing their concerns and opinions about the world around them—through performance of ritual laments.[10]

The senate clerk covers the microphone with his hand to mute the women's voices while Mike Pence calls for order. The vice president strikes the gavel to sound-block. He remains impassive, his white hair perfectly combed. "Sergeant-at-arms will restore order in the galleries." Another woman calls to the senators, "Where is my representation? I do not consent!"

The clerk again smothers his microphone, muting her words.

In these songs of mourning, Greek women are empowered through their pain

[9] http://www.c-span.org/video/?c4753945%2Fsenate-votes-50-48-confirm-brett-kavanaugh-supreme-court

[10] Olivia Dunham, "Private Speech, Public Pain: The Power of Women's Laments in Ancient Greek Poetry and Tragedy," *CrissCross*, no. 1 (2014):2-6.

to address publicly issues of social importance; the most successful performers skillfully weave their narrative, sometimes abrasive, often persuasive, and always charged judicially and politically.[11]

Women in the senate gallery rise one after the other throughout the vote. "This is a stain on America. Do you understand?" Each time their words are blurred by a hand on the microphone, but the guttural anguish that lies beneath the women's words is heard.

The words of the laments...mixed with cries and shrieks must not be perceived simply as sounds, but as actions displayed before witnesses in an open strategy of..."truth-claiming." The laments are directed toward the doomed.[12]

You cannot see the women in the galleries, but your body responds to their voices the way it did to your newborn: immediately, with everything you are. Their voices command you to action.

There is a Catholic way of silencing women, but you will be restrained no longer.

&

Mary Catherine Ford is a writer based in Queens, New York. Her work has appeared in such publications as *The Chicago Tribune, Entropy Magazine, World Literature Today,* and *The Mass Review.*

---

[11] Ibid.
[12] Ibid.

WOULD MY HEART SURVIVE DONALD TRUMP?

By Lisa L. Kirchner

The day Donald Trump was elected I went onto Match.com and changed my dating profile. Right at the top I wrote "NOTE: If you voted for Donald Trump, keep scrolling." I wasn't sure why I bothered, I rarely looked at the account anymore. I didn't make the change to winnow potential partners so much as to announce how sickened I was by the officer-elect. That turned out to be prescient.

Two days after the election, I crumpled over on my mat in yoga class, reeling from chest pain. After Googling the symptoms—soreness in my chest, difficulty breathing, numbness in my left arm—I took myself to the emergency room. There I was diagnosed with costochondritis, which sounded like a fancy form of hypochondriasis but is in fact a swelling of the cartilage around the sternum brought on by anxiety. "Anything stressful happening?" the doctor asked.

Was she kidding? Anything stressful? How about the end of my personhood as a woman? A shove into cement for all women who've experienced sexual abuse? The horror of an inarticulate man with a microphone? Who wasn't feeling stressed out? As to the latter question, I had my suspicions, starting with the doctor.

I had recently moved to St. Petersburg, Florida, a red state I'd never planned to call home. But when my mother died, the house I'd been renting out for twenty years felt like too heavy a burden to keep. I knew if I took the profits from its sale back home to New York City, they'd disappear. The move to Florida was meant to be temporary, only a year, until I fulfilled the obligation set forth by the condo association, which prohibited me from renting the place for twelve months.

It turned out Florida was good for work. I had just enough

business to keep me afloat, with ample time for my own writing, friends, and beach-going. After ten years in the city, the simple fact that I could drive to the grocery store made life feel luxurious. It mattered little that the dating scene was disastrous; I'd been single for most of the decade since my ex-husband surprised me by asking for a divorce over the phone. It was as easy to not get involved with the party-all-the-time guys in Florida as it had been to eschew the work-all-the-time guys in New York. I preferred being on my own to being in a union that had any room for secrets.

So it was a real surprise that my edit drew fresh attention to my account. After all, one of my profile pictures was of me with a Hillary Clinton cutout, taken at the Democratic headquarters in St. Petersburg. Didn't most men look only at the pictures?

"You voted for Trump?" came a message.

What? I clicked. Cute guy. No pictures of guns and only one on a boat with a dead fish. When it came to online profiles near me, this made him a screaming liberal. *He must be joking.*

"Oh, hells no!" I replied.

Nothing more from him, but that didn't bother me for two reasons. One, if I'd learned anything from online dating in the past ten years, it was not to take anything personally. Two, I was getting plenty of other messages. Mostly I ignored them. There was a mind-numbing similarity to the messages—"Hey"—and I could not bear to read how another man in his 40s lived for the weekends and couldn't wait to retire. Besides, my health had moved to front and center on the priority list.

To eliminate stressors, I started on Facebook, leaving all the political groups I'd joined. That sounds so much easier than it was—I'd come to look forward to seeing what my new Facebook acquaintances were posting and getting their responses to my posts. After that, I went on Twitter and unfollowed political accounts and newsgroups. That was less difficult.

I worked from home at jobs I chose. Thanks to Obamacare, the only anxiety-producing thing in my life was the fact that the liberal ideals I'd campaigned for since high school had just been crushed… just when I'd finally let myself believe that a highly competent woman would win the day. The fact that she did not prevail over such an ignoramus was not something I could discuss lightly, so finally I told my friends I couldn't discuss politics anymore. Those were awkward conversations. We LOVED tearing through the foibles of our president-elect, and I was a ringleader. But those conversations got me riled up, and I couldn't see any other way to de-stress.

Then came the revelation.

As more messages poured into the dating site, I realized that my profile message was unclear. The messengers had misunderstood "keep scrolling" as "keep reading." *Jesus H. Christ, I have to delete that thing.* I logged in to delete and glanced at the accumulated messages. Some of them seemed to have read my message correctly, but nobody I was into. Something about the election had brought on a surge of desperation. I needed a break. And just then—while online to deactivate my profile—came the most intriguing message I'd ever received in my ten years of online dating and five years of being a dating columnist.

The message opened with: "Nice use of the parenthetical." NICE USE OF THE PARENTHETICAL? The guy not only knew what such a thing was, he had recognized it and had spelled it correctly? The rest of his message referenced my profile. He read my profile? And his screen name referred to a poem. I had to write back. After a few witty back and forths, we moved to text messages. The conversation kept rolling until he mentioned something about pinot and pizza.

"Could be a deal breaker," I wrote. "I haven't had a drink since college."

If there was one thing I'd learned, it was that it was best to get deal breakers out of the way immediately. He said it wasn't, so I asked what his was. He wrote: "Not really sure…getting shit for not texting/calling every five minutes. Trying to make me find Jesus. No physical, emotional, or intellectual attraction. Extremism. Putting toilet paper on the roll backwards. That's all that comes to mind. You?"

I was already a little bit in love. "My only deal breaker is lack of ability to communicate. Things, unanticipated things, will surface."

"Things?" my poet asked.

"Who knows what things?" I wrote. "You do need somewhat of a shared value structure, but there will be variances there. I don't need a replica of me, I'm already here."

The messages flew. That was over Thanksgiving, so we had more time than usual to flirt via text. He was funny without being overly familiar, interesting and interested, so he didn't seem full of himself, and both of us had made our way in life without much parental support. That was the tripping point.

I told him my dad wasn't a monster, but that he'd voted for Trump. That's when he let me know that he, too, had read my profile differently than I'd intended. "I actually did vote for him."

On the one hand I was horrified. And yet, while canvassing for Hillary, I'd developed a genuine interest in objections to the idea of Hillary as president. I wanted to hear what he had to say.

He said he liked Trump's economic policies better, which struck me as ill-informed. I complained about Republican economic policies but didn't cut off the conversation. "I voted for Bill, but I'm not a fan of either of the Clintons," he wrote.

Again, I couldn't end the conversation because he'd not said the magic words: I hate Hillary. In my book that's not-so-secret code for "I hate women." He told me he wasn't sure he'd have voted for him if he'd actually thought he had a chance of winning. That gave me pause.

I desperately did not want to talk about politics—my chest pains had eased considerably since the news drought. And I did want to meet him. I'd come to trust myself enough in the dating world to know that if we went out, I'd spot a misogynist quickly. Nothing about him said "classist, woman-hating racist," so what was my objection? Legislation I wasn't going to talk about? After a moment's reflection, it felt like the most natural thing in the world to reply. "Already we have a thing," I texted. "And I like how we're able to talk through it."

Our first date was furniture shopping. If he was cheap, had bad taste, or was rude to the salespeople, I was ready to bail. Why give the guy any slack? "This one," he said, sitting on a gorgeous retro modern couch. "Can you treat it for stains? This one can be a total slob." He was pointing at me; I found the pretend familiarity hilarious.

For our second date, he came to a storytelling show I host. I invited him, thinking he might not come since it was a weeknight, but I was disappointed when I didn't see him until intermission.

"Your opening song was fantastic," he said. The fact that he'd been there without needing anything from me was impressive, but when he finished the night with a rendition of Frank Sinatra's "Fly Me to the Moon," I was all but on the second date with him.

After we'd gone out for a couple of months it was time for the real test—I took him to my yoga studio. Would he talk during class or try to touch me? "Listen, I don't have any reason to think we won't be together awhile, or I wouldn't be bringing you here at all," I told him. "But this is my yoga studio. No matter what happens with us, I claim this place." The next day he told me that I'd earned his colleague's seal of approval for that comment. Not only was he talking about me to his peers, he wasn't afraid to show himself as submissive. I swooned.

We are very different, but my poet has shown me time and again how much he respects and values women. He is the only man I've ever been with who views my time as equally valuable. To write is to require great swaths of unprofitable time alone, and he gives me that without hesitation. He is remarkably unthreatened by my work and even pitches in at every story show to make sure it runs smoothly. In short, I could not have dreamed up a more supportive partner.

My poet and I got married. He has shown me repeatedly that we share a value structure more aligned than I would have believed if I'd rejected him based on what turned out to be cursory evidence. What is my activism about if not to avoid falling into this very trap? At our wedding, there were rabid Republicans and die-hard Democrats. None refused to celebrate love.

In a recent yoga class, the teacher was talking about how the practice of yoga is more than exercise; it's about seeing what binds all beings rather than what separates us. It reminded me of a quote from the spiritual leader Ram Dass.

"If you close your heart down to anything in the universe," Dass once advised parents grieving the loss of their child, "you are then at the mercy of suffering. And to have finally dealt with suffering, you have to consume it into yourself. Which means you have to—with eyes open—be able to keep your heart open in hell."[1]

By learning to keep my heart open in hell, my heartache finally disappeared, along with the costochondritis.

෨

Lisa L. Kirchner is the author of *Hello American Lady Creature: What I Learned as a Woman in Qatar*. Her work has appeared in *The New York Times*, *The Washington Post*, and *Salon*, among numerous other outlets. She currently writes an advice column for *Creative Loafing Tampa Bay*, "Love Confidential." She found love thanks to a grammatical error, and is currently at work on her second memoir about learning to embrace her imperfection.

---

[1] Ram Dass, "Dealing with Suffering and Seeing it as Grace," Ramdass.org, August 19, 2018.

Letters Between Two Women Following the U.S. Presidential Election of the Man Who Grabs Pussy and Lost the Popular Vote

By Beth Couture and Renée E. D'Aoust

From: "Renée E. D'Aoust"
To: "Beth Couture"
Subject: Letter from Renée
Date: Saturday, November 12, 2016 at 12:14 PM
Lugano, Switzerland

Dear Beth,

And so the U.S. Electoral College elects the sexual assaulter-in-chief—Trump. I'm gutted. Devastated.

How are you feeling, my beloved friend? I think of you on the front lines, serving people, finishing your MSW. How can I support you better? How does it feel in America?

Today Tube of Fur woke at five a.m., as she does, and grunted. Last night, we walked our chestnut trail—*Sentiero Eden*. Waddle up, waddle down. It is small comfort to me that Tootsie does not know how screwed we are. She has stayed close by me all week, as I get out of bed to teach, to write, to go to physical therapy. Wednesday after the election results were clear, my physical therapist (she's Dutch) said, "This affects everyone!"

This is the normalization of racism, hate, sexism, climate change denial, the denial of responsibility we have to our brown and black and every color and LGBTQ sisters and brothers. The sham that I'm supposed to get along, the idea that I'm supposed to normalize the sexual assaulter-in-chief, the idea that I'm supposed to support a system of white supremacy in the country whose passport I carry. This is the normalization of excuses that favor fascism.

I say, white people, this is on you. Squarely. I'm a white woman. This is on me.

Our black and brown and LGBTQ brothers and sisters have been terrified to live in America. We have killed our First Peoples through genocide and called it assimilation. No more. I'm now terrified, too. I never wanted to leave America to live in Switzerland. Now, I do not want to come back. Why? I don't feel safe. Know: I've been raped, sexually abused, harassed, stalked. A friend told me last summer that I did not understand domestic violence. I wondered, *have I done such a great job of normalizing myself? The violence in my past?* Twenty-five years ago when I spoke up, my extended family stopped talking to me. My mother's two sisters shunned my mother. My aunt told me I was "precocious" and "guilty of everything [he] would do from now on to any other girl" if I didn't report. Another abuser stalked me online. Another woman told me, "You wanted it." Have I spoken of how my body is a locus of assault? Have I written about it? In obscure terms. I will now speak up. I am terrified of global climate change. Global climate change affects my body and the earth. But brown and black and LGBTQ bodies have been terrorized for years. So, my fear is privileged; I am a white body. I am terrified that the sexual assaulter-in-chief has normalized ignorance, normalized grabbing pussies, normalized grabbing my pussy.

I have been practicing a potpourri of radical self-care that includes drinking too much coffee, eating too many Italian cookies, breaking up with Facebook so I can freak out on Twitter, and grabbing Tube of Fur to cuddle. Kindness is my religion. Being a doormat is not. My belief in kindness has meant I keep my mouth shut. As a white woman, it has been my privilege to keep my mouth shut. But when my brother killed himself, I swore I would not abide bullshit. I have not kept my pledge. In Ian's name, I will speak up.

Thanks for suggesting I read Bessel van der Kolk's *The Body Keeps the Score: Brain, Mind, and Body in the Healing of Trauma.* Spot on. Please continue to help me see my own blindness, to break down my privilege, to serve.

Give my love to Esteban, too. I send you love. Much love,
Renée

From: "Beth Couture"
To: "Renée E. D'Aoust"
Date: Thursday, Nov 17, 2016 at 9:19 PM
Subject: Letter to Renée
Philadelphia, PA, U.S.A.

Dear Renée,

The other night I dreamt about dying. In the dream, I was some-how certain that I was going to die, and I was so scared and so angry and sad. I kept saying I wasn't ready, I had so much left to do, I couldn't die. Not yet. It reminded me of when Ed and I talked about death, about the afterlife, and it hit me in such a powerful way that maybe there wasn't anything after this life. Maybe we really do just die and rot, and that's it. I have never been able to accept that idea. I don't believe in heaven or hell, but I've always believed that we don't just stop, that there must be something after this and we will be aware of it. I don't know if I believe this because I *actually* believe it, or if I'm just too scared to think about the alternative. In that conversation with Ed, and in the dream, I faced it. I allowed myself to think that maybe that's all there is—death and no longer being. And I sobbed like I have never sobbed. I couldn't stop. It felt like someone was tearing out my insides. That's what it feels like now, almost all the time. Like I am looking into the face of something too horrible to comprehend and I can't stop sobbing. Like I am seeing the possibility of death for the first time. And I'm not ready to. I'm not ready to look, but I have no choice. I'm not ready to face the possibility that this is all there is.

Esteban and I decided a few months ago that we wanted to have a baby. This was such a big decision for us. I don't think it was some-thing I had ever allowed myself to imagine, because I am terrified of being a mother, of fucking the kid up, of raising a kid in such a scary world. Getting pregnant always felt like such a selfish thing. There are so many kids in the world who need parents, so few resources to go around, so little certainty that the world would be okay for the kid. But we decided that to have a kid, to make one ourselves, would be an act of hope.

The day after the election, I realized that I could not bring a child into Trump's America, that I no longer believed enough in the good in the world to get pregnant. I think about having a baby now, and it feels so cruel, so absolutely harmful, and I can't do it. I think Esteban could still do it even though he understands my feelings, but I can't. I don't have that much hope. It breaks my fucking heart every time I think about it. It feels like death, and the grief is so big, so powerful that I don't know what to do with it at all. We are looking into adoption now, and that may be the most ethical decision anyway. Certainly we can love the child the same. But it hurts so much to think that we don't, *can't* have the same hope we used to, the hope we worked so hard to have.

I guess that's what I'm feeling most of all—hopeless. For the first time. I've always been—in spite of my depression and anger and fear, in spite of the reality I see as a social worker—an optimist. I have always believed that no matter how bad things are, they can and likely will get better. Not without a fight, of course, not without a hell of a lot of work, but they will get better. Things will be okay. I'm not sure I believe that anymore. I know the United States is a country built on slavery, on genocide, on greed. It's a country that claims values it so often acts in direct opposition to. Trump really is no surprise. But the loudness of his bigotry, his fearmongering, his stupidity, still surprises me.

My sister got married a little over a year ago and is now afraid that her marriage will be nullified, that the woman she loves will no longer be seen by those in power as her family. My three black nephews now have even more to be afraid of when they walk down the streets, because of the violence Trump endorses and encourages in his supporters. I work with students who are afraid for their lives, the lives of their families, their futures. This isn't how it should be. And I'll fight for how it should be, for how it will one day be. Because there's no other choice. Right now I'm grieving, and I feel there's no other choice but that either. I'm so grateful you're with me in the fighting, in the grieving.

So much love to you, and please give my love to Daniele, to your sweet dad, to the Tube of Fur (who always gives me hope).

Beth

From:"Renée E. D'Aoust"
To: "Beth Couture"
Subject: Letter from Renée
Date: Friday, January 11, 2019 4:40 PM
Lugano, Switzerland

Dear Beth,

Wanted to tell you—I re-gifted the dachshund skeleton "Bones" that you gave me. My dad was freaked about having the tube of fur (with no fur) in his home, and my husband didn't want the skeleton here in Switzerland with Tootsie. (I did.) I bought Bones a leash (pink) and a collar (green) with a bright pink bone-shaped ID tag; now she's in her forever home in Upper Manhattan. My friend Stacey has a life-size skeleton named Sligo (named for an uprooted medieval skeleton found in Ireland), so now Sligo has a dachshund companion, Bones. I feel guilty about all the work you did finding me Bones at Target; I'm sorry, and thank you so much. Stacey loves them together! (Stacey told me that when the cops came by recently to ask about an incident in her building, the eyes of the male cop kept sliding away, looking over Stacey's shoulder to Sligo and Bones, with an expression somewhere between anxiety and disgust.)

This is only the second trip I've made to northern Idaho, to the USA, since "45" was elected. It's strange to shop in a grocery store with a man wearing a Confederate flag jean jacket and a hip holster with a handgun. Was I ever used to that? I abandoned the cart in the store. Walked out without my tortilla chips and salsa. It's really hard to find good tortilla chips and salsa in Switzerland. I've applied for permanent Swiss residency, and the FBI signed off on my necessary criminal background check.

Today I spent all day with my hands on my mother's stories, poems, papers, journals, novels, cookbooks, and newspaper articles. Susan Saxton D'Aoust wrote her entire life. I miss her. May she be blessed. May you be blessed. May we survive "45."

I've been thinking about how Taylor Swift's mom wished that she hadn't taught her daughter to be so nice. Did my mom teach me to be too nice? I don't think so. My husband got really excited once when this strange man—a friend of a friend of my mom's—was making the moves on my mom.

"Did your mom just walk away without a word?" he asked.

"Yes!"

"That is freaking amazing. Your mom is awesome."

That dweeby guy who was making his moves on my mom just kept drinking his rat-piss beer when she walked away.

Rat-piss beer brings me to the "Kavanot" hearing. Watched the entire spectacular shitstorm. It pained me to see how helpful, how collegial, how nice Dr. Blasey Ford was to the whole committee. Such a bizarre contrast between her professionalism and Judge Kavanaugh's rants. I want to know what you think—from your perspective as a working therapist, a writer, a woman, a teacher, a human.

The next time I visit my dad, if our neighbor comes over and once again uses his slur to refer to House Speaker Nancy Pelosi, I will yell at him the same way my mother did fifteen years ago.

Tootsie is now our Senior Dachshund. What a waddler! All my love to you and E. and the kitties four.

Yours with love, always,

Renée

From: "Beth Couture"
To: "Renée E. D'Aoust"
Date: Wednesday, January 16, 2019 at 2:42 PM
Subject: Letter to Renée
Philadelphia, PA, U.S.A.

Dear Renée,

I'm so fucking sick of niceness. I'm so fucking sick of women being afraid to take up space, to walk down the street, to say something not-nice to a very not-nice guy who is going to rape us or kill us or at the very least threaten us because we threatened his ego. I am so sick of women being afraid to have sex, to have human bodies, to do human things with those bodies. I am so fucking sick of men who think they can do what they want with our bodies. I can't tell you how many students I work with who came into my office terrified and anxious and so, so angry during the Kavanaugh hearing.

Eighteen-year-old girls who barely know what the Supreme Court is but who know what sexual assault is because it happened to them or their friend—or, more likely, them AND their friend. Eighteen-year-old girls who were not believed when they told their parents, their friends, their boyfriends, girls who told me I was the only one who had believed them, and ALL they wanted was to be believed. Watching Dr. Ford made me so sad, but it also just pissed me off. I want to tear these men apart. I want to show them that their time is up, that we're not letting them get away with hurting us and hurting us and hurting us anymore. Except. We ARE letting them get away with it. We let Kavanaugh get away with it, and Brock Turner and Clarence Thomas a long time ago (but not) and so many others. We let them get away with it. The guys who assaulted my students got away with it. And I don't know what to do with this. I don't know what to say except *WE HAVE TO CLAIM OUR POWER*, but I don't even know what that means. We have it, right? I know we have so much more power than we use, so much more power than we even know. And I know we can take it back. We've started to, maybe? But we need to stop being so nice. It doesn't serve us. I'm so angry all the time. I know that doesn't serve me either, not when it keeps me up at night and makes me yell at my dad at Christmas because he said something I didn't like and he's an old white guy. But I don't know what to do with my anger either. I'm done being nice, but I don't know what else to be right now. The anger at least keeps me from feeling sad all the time, from despairing.

Working with college kids breaks my heart in so many ways. I love these kids. I absolutely adore them. I want to hug them and make them tea and tell them everything is going to be okay. I want to believe it will. I want to apologize for being part of what got us into this mess. So many of them are working so hard to create the world they need. They're protesting, making good decisions, voting. They're doing the work to make things better, work so many of us should have been doing for so long. They deserve so much better. I think we do too.

I wish I could be there when you yell at your neighbor. I know your mom will be.

25

I'm in my office at work, in the middle of the city, and there is a woman screaming her head off on the street. I can't see her, but she keeps screaming—the kind of scream you hear in a horror movie. No one is doing anything. People keep walking and don't stop, they keep driving, no one seems to even notice her. There's a metaphor in this, don't you think?

I love you. You and Daniele and Toots the Old give me so much hope for the world. Thank you for that.

XOXOXO,

Beth

P.S. I'm so glad Bones has a forever home and is no longer freaking your dad or Daniele out! It sounds like she's met her person, but I know she loved spending some time with you along her path. LOVE.

&

Beth Couture is the author of *Women Born with Fur* (Jaded Ibis Press, 2014), and her fiction has appeared in various journals and anthologies. She is a therapist at the University of the Arts in Philadelphia, and she and her spouse live with their four ridiculous cats in West Philly.

Writer and teacher Renée E. D'Aoust is the author of *Body of a Dancer* (Etruscan Press). Follow her @idahobuzzy where she tweets about writing and her tube of fur Tootsie.

Trigger Warning: The Supreme Court May Be Dangerous to Your Mental Health

By Alissa Hirshfeld, MFT

Since the 2016 presidential campaign and subsequent election, I've witnessed rage and fury in many of my women clients. Those with narcissistic fathers and partners in particular are traumatized when they see President Trump display the abusive behaviors of demeaning and humiliating women, behaviors that they have experienced personally from the men in their lives. Those who have been raped or molested believe that rape is being condoned by this administration, a belief first formulated by Trump's minimization of the *Access Hollywood* tape, further grounded by Betsy DeVos's decisions that hinder the ability of rape victims on college campuses to seek redress, and established by the subsequent nomination and confirmation of Judge Brett Kavanaugh to the United States Supreme Court.

Judge Kavanaugh's confirmation process had a particularly deleterious effect, both on me and on my many female clients. Dr. Christine Blasey Ford recounted her memory of being sexually assaulted by Kavanaugh. Moved and shaken by her vulnerability and the obvious trauma resulting from the assault, I was impressed that, despite her visible distress, she was able to explain the neurology of memory encoding, the process by which traumatic memories are stored in the hippocampus. I was glad viewers were educated about these facts as it helps people to understand how traumatic memories can remain so vivid, although fragmented, and how sensory experiences, like hearing the laughter of her tormentors, could be seared into Dr. Blasey Ford's awareness. As someone who has heard the stories of many assault and rape victims, Dr. Blasey Ford's testimony was compelling and believable.

While I felt some sympathy for Judge Kavanaugh's discomfort, his demeanor was defensive and unpersuasive. He dodged questions and claimed to be certain that he had never blacked out after drinking to excess, despite his friends recalling him having done so. The very experience of blacking out in this fashion, after an excessive amount of alcohol consumption, is characterized and defined by a loss of recollection by the drinker. Judge Kavanaugh was arrogant and disrespectful to the Democrats questioning him, in stark contrast to Dr. Blasey Ford's accommodating demeanor toward all of her examiners.

In short, Brett Kavanaugh reacted as perpetrators of sexual assault often do when confronted with their crimes, by engaging in DARVO—Deny, Attack, Reverse Victim and Offender. He denied Dr. Blasey Ford's rape-attempt charge with absolute certainty, despite the strong possibility that he was drinking heavily on the night in question and that his memory was likely to have been impaired. Too savvy (or perhaps well advised) to attack Dr. Blasey Ford directly, Judge Kavanaugh proceeded to attack the Democrats for their investigation of him, turning himself into the victim of a liberal conspiracy.

After the proceedings, the American Psychological Association issued a statement reminding us that sexual assault is likely the most underreported crime in the United States.[1] Two-thirds of sexual assault victims don't report their attacks to the police. Many victims are afraid to confide even in members of their own family, due to feelings of shame, fear for their own safety, concerns about being believed, and wanting to avoid causing pain. Since giving her own testimony, Dr. Blasey Ford has been blamed, shamed, and attacked. Her life has been threatened and, together with her family, she has had to go into hiding for an extended period of time. These are the grim consequences of speaking up and speaking out after suffering a sexual assault that scare so many victims into remaining silent. Based on my decades of clinical experience, left to grapple with the legacy of assault, victims often suffer from low self-esteem, have difficulty

---

[1] Jessica Henderson Daniel, PhD, *Statement of APA President Regarding the Science Behind Why Women May Not Report Sexual Assault*, September 24, 2018.

trusting others, and struggle to form intimate relationships, *often for the rest of their lives.*

Since the Kavanaugh hearings, my clients, and those of my colleagues, have been emotionally triggered—having feelings of anger, fear and despair evoked—to a degree I've not seen since the onset of the #MeToo movement and the demonstrated ubiquity of sexual harassment across a multitude of industries.[2] Many of our clients express fear that America is no longer safe for women, recalling how they were greeted with suspicion or punished when identifying their assailants. Inevitably, some victims question whether reporting their assaults is worth the emotional toll it takes on them. These women were sickened by the Republican men on the judicial committee who made little attempt to empathize with the position of a sexual assault survivor, but spoke instead of "plowing through" the confirmation of Kavanaugh, words that are suggestive of raping the country or violating the will of the people.[3] Women angrily point out that our president—himself accused by *twenty-three* women of sexual misconduct—should not be allowed to nominate another alleged offender who might be in a position to let the president off the hook for his own varied crimes.[4] Lindsey Graham's demeaning remarks on FOX News that Dr. Blasey Ford needs therapy are a further example of the derisive manner in which sexual assault survivors are frequently treated.

Dr. Blasey Ford, desiring to put her trauma behind her, sought therapy to assist in her courageous effort to reestablish a happy and productive life for herself. Her emotional testimony before the judicial committee spoke eloquently to the depth of long-held pain suffered by sexual abuse survivors. As a professional in the mental

[2] It is not only women who are victimized. According to the National Sexual Violence Research Center, one out of three women and one of six men experience some kind of sexual assault during their lifetimes. Some of my male clients have been triggered by the Kavanaugh hearings as well.

[3] https://www.newsweek.com/mitch-mcconnell-brett-kavanaugh-allegations-1134001; Thirty-eight percent of Americans opposed Kavanaugh's nomination, compared to thirty-four percent who supported it. The remaining were undecided. https://www.nbcnews.com/politics/first-read/poll-opposition-kavanaugh-s-confirmation-grows-n911581

[4] https://www.businessinsider.com/women-accused-trump-sexual-misconduct-list-2017-12

healthcare industry, it is my firm belief that Congress would be an improved, more evolved institution if *all* of its members received psychotherapy to enhance their capacity for empathy, to improve their ability to communicate and negotiate, and to enable a better understanding of the psychology of their colleagues and the individuals over whom they legislate. President Trump's erratic behavior in office has prompted some mental health professionals to propose that all presidential candidates undergo a mandatory competency evaluation by a mental health expert—similar to that required of those entering the military—prior to being sworn in.[5] In April 2017, Congressman Jamie Raskin introduced H.R.1987, a bill to establish an Oversight Commission on Presidential Capacity. The primary task of this committee would be to determine whether a president is mentally or physically unable to discharge the duties of his office.[6]

I am Judge Kavanaugh's age, and I grew up in Washington, D.C. My best friend from high school was acquainted with one of the friends Brett Kavanaugh had mentioned on his calendar. Others among my high school classmates attended parties with him and his group of friends. In college, I worked as a peer counselor and was responsible for leading workshops in university dorms to educate incoming freshmen about the prevalence of date rape—a term just coming into common usage in the late 1980s. We warned young women not to go to parties alone where heavy drinking was taking place, and once there, never to venture into a room alone with a young man. It is disheartening, demoralizing, and infuriating to witness the lack of progress regarding the prevalence of date rape, and the impunity of its perpetrators, over the past thirty years.

The National Sexual Assault Hotline reported a two hundred percent increase in calls during Judge Kavanaugh's hearing.[7] This suggests that in witnessing this administration's contempt for abuse survivors, and its inclination to protect, excuse, and even elevate those accused of assault—like Judge Kavanaugh and, indeed, the

---

[5] https://www.theatlantic.com/politics/archive/2018/01/bandy-lee/550193/.

[6] https://raskin.house.gov/media/press-releases/raskin-introduces-bill-establish -independent-commission-presidential-capacity.

[7] https://www.cnn.com/2018/09/24/health/national-sexual-assault-hotline -spike/index.html

president himself—victims are advocating for themselves in record numbers. The midterm results—which saw a record-breaking number of women from diverse backgrounds elected to Congress—also demonstrate that our voices are resonating powerfully with the electorate—a cause to celebrate. One can only hope that the media attention generated by Judge Kavanaugh and Dr. Blasey Ford bends the arc of the moral universe toward awareness, empathy, equality, and justice.

છ

Alissa Hirshfeld balances a psychotherapy practice with parenting and writing. Her academic articles have appeared in *American Journal of Psychiatry, Creativity Research Journal,* and *The Therapist Magazine.* She is the author of a memoir, *This Whole Wide World is Just a Narrow Bridge,* and a novel, *Living Waters: From Harvard Halls to Sacred Falls.* Ms. Hirshfeld is active in the Duty to Warn movement, warning about the danger this president presents to the public mental health.

Hauntings

By Dawn Marlan

I. "On Becoming "Nasty"

It's 1977, the year I lose my innocence, the year that *Saturday Night Fever* makes us feel a little sorry for the guy with the disco strut and the rape moves, and Roman Polanski strikes a plea bargain, reducing his rape indictment to unlawful sex with a minor. I'm eleven years old and barely pubescent and already I hate the concept of innocence, which celebrates the state of powerless bewilderment. Eternal childhood is not my goal.

I'm a sixth grader at Nixon elementary in the suburbs of Pittsburgh, Pennsylvania. I live with my mother and sister in an apartment complex where kids roam around playing kick-the-can and smoking monkey-vine, tiny curled branches that simulate cigarettes by producing a thin ribbon of smoke when you light them. I am in a hurry to be grown. And maybe that's why I follow some neighborhood boys into a walk-in closet one day and don't object when they divide up my body, upper and lower halves. I am vaguely aware that I'm not supposed to be here. I am not actively scared of the older one, who is fourteen and looks like a man, but he is in charge, because he is older. His younger brother is my boyfriend and he doesn't seem to want to be there either, because for a while he hides behind a row of hanging clothes. He's a bit of a baby. I'm not sure why I'm here, except that I am vaguely curious about this netherworld, and I can't find an excuse to say no. It takes longer than I want it to, this odd, detached, formal experiment, and I distract myself, avoiding the disgusting things, like tongues. When I emerge from the closet, body still miraculously "intact," I am another kind of creature, a despicable, sullied thing.

There's no way to tell by looking at me, but my body is a tainted body, and everyone knows it. What's worse is that *I* come to know it, and this knowledge shapes the way I understand myself and how I respond to the constant onslaught of solicitations that belong to being a girl.

They happen everywhere, like the time I'm at my mother's friend's apartment in a bedroom with her son. The adults are chatting in the next room, unsuspecting. They can't rescue me from a situation they can't imagine, and I don't know how to extricate myself. I am too embarrassed by the predicament of my weakness to draw attention to it. And I don't quite realize I have a choice in the matter.

There's another thing I don't realize. It's possible to lose your innocence more than once. It's something I won't learn until many years later. Innocence suggests something beyond or other than an untainted body. It suggests a state of not-yet-knowing and perhaps not-even-suspecting. And what I do not yet know has nothing to do with sex directly, but only with how sex is connected to cruelty. Before I walk into the closet and before Donald Trump secures the Republican nomination, I do not yet know how cruel the world is.

An experience of unwanted "contact" is not usually something that happens just once, and its effects are not easily contained. I am still not sure why I went with boys who disgusted me, or why I repeated such experiences. I only know that in matters of sex, there isn't a self-protective reflex you can rely on when your finger gets too close to the flame. Children don't learn to avoid situations of discomfort or disgust. They learn to adapt to them. At eleven years old, I adapt to a feeling of violation. I develop a habit of overcoming disgust.

While I am busy becoming worldly-wise, a species of woman, I still consider myself a tomboy. I play softball, collect stuffed animals, invent Communism. I am fascinated with extra-sensory perception, unidentified flying objects, the escape artist Harry Houdini, and the world of Narnia—magical, faraway places, extraordinary powers, escape routes. But reduced to a tainted body, all this disappears in an instant. I am a notch on a belt, humiliated as a body before it can even become itself. The word "whore" can snuff out a world alive with possibility and value.

Most of the time I do not believe in the story of my worthlessness.

But another part of me is not so sure. I accept both that I could have refused those boys and that I should have refused them, because I keep it secret. I suspect that what is said about me must be true: something about me is nasty.

There are only so many stances you can take toward your own nastiness. You can deny it and call it a lie, while inculcating shame; you can embrace nastiness, rejecting wholesomeness as the real lie; or you can accept that what happened to you, whether or not you allowed it to happen, is pain that adds depth to your soul. I try to adopt some combination of these positions, none of them wholeheartedly, because the truth lies in some foggy space between them that makes it hard to know if I am guilty or innocent, meek or defiant. I cannot account for what happened to me. I cannot claim to be a victim any more than I can claim to have been a willing participant.

I try to adopt a tougher attitude than matches my feeling. Someday, I will raise my hypothetical children in New York City, where they will learn to step over the homeless without feeling shocked, because it is dangerous to be naïve about the world's goodness. I will take them to parties in the countryside where purity is not worshipped and where people dance naked around bonfires.

While I am waiting to grow up enough to do such things, I console myself with songs that tell me I'm not alone, like Gloria Gaynor's "I Will Survive." When *Grease* comes out in 1978, I am moved to tears by Rizzo's song "There Are Worse Things I Could Do." It's about how the worst sin isn't being "trashy," but being a bad person. But her example of a bad person, a tease, is an irony that is lost on me. At the very moment when she sings in her own defense with so much power, she is condemning herself to follow through with whatever she started.

II. Trumpian Nasty

I'm watching the final presidential debate of 2016. Hillary Clinton is talking about her tax plan and how it would affect the wealthy. Her own taxes would go up, she says, and so would Donald Trump's, "if he can't figure out how to get out of it."

"Such a nasty woman," he responds.

What he means, of course, is that it's unfair to insult him for enriching himself at the expense of others. It's not nasty to abuse people. It's nasty to speak of abuse. But his strategy can't be effective, because it's too transparent that he's trying to shift the terms of the discussion, trying to unravel the link between character and behavior and reassign it to gender: a man is strong and deserving, a woman weak and mostly unpalatable. He does it again when she's a second late to the stage after a commercial break. "I know where she went—it's disgusting," he says.

He knows that as long as Clinton can speak, she's going to win. So speaking itself becomes a hallmark of nasty. But it's better to find a way to reduce her to her body, to reduce all women to their bodies. She's too formidable in her pantsuit, so he puts her in a bathroom stall and pulls her pants to her knees, making her ridiculous. *Consider her bottom*, he seems to say, *consider her bottom as something disgusting*.

It's what he did to television anchor Megyn Kelly almost a year earlier when he was just getting rolling. To his fury, Kelly had questioned his treatment of women. *Forget her words. Consider her body.* And lest anyone get too excited about a body that conforms to the reigning ideals of beauty and proportionality, he asked us to consider that body bloodied.

I listened to him talk about "blood coming out of her...wherever," with a sort of amused horror, a kind of "fascination of the abomination." I suppose I shared with his supporters a disgust with the canned, clichéd quality of political discourse, the smarmy, polished rhetoric, the Ken-doll demeanor so integral to political packaging and posturing. And there was a thrill in suddenly realizing that Trump wasn't going to play that game; he was going to blow the whole thing up. I felt the wild joy of destructiveness, but only because I believed—how could I not?—that he was destroying himself. He would bring the whole lot down with him, and only the truth-tellers would remain.

With the second debate, I still believe he'll self-destruct, because look at him looming over his female opponent, stalker-like, breathing heavily and grimacing. I am giddy with outrage, giddy with something resembling happiness, because his weakness is exposed. Everyone will see that only his emptiness could produce such theater, such embarrassing clownish bluster. Everyone will see his unfathomable immaturity, even if its level is hard to gauge. Is his true age fifteen or is it five? Either way, it can't be humored for long. His taunts are a dazzling act of self-immolation. Who could possibly fall for him? Who could fail to notice his abiding insecurity and the colossal, cruel joke of such a candidacy? But I have not yet learned that everything is reversed under Trump; that bad is good, that weak is strong.

By the time the Access Hollywood video comes out, I'm far less giddy.

"You know I'm automatically attracted to beautiful—I just start kissing them. It's like a magnet. Just kiss. I don't even wait."

He calls it locker room talk, by which he means that it is *only* talk and therefore innocent, while also suggesting that such behavior is ordinary and even intrinsic to all-American masculinity. His grabbing and kissing is magnetic, just doing its thing, conforming to natural law. There's no need to read another's desire because what matters is *his* attraction, *his* desire, *his* will.

Not our locker rooms, they say, a reassuring sign that this is still a world I recognize, a world in which it is not respectable to force yourself on a woman. And yet this strikes me as an eerie repetition.

"And when you're a star, they let you do it, you can do anything… grab them by the pussy."

I remember overhearing some twelve-year-old boys on the school bus talking about a girl from the neighborhood. They were describing what they would to do to her if only she'd put a paper bag over her head, if only she'd expose her Barbie-like body and spare them the sight of her face. I don't remember whether she had a case of acne, or a nose a touch too big. I only know that they were fantasizing about getting rid of her face, the place where feeling is most legibly registered. They wanted to use her body without having to worry about her person.

And it wasn't just talk. They grabbed. I came to understand grabbing as something inevitable. There were so many instances of it that the memories bleed into each other: a man in Paris who grabbed me in an underpass; a Tunisian shipowner who gave me a ride and put his hand on my upper thigh; a clown in Berlin who was dating my teacher, and who refused to drop me off at my apartment when my head was splitting, because he wanted to draw me a bath; a bath would do me good; the boys and the men trying to push my head into their crotch, their hands heavy, my head straining against them; the teacher who started to kiss me just as I was confiding to him how heartbroken I was about someone else.

For Trump, there's nothing wrong with grabbing bodies or grabbing money, because other people don't exist for him. But no one who understands the basic principles of human decency will ever vote for him, I tell myself. They can't hate Hillary enough to sacrifice us.

Then again, I remember how they vilified her when, as First Lady, she said she wouldn't spend her time baking cookies. I remember how they skewered her for proposing universal health care. And I remember that for ten years Congress failed to ratify the Equal Rights Amendment—*Equality of rights under the law shall not be denied or abridged by the United States or by any State on account of sex*—killing it in 1982 when I am sixteen years old. This tells me a lot about how inequality is not only acceptable to powerful men, but vital to them.

III. On Becoming Untouchable

It's on the school bus as a kid that I learn the word, *kike*, but I'm not particularly worried about it. There are certain things I believe about this country—that it's democratic, that it's embraced its Jews, that it despises anything smelling of socialism, which is a dirty word here. It means we don't have to worry about descending into fascism but we can't become truly progressive either. I see a fixed range of possibilities, which partly keeps me safe. Because everyone accepts the tenet "Never again," I don't believe that anti-Semitism is a real problem anymore. I resent it too, resent the fact that the only thing I'm taught about being Jewish is that we were always hated. No one I know talks about Jews and money, or Jews killing Jesus, or Jews being sex fiends. It's the other things the kids in the Pittsburgh suburbs don't like, the bookishness, the verbosity, the tendency to talk about feelings, which is embarrassingly feminine. And I suspect that something about this aversion to talking makes my school a place of posing and swaggering and shaming.

It's the spring of 1978 when I go into the closet with those boys and the shaming begins, but in the summer I go to sleep-away camp in West Virginia. And after that I'm okay because the kids who go there are different. Most of them are from the Jewish community in Squirrel Hill, where my father and stepmother live. I am in love with summer camp, astonished at the camaraderie that seeps into everything we do. We swim in the lake and shoot arrows and ride horses. We go on survival overnights. We stand on picnic benches in the dining hall, singing our hearts out. On Shabbat, we set the table with the meat dishes (it's usually chicken). We dress up for dinner. Services are held in a clearing in the woods. The light is streaming through the trees; the leaves are fluttering. We are bound together by the beauty of this moment—the dappled shadows on the ground, the leaves fluttering, the melody rising. I am grateful that we have the freedom to think out loud here. We talk about everything, like what we would do if there were only one boat and we had to decide who would start a new civilization, or whether we would marry someone who isn't Jewish. I say I would, because my parents are divorced and I already know that love is rare and fragile. We are not afraid to say anything, even when we disappoint each other.

Squirrel Hill is a place where I am not afraid. And that's why I escape there on the weekends when summer camp is over. It doesn't matter whether I'm getting a slice with friends at Mineo's, chomping on chewy, thin-crust pizza dripping with East Coast grease, or, when I'm older, standing in front of Rhoda's, the Jewish deli, waiting for some nice person to buy us beer, or watching basketball at the JCC, or volunteering there; I feel at home. I'm one of the teens running arts and crafts classes for people with certain disabilities, accompanying them on a field trip to Philadelphia. They are part of the fabric of the JCC. They hang out here like we do, and kids greet them warmly. This is my first introduction to a culture that doesn't punish people for their deviations.

I am strong here. Untouchable.

I live for my weekends in Squirrel Hill. But on Sunday, I'm back in the suburbs, where football players preen on the ramps, whispering and laughing, and where the kids will grow up to be Trump voters.

IV. The Bubble

Squirrel Hill has taught me that there are alternatives, and I pour through the college books until I find one. The school I discover is a tiny experimental college of six hundred students near the green mountains in Bennington, Vermont. I spend my college years in a kind of sanctuary, in a school that celebrates artists and misfits, as if one's prior abjection, real or imagined, were now a thing of value and consequence. There are no grades, which might account for the boldness here, the passion for learning that animates everything. We are on a first name basis with our professors, who invite us to their homes for wine, conversation, and occasionally, for sex.

This is not a safe zone, but that's not what I'm looking for. I don't want to be protected from entanglement with my professors, which would constitute an assault on my agency. But I am better able to protect myself now, and maybe the difference is that I'm older, or that, in a place pulsing with Dionysian excess, my shame has receded, and it's easier to know my desire and to recognize when it is missing.

The age of identity politics is dawning and I am no exception to the impulse that fuels it. I am hungry for literature written by and about women and Jews. I am studying German modernism, an era of moral limbo between the death of one ethical system and the birth of another. From Hermann Broch I learn about this age of somnambulism, of sleepwalkers flailing about without common values to orient them. Workers and women and black folks and Jews are rising up, terrifying those in power. Their terror is hard to imagine from our ivory tower, where we mock such anxieties. We hold our truths to be self-evident. I perform mental acrobatics to conjure a mindset in which the self-determination of the marginalized is actively threatening.

Here are the books that stand as evidence. Here are the Jewish vampires, international conspiracies, control of the press, and globalist money. Here are the placards featuring men with long hooked noses poisoning the wells, rats carrying the plague. It is ugly, but it is fifty years ago. That's ancient history, like my childhood of whoredom.

Maybe that temporal distance is also why I am caught off-guard one day at the sight of a table in the quad, where women from the Feminist Union are handing out pamphlets about sex-positivity. They are selling T-shirts with the words, "This is the face of a Feminist." What stuns me is that I feel nothing beyond mild appreciation for the women behind the table. I like their T-shirts. But I have no urge to wear one. It's as if the energy of activism requires not just the knowledge of injustice, but a sense-memory of pain. I have spent enough time in a shimmery bubble among compatriots that my pain is healed, or at least buried.

The bubble travels with me. For thirty-two years, it is possible to remain cozily tucked away in an alternative America. I don't need a T-shirt anymore. Until I do.

V. The New Nasty

The day after the election, the swastikas start to appear. The first one I see is spray-painted on an underpass somewhere. It's circulating on my feed. That's all I remember, just the fact of it, black paint on a concrete wall.

I scroll further and find a post of a woman I know from the soccer circuit. It features her son on a golf course: "this day is about Jack," she writes. On a day when the white supremacists are celebrating and men are reminded that neither their ignorance nor cruelty is a barrier to power, it's a day about Jack.

I follow her threads for days afterwards, from the posts where she says that Hillary still just "bugs" her, to the expressions of unmistakable *Schadenfreude*, to the ones urging us all to "get over it." But I will not get over it. I am too old to override my disgust.

We are now pitted against each other. The fishmonger I used to chat with, the doctor I need to consult with, the charmingly unguarded used car salesman with the big smile and the closely shorn, military -style hair all look suspicious, and it is a loss. I cannot look at the stranger without mistrust or at my neighbor without wondering whether he voted to do me harm. I suspend my generosity, and my world is narrowed and impoverished.

With each abuser-of-power who is rewarded and lauded, I realize that I live among enemies. The voices on our feeds and on our air waves belong to the sneering, puffed-up boys who roamed the ramps in high school. They are risen from the dead. They are returned to power again and they stand with Cosby, Assange, and Weinstein; they stand with the Catholic priests who abused their power and the men who roam the halls of Congress, their crimes invisible. Ask me if I am surprised at the sheer numbers of such men multiplying before our eyes. I am not surprised. I am only surprised that in this thug nation some are falling.

This is the past to which Trump promised to return us. We are not returning to the age of shame, but to something possibly more brutal that has emerged in its overcoming. The cruelty that was hidden away is exposed. The veneer of decency is stripped away. The limit to acceptable, social behavior has been breached. There is no more pretending. In the president's support of accused child molester Roy Moore is the ghostly return of an American ideal of the cowboy outlaw, a Billy the Kid who rapes a woman and is rewarded by her love. But there is no fade-out concealing the scene of these new crimes. It is our job to keep them there in the open, to name them properly, to embody nasty anew.

In Charlottesville, white supremacists march in the open, brandishing torches and chanting, "Jews will not replace us." One of them plows his car into a crowd of protesters. Through someone I knew from high school, I find myself on a thread filled with people who are condemning protestors. Not the white supremacists protesting against the Jews, but the counter-protestors. Hatred of Jews, hatred of people of color, and hatred of women converge here.

I write to a soldier, who seems to cheer Heather Heyer's death, but I cannot quite believe it. I irrationally hope to find some common, moral ground. After all, he fights to protect the idea of America.

Surely you recognize Heather Heyer's right to speech, I persist, *surely you believe in the right to assemble. Surely you're not for transgressing democracy itself, good soldier.* But nothing is sure any more.

From the small screen glowing in my hand comes his response, supported by the thread. They have no regrets. She was a *libtard.* She was not what they consider a "ten."

VI. What Ghosts Whisper

Old tropes are back in circulation. *But, George Soros,* they say. He is the face of global, Jewish power. *But, Hillary Clinton meeting in secret with international banks to plot the destruction of U.S. sovereignty.* She is pictured with a Star of David on a pile of money. *But, bloodsuckers.* A picture of Trump's enemies behind bars—Soros, Clinton, Comey, Rosenstein. "Contrary to what are surely prevailing assumptions, anti-Semitic incidents constitute half of all hate crimes in New York City," says the *New York Times.*

Now, every time I read the *New York Times,* I hear his taunt, "The Failing *New York Times."* He steals our language. He fills our head with lies. *The press is the enemy of the people.* There are algorithms that shield us from our enemies, which tell us that truth is what we fantasize, that facts are what we believe.

I'm sitting in synagogue for a bar mitzvah. I don't attend much since Rabbi Yitzhak retired. Rabbi Yitz has a strange power. He makes it possible to transcend the ordinary. Or elevate it. I can't tell the difference. I finally understand that prayer is like magic. It is like art. He chants and his voice—joyful, mournful, hopeful—opens up access to the mysteries of this ancient tradition that is somehow also mine, transporting me to a place where, for a few minutes, I participate in carrying the collective sorrows of the world, in making them meaningful.

Maybe I also love him because he is from Squirrel Hill, and it's all intertwined for me—his familiar, Pittsburgh accent, like the one I cultivated as a kid, but later lost; his rootedness in Hobart Street, where he grew up *davening* in a Hassidic *Schul,* and where, steps away, my family lives in a house that was built by the rabbi from another Squirrel Hill synagogue.

I am sitting in Temple Beth Israel in Eugene, Oregon, and Yitz is not there and the new rabbi mentions Pittsburgh. The tragedy that happened this morning in Pittsburgh. My heart stops beating.

It all comes out when I'm standing in the social hall—the blood-bath in Squirrel Hill, the man shouting, "All Jews must die" as he sprays the synagogue with bullets. I remember that my father is at a conference in Denver. My stepmother and brother would not be in synagogue. But they might be "up-street" running errands. I try to calculate whether they are at a safe enough distance from the danger.

I learn that Rabbi Yitz is there this very morning, that he gave the sermon at the Tree of Life the night before, that he is rushing toward the shooter, because his friends are there. The police stop him in the parking lot. Because he was running a few minutes late, he is still alive, outside of the synagogue, waiting.

I read the names of the victims and for a minute I think, *no one I know.* I read the list again and linger over two names, hauntingly familiar, as I fight through the haze of thirty-five years. I scour my feed, post after post from Pittsburgh. Everyone I know from Squirrel Hill is in mourning, and it is confirmed, two of the victims are David and Cecil Rosenthal, who used to hang out at the JCC, and, I'm pretty sure, were in the arts and crafts class and on the trip to Philly. I recognize them now in the pictures, the faces of the young men shining through the faces of middle-aged men, embraced by a community that does not punish difference.

I am learning that there are different kinds of hauntings. There are the ghosts of the Sleepwalkers, the vermin-hunters, the thick-necked boys I thought were buried. And there are the other ghosts following you into the darkness, reminders that there were and are alternative communities.

From my earliest years, my strategy is to seek out alternatives, to cede the center and find solace somewhere else. My suburban school is the site of shaming, so I escape to Squirrel Hill. Mainstream ed-ucation is alienating, so I find Bennington. Masculinity is reduced and sold as blustering, self-centered, pseudo-toughness, so for a while I reject masculinity. Anti-intellectualism is rampant, so I make my home in the university, a place that does not count as "the real world." "Real Americans" are rural (apple-pie-baking, truck-riding, and gun-toting), so I must not be a real American; I must not be real at all. If I cede the center and stay put in my small corner of the country, they might leave me be.

But it is not enough. And it is no longer possible. Charlottesville reaches Eugene, Oregon. Each world acts upon the other.

There's something comforting and seductive about insular communities. It's terribly difficult to resist the temptation to retreat into our bubbles. Look at them, iridescent and gleaming! They are buoyant, floating high above the bleakness of the earth. And yet, it might be time for them to burst. They do not protect us sufficiently and they protect us excessively. We are not far away enough from those who would harm us and we are too distant and separate from potential friends.

It is a state of emergency.

He is an emperor-without-clothes except his red tie wagging as he struts through the streets; he is a small boy in his daddy's dinner jacket, a sun-king impersonator in a tanning bed; he is trapped in a gilded tower with nothing but burnt steak on offer; he is puffed up like a sick bird, a helium balloon baby flying over London; he is his most animated cartoon self before a rally, site of simulated love, where he gives his one-and-only speech about how they adore him; he has the best words and knows more than all the generals he wants to own and then fire; he deflates at the proof of a scant inauguration crowd; he cheers himself with the unparalleled pleasure of eye candy; he is a prisoner of his glory, barely perceiving that he's being pelted with egg in his pillory; he plays with rocket man, an action figure in his toy-chest and holds us hostage for his beaded curtain on the border; he is banging his fists on the ground at the check-out counter; he is an expert attention-getter, flanked by thugs; his authenticity is fake news. He is all this and he is a match near a gas leak.

This, they have done. But we are the deciders.

It is hard to focus from the bleachers of the carnival. But we cannot cede power to those who claim him. Trump-world corrupts our language, our culture, our planet. What choice do we have but to abandon our cocoons, and move into the uncomfortable space in the center? Not the center of the spectrum, but the center of power, the virtual polis, the place where the range of the acceptable is adjudicated. We must not imitate him. We can face him down by force of grit, because we are not wooden puppets; we know how to be real. If we are brave, we can occupy the center and the cruelty of the world can take the margins.

꙳

Dawn Marlan is a Senior Lecturer in Comparative Literature at the University of Oregon. She writes personal essays, novels, and cultural criticism. Her work has appeared in anthologies, literary journals, and national magazines including, *Lilith*, *The Evergreen Review*, *The Atticus Review*, *PMLA*, *Modernism/Modernity*, *The Chicago Review*, and *The Oregonian*.

Our Selves

From Reaping to Reckoning

By Reema Zaman

I am my own.

I run through these woods, cocooned in somber reflection. Known and seen only by the trees, my limbs pulse with hard-won agency. How sublime to be safe from the wet, hot suck of others. How luxurious to be preoccupied solely by a role and design I assign myself. At thirty-three, I feel the occasional ache in my knees and lower back. Three decades of committed motion can have that effect.

I meld well with the woods' palette. My color is that of my skin, the only hue I've ever desired. It defies name for I cannot be rooted in place. The most accurate description is:

I am my own.

When you are anything but Caucasian, you are frequently reminded of your difference, which ensures you cannot forget your alleged otherness. Otherness is the mechanism behind exoticism of any kind, but you only know otherness when it is pointed out to you, and, if you allow it, the pieces of you will become politicized. It is then your burden to regain authorship.

Fall delivers the uncanny; in the leaves, we witness both sunrise and sunset. We fall to our knees, humbled by majesty we can never replicate, only exalt. Like the trees through which I run, my skin shifts with the seasons. I move through honey to caramel to amber to toasted sesame. During my twenties, as a girl, as a fresh immigrant, as an actress, my skin existed only as extension, as determined by others: by their nearness, their gaze, their decree. *We're looking for someone lighter. You don't fit with the cast line-up.*

Such were the waking hours. Self-preservation demanded disassociation. The slicing of self to trade as commodity.

In the evenings, my skin was that which pleased, a landscape licked clean, and paradoxically in the process, dirtied. Him after him after him, each man burrowing with such fervor, furrowed brow, clenched jaw, knotted heart, foraging through my pieces, kidnapping any errant bit he could to spackle his jagged form. As if the harvest of my parts could complete him. Scrolling down and along the walls like the stock exchange sprinted my orphaned self.

What is the way forward when one's pieces are taken, rewritten, or threatened extinction by a person, a country, an ideal? How does one heal the reaping?

I run. I run fueled by a fire sourced and sustained from within, lit from a wick only I match. I run, remembering that in the deepest ink of night, the one thing we each can claim is sovereignty over our sense of self. I run and recover the taken, the misplaced, the surrendered. How I adore that word: recover. To retrieve, to unearth, to heal. Each day, I lay to rest what needs tender burial. Hopes that have been pierced. Losses that haunt. Characters I no longer need. Those I love but cannot have.

Today, I lay first to rest a miscarried daughter. With crystalline certainty, I know she looks identical to me, which is to say, identical to my mother. Ours is a fierce thread. Every feature emerges. Miscarry. How like Western medicine to invent such a word. Through a pert trio of syllables, it paints blame; it says a woman fails to handle, perform, correctly.

Beside her, I lay down another memory, one I thought was healed long ago, but it reemerges to hunt me. It is a memory of a night when, at age twenty-three, I was raped. My assault was swift. I was one of the luckier ones. My rapist was frugal with time, pain, and me. After his criminal acquisition, I sat in the dark, listing my options and weighing the cost of each. Back then, I was on my Optional Practical Training visa. If I accrued enough professional credits, I could, hopefully, obtain a green card.

To negotiate any legal retribution for rape is a brutal ordeal, for any woman, any nationality. The fine print of my immigrant status claimed I was—am not to be treated any differently than an American woman, but often, the fine print fails to inform reality. Similarly, the minutia behind immigration included nothing to suggest pressing charges against a rapist could compromise my status or my future application for permanent residency. But if my case landed in the wrong hands, say of that one deciding authority who found pleasure in turning the innocuous into injury, all my work would have been for nothing.

I had been working—and I continue to work—so hard to live in America. I loved and continue to love this country beyond words. I haven't a place in Bangladesh. But here in the United States, I can pursue the life I want, to be a voice for those without one.

Thus, after the rape, I decided I would not harm my chances for staying in the United States. The irony was acutely painful: I had to be quiet in order to be a voice for others later. The injury that hurt most was the fact that my silence would allow my rapist the wicked freedom to assault other women. The thought of hypothetical "others" branded me with guilt.

Today I am a permanent resident of the United of States of America. I am not a citizen but I will be soon. Today, November 8, 2016, I lay to rest, along with that memory from ten years ago, what happened last night, the howl of our collective anguish after the election of Donald Trump. I stand by an invisible tomb, feeling both alone yet tethered, tiny yet enormous. This latest loss feels significantly different. All around me, I feel the shimmering presence of brothers, sisters, siblings, as we mourn our tragedy and stand today in our connected conviction that we will bury and honor what needs rest, and then rise anew.

I breathe, swelling with a feeling of togetherness that is vast, sacred, and comforting. I close my eyes and reunite my fractured selves. I claim skin, limbs, lips, hair, identity, which are no longer things to alienate, demean, monetize, or consume. They are simply mine and part of a grander choice. I know now more than ever before that we either orphan or own our truth. Our disappointments and lashes can never fully mute us but rather, they are invitations to speak.

Fall reminds us that from decay, we grow. The grim truth behind loss is that with each one, we become better at coping. As we move through the passage of time, our wounds stack. It is not that the losses dull or lessen each other. Each blow is like that of a blacksmith's hammer, pummeling iron. Each hit fortifies our metal.

No group knows this better than women—we are privy to unique grief, singular hostility. Thus, forged in fire, we are all the more prepared and capable for leadership, resilience, grit. We know, despite and in the name of our many shocks, the few things we do have are paramount. We have autonomy over sense of self. We have the choice to persevere. We remain, as ever, voices for the stories and souls that have been silenced.

The darkening light alerts me. It says, *Sister, return home. Don't let yourself be caught by the shadows that roam.*

I run home, racing the setting sun. At the door, I turn to breathe in the fading light. Looking into the sky, I wonder of the things I cannot know. I cannot know and yet I do sense that tomorrow, voice after voice after voice will rise as a roar. I cannot know and yet I do feel that next year a riotous movement of women will swell, millions deep, chanting, *Me too.* I cannot know and yet I do see that in two years, my first book will be born. A memoir holding the wounds of years, their hard-won healing, my triumph over the past, a love letter to my kin. I cannot know and yet I do that upon its birth, all the losses of the past will have made sense. They will—I will—have transformed from pain into poetry and poetry into power.

Thus, as the fiery eye bids the day adieu, I decide: this is not our reaping, it is the beginning of the reckoning. Those who refuse to accept our value as women do not know and yet I do: our time has come. I know, for I am woman. I embody inherited wisdom from my mother and hers and hers. They remind me, *To speak is a revolution. It is time.*

I enter my home, shower, eat, write, read. I soothe my ache with the lullaby my inner voice has recited to me from the time I was a toddler: I love you. I am here. I am yours.

Before sleep arrives, I repeat again our song, adding a new refrain. I love you. I am here. I am yours. I am my own.

❧

Reema Zaman is an award-winning writer, speaker, actress, and author of the critically acclaimed memoir *I Am Yours*. *I Am Yours* has been adopted into the curriculum of several high schools through an Innovation Grant from the Oregon Department of Education. Reema's work has appeared in *Vogue*, *Ms.*, *The Guardian*, *Salon*, *Guernica*, *Longreads*, *Shape*, and elsewhere. She is the 2018 Oregon Literary Arts Writer of Color Fellow and is currently partnering with the International Rescue Committee and Girls Inc. to serve crucial causes and empower the next generation of leaders. Born in Bangladesh and raised in Thailand, she currently lives in Oregon. As the only Reema Zaman in the world, she is easy to find on social media. You can follow her on Instagram, Facebook, and Twitter and learn more at reemazaman.com.

New Normal

By Amy Roost

October 28, 2016

Yet another woman has accused Donald Trump of touching her inappropriately. He dismisses her as a "porn star" and says sarcastically, "Oh, I'm sure she's never been grabbed before." At a rally, Trump revels in the news that the FBI is reopening Hillary's private email server investigation. "I think this changes everything," he tells the jeering crowd, who shout "Lock her up! Lock her up!"

October 31, 2016

I spend the day readying the condo and burning off nervous energy in anticipation of my son's arrival. I place Post-it notes everywhere I can think of. The Post-it on the kitchen cupboard reads "bowls and plates." The drawer below is labeled "silverware." The toaster is simply "toaster." I roll up the throw rug in the entryway, afraid it might pose a tripping hazard. I hang a whiteboard and calendar in Spencer's old bedroom while awaiting delivery of the hospital bed, and then I remember the doctor's advice that Spencer should avoid alcohol while recovering from his strokes and subsequent brain surgeries. I empty the refrigerator of beer and wine so as not to present a temptation. While hiding it in the storage locker beneath the stairs, I decide that as an act of solidarity, I, too, will refrain from drinking.

A new normal is about to begin, one that is outside the protective womb of the hospital where I spent forty-eight out of fifty-six days at Spencer's bedside waiting, tending, and advocating. I'm relieved he's been discharged and also terrified to think that I'm about to assume the roles of doctor, nurse, and therapist, in addition to full-time cheerleader. I haven't yet managed to overcome the shocks to my body and psyche from his hospitalization, much less gather my own inner strength. How will I help him gather his?

I make pumpkin spice whoopie pies, a Halloween tradition in our family. Perhaps tasting these will jog Spencer's memory of Halloweens past. Like the year he was Buzz to brother Stuart's Woody. Or the time he sat patiently while I painted his face to look like Gene Simmons of the band Kiss. Maybe he'll be reminded of the annual pumpkin-carving parties we hosted in our driveway. Surely he'll recall the carving party that was canceled on the day we were evacuated ahead of the wildfires clawing their way toward our backyard.

My husband, Ain, arrives home from work, followed in short order by his daughter Lindsey and her two children. Matty is dressed as The Incredible Hulk. Baby Grace is a tiny pea-in-a-pod. I find an old T-shirt and write NASTY across it with a black Sharpie, don a witch's hat, and we all head out for a quick round of trick-or-treating prior to Spencer's arrival.

Finally, Spencer is home, along with Stuart—who has accompanied Spencer on the flight from Seattle. My two sons, one tall and athletic, the other short and brainy, have both survived multiple brain surgeries. They each grab a whoopie pie, plop down on the sofa good-naturedly, and compare the scars across their respective skulls to see whose is longer. Brain malformations—etiologies unknown and, according to doctors, unrelated—and near-death experiences have brought these two very different brothers closer.

My personal cheering squad, Ain and Lindsey, pull up chairs, and Matty and Grace—two sources of joy during what has been an otherwise joyless time—spread their candy out on the floor. I sit down for the first time all day, look around the room, and contentedly bite into my own pie.

November 1, 2016

I feel a sense of generalized anxiety coming on. Maybe it's my new normal. Or maybe it's the news that Hillary's lead in election polls is shrinking following the FBI's reopening of the email investigation. Plus, there are the reports from early voting sites that African-American turnout is down sixteen percent while white turnout is up fifteen percent. I watch pundits on CNN speculate as to the reason for this, given the Clintons' longstanding popularity among black voters.

One points to the "almost surgical" curtailment of early voting sites in predominantly black precincts. Another blames voter ID laws. A third speculates about the cumulative effect of social media attacks on Clinton. I pray that Hispanics, whose undocumented brethren Trump has maligned as "murderers" and "rapists," will bridge the gap come election day.

November 2, 2016

The director of the brain rehabilitation center calls to inform me that Spencer qualifies for their outpatient day program. The final hurdle is getting his health insurer to authorize the recommended treatment plan.

A United Health Care representative confirms over the phone that Spencer's coverage allows him only forty hours of rehab per calendar year. I explain how and why this is insufficient, and I can tell by her sympathetic tone of voice that she has done the math. She understands that forty hours translates to less than three weeks of rehab for Spencer, who is seen by three therapists a day. Meanwhile, the doctors are recommending six months—or over five hundred hours—of rehab if he's to have any chance of being a fully function-ing member of society again. I want to hang up on her but instead thank her for her time and move on to Plan B—finding Spencer a new healthcare plan for the upcoming year.

Meanwhile, the first hospital bill arrives in the mail. It covers only the first day of Spencer's care, which includes the air lift from Bell-ingham to Seattle and totals $10,270.

November 3, 2016

Trump is praised by members of the media for "disavowing" the support of the former KKK leader David Duke. Strange what passes for presidential material these days. The *Times* reports that Trump's income isn't what he says it is. The story is hard to follow. Which is, I suppose, why no one does.

He flies from rally to rally aboard his gold-plated jet, announcing to anyone who will listen how much the crowds adore him. This man-boy-who-would-be president has a seemingly bottomless need for attention.

I constantly check my newsfeed, hoping for something—anything—positive to mitigate my sense of impending doom. I'm buoyed by an article describing how narrow Trump's path to victory is; Hillary could lose Florida, North Carolina, and Ohio and still beat him.

November 5, 2016

Some mornings when I wake it takes a few seconds before I remember what happened, and how I arrived at the world I'm living in now. Once I do remember, I stare at the ceiling and resist getting out of bed. But I know that I must, because Spencer can't manage on his own. He might get so far as taking the eggs out of the refrigerator, but then forget why. I need to be there for him and so I rise.

I strain to read the fine print of the health insurance options the broker has emailed. After compiling a comparison matrix, I choose a plan for my twenty-two-year-old that comes with a $605 per month price tag. It's worth it because the new policy has no cap on rehab visits.

November 8, 2016 (Election Day)

Dear Donald Trump,

There are a few last things I'd like to say as voters show you the door that I hope hits you on the way out: You have been terrible for our country, and I look forward to healing from the wounds you've inflicted. You know that expression "You give [blank] a bad name."? Well, I don't know how you did it, but you somehow managed to give men, white people, Americans, New Yorkers, moguls, and douchebags a bad name. The bigger you lose tonight, the happier I'll be. You are a scab, a wart, a boil on our nation's tough hide, and I thank God the sensible people of this country will finally excise you.

November 9, 2016

For the second time in ten days, I'm faced with a new normal. Donald Trump is the president-elect.

While waiting for the coffee to brew, I glance at Facebook on my phone. The first thing I see are celebratory remarks about Trump's victory from a Christian fundamentalist high school friend who rarely posts to social media. Each post ends with the words "Praise be to God," as if God somehow ordained the election results. I unfriend her.

Next, I come across a comment by a friend of my stepson's, a white male millennial. It reads, "Apparently lots of women like having their pussies grabbed." I respond:

> Dear White Men,
>
> Seriously, for just one day, shut the fu*k up. Take some time to reflect, "bros," and have a good LONG look in the mirror. What have you done in your life to set women back? Or kept them from rising up? Have you, too, stereotyped women in your lifetime? Have you consciously or unconsciously objectified women and contributed to voters having such a low regard for women that they would elect a race-baiting, misogynistic, liar-to-be president?

Later in the morning, Stuart texts me photos of his college library where overnight someone spray-painted swastikas on the bathroom walls.

I can't take it. I also can't look away.

November 10, 2016

I listen to Trump's press conference on my way home from dropping Spencer at rehab. He mentions that he's considering keeping two provisions of the Affordable Care Act: the prohibition against insurers denying coverage because of a patient's preexisting condition, a provision both Stuart and Spencer will depend upon their entire lives; and the one that allows parents to keep their children on their insurance plans until they turn twenty-six, which currently applies to both my sons. Hearing that Trump will preserve the key components of Obamacare is a massive relief until a commentator points out that Trump's plan will never work. Without a mandate for everyone to purchase health insurance, the preexisting condition provision would send insurance companies into a death roll.

I've gone through life blithely assuming I could handle anything thrown my way. Now that I'm forced to prove it, I'm not sure I can.

My reserves are all used up. I just want someone to hug me. Hold my hand. Leave flowers on my doorstep. Bring me a hot roast beef sandwich with extra cheese or simply text me a funny cat video. I've suffered a crack or two or three, and I'm afraid I won't be able to hold myself together much longer.

Spencer, who knows nothing of my gossamer-thin nerves, arrives home depressed. Who can blame him? One day he's working his way toward a college degree in engineering, mountain biking and snowboarding on the weekends, and the next day he's using a walker and can't find his way to take out the trash. I suggest we go to the beach and let nature work its magic. As we amble north along the shoreline, mist settles on our matching curls, salt rims our lips, and the rhythm of the waves steadies our breathing. When the stars come out, we turn back for home, ready to once again face reality.

A dear friend calls to check up on me. I confide, "I'm barely hanging on." She, a recovering alcoholic, offers me some ironic and excellent advice. "It's okay for you to have a glass of wine. Spencer would want you to."

I cuddle with Ain, apologize for my recent testiness and for having triaged his needs into obscurity these past several months. He takes my hand, kisses it, and forgives me. I pour that glass of wine and savor it in small sips. Dinner consists of a warm baguette with a wedge of Brie cheese. I read for a while, a quiet novel by Wendell Berry, and then head to bed early, because I'm tired and because there is nothing noble or pretty about an exhausted martyr.

December 9, 2016

Trump picks a climate change denier to head the EPA; his nominee for labor secretary opposes minimum wage hikes; the incoming treasury secretary is a Goldman Sachs alumnus who is best known for aggressively foreclosing on home loans.

Meanwhile, speaking at a "victory rally," Trump stokes the flames of fear, calling the stabbing attack by a refugee at Ohio State University "yet one more tragic reminder that immigration security is now national security."

Elections have consequences.

December 13, 2016

I'm awakened from a fitful sleep by the supermoon's penetrating reflection off the ocean's surface. I stare at the spectacle outside my bedroom window and debate whether to wake Spencer to show him too. My mother's voice reasons, *He's exhausted from rehab. Let him sleep.* My cynic's voice asks, *He won't remember it, so why bother?* But my optimist's voice interrupts. *Whoa, Nelly! That's no way to think!* Resolved, I go downstairs and rouse him. Together, we watch from the living room balcony as the moon slides into the ocean's cradle. Satisfied and sleepy, we each return to our beds.

The next morning as Spencer stands at the stove turning the bacon, I ask, "Do you remember my waking you?"

After a pause he answers, "Yes."

"Do you remember why?"

He thinks for a moment longer before asking, "The moon?"

That's how we interact these days, going over events again and again, point by point, trying to trigger the memory. But the image of the supermoon setting has so imprinted itself on Spencer's healing brain he needs only the tiniest prompt to recall it. No matter how sluggish he is at rehab today, I feel vindicated for having wakened him early for some nature therapy.

December 15, 2016

I suspend a self-imposed news and Facebook diet just long enough to hear Trump dismiss as "ridiculous" claims by the U.S. intelligence agencies that Russia intervened in the election to help him win the White House. Also, Kanye West paid a visit to Trump Tower. I return to my diet.

December 23, 2016

Dear Spencer,

Happy Golden Birthday—twenty-three on the twenty-third!! I'm tempted to talk about how this year has sucked something awful for you and how I hope for a much better year ahead. Instead I want to talk about what a truly amazing year it has been. How the trauma you've endured has become the incubator for your greatest strengths. Because of your injury, you are more compassionate. You see people you would not have noticed before and consider another's circumstance with love rather than judgment.

You have learned that life occurs in the present moment. The experience of joy happens in the present moment. Your perception and experience of connection with something that is greater than yourself occurs in the present moment.

You've proven to yourself and others that you have the courage and the strength to overcome your injury and fight your way back. With that knowledge to draw upon, it is unlikely there will ever again be a challenge that you don't have the courage and strength to fight.

Having come so close to losing everything, you will now give up considering if a cup is half full or half empty and simply be thankful for having a cup to drink from. You understand that what matters most is people, not things. You understand that the right perspective makes the impossible possible. You learned that the try is everything. The try is you saying to your brain, Hey, I value this connection and I want it to happen. You may have to try, try, and try again with no results for a thousand times before you get even an inkling of a result but you know that if you don't try, it may never happen.

Most importantly, you understand what I knew the instant I held you in my arms twenty-three years ago today: that life is a gift to be cherished. And you, Spencer, are a gift to so many who have watched on this past year, teaching us all through your actions, your spirit, your will, and your grit what this spin on the big blue marble is all about.

You are my hero, my teacher, my friend, my son.

Love, Mom

January 6, 2017

The director of National Intelligence releases a declassified report that concludes Russia interfered in the 2016 election. Trump responds to the findings on Twitter maintaining that Russian interference did not affect the election result, and claiming he has "nothing to do with Russia."

61

January 24, 2017

At a family conference today with Spencer's care team, we all agree that Spencer's affect is improving and he's more self-aware, especially of how long this dang recovery process is taking. The most difficult moment of the meeting is hearing the case manager say the words I've been defending against for months: "Spencer probably won't ever be the same." In other words, Spencer 2.0 is here to stay. It's a struggle letting go of the old Spencer and accepting the new. Part of me is not ready to let go, because I haven't finished grieving. Another part of me recognizes the need to move into the present and deal with what is.

Later, when I pick Spencer up at rehab, I ask, as I do every day on our drive home, "What did you have for lunch today?"

"Chicken tenders and a cookie," he answers.

I pull the car over to the curb and begin to cry.

"What's wrong, Mom?"

"Today is the first day you've been able to answer that question."

Spencer breaks into a crooked smile. "Well, there is that," he says. "Even if we do have Donald Trump for president."

৵

Amy Roost is a documentary podcaster and freelance journalist. She is an Annenberg School of Journalism 2019 California Health Journalism Fellow and recipient of numerous journalism awards for her op-ed columns appearing in *San Diego Union Tribune* publications. Her forthcoming memoir is based on a 2017 Snap Judgment podcast she wrote and produced about how she replaced a black child that her parents adopted and later returned in 1962.

THE PARALLELS BETWEEN SOCIAL MEDIA AND PTSD IN THE AGE OF TRUMP

By Michele Sharpe

Survivors of family and intimate partner violence adopt many strategies for self-preservation, both with and without conscious intent. Two strategies I have adopted in the past were numbing myself with alcohol and drugs, which was not very effective, and volunteering with battered women's service organizations, which both educated and healed me.

In the 1970s, following my escape from violence at the hands of my adoptive parents and, later, my high school boyfriend, I worked to prevent future abuse by closely monitoring cues, like the heaviness of a footfall or the tone of a voice.

Back then, I didn't know I was suffering from PTSD, a diagnosis that didn't enter the *Diagnostic and Statistical Manual of Mental Disorders* until 1980[1] and wasn't applied to survivors of child abuse and intimate partner violence (IPV) until the 1990s.[2] Today, I recognize my earlier responses as "hypervigilance,"[3] a common symptom of PTSD that's described as the "experience of being constantly tense and 'on guard,'" acting "on high alert in order to be certain danger is not near."[4]

Hypervigilance wasn't the only trauma symptom I experienced.

[1] M.A. Crocq & L. Crocq. "From shell shock and war neurosis to posttraumatic stress disorder: a history of psychotraumatology." *Dialogues in clinical neuroscience* 2, no. 1(2000): 47-55.

[2] J.P. Wilson "The Historical Evolution of PTSD Diagnostic Criteria." in *Psychotraumatology: The Springer Series on Stress and Coping*, ed. G.S. Everly and J.M. Lating (Boston, MA: Springer, 1995).

[3] T. Mignone, E. Papagni, M. Mahadeo, K. Klostermann and R.A. Jones. "PTSD and Intimate Partner Violence: Clinical Considerations and Treatment Options." *J Addict Med Ther Sci* 3, no. 1 (2017): 001-006. DOI: 10.17352/2455-3484.000018

[4] PTSDUK. "What is PTSD Hypervigilance?" (Accessed January 12, 2018. https://www.ptsduk.org/what-is-ptsd-hypervigilance)

I also endured recurring nightmares, intense anger, and startle responses to movements near my head, but hypervigilance is the one I've been thinking about a lot lately, especially in the context of our current political climate.

It's not a stretch to say Trump behaves similarly to abusers. Many characteristics of batterers—grandiosity, alignment with traditional gender roles, using sex as an act of aggression, blaming others for their actions, denying or minimizing their own bad behavior, losing their tempers explosively, insisting on control[5]—aptly apply to the leader of the free world.

In turn, I've seen many people respond to Trump—and, for that matter, to other politicians acting in abusive ways—with the same kind of alertness I adopted while experiencing PTSD as a survivor of abuse. Only now, instead of taking place in real life (IRL), this hypervigilance plays out on social media.

As the 2016 American presidential election drew near, my relationship to social media intensified. I checked multiple feeds for news each morning and again each night. Every new misogynist revelation, every new racist pronouncement, left me enraged or numb. I felt fearful. I joined secret Facebook groups for survivors of domestic violence, where I read other women's posts about being triggered by political rhetoric and disclosures of abusive behavior. My morning writing practice fizzled out in favor of huddling under the quilts with my phone, tapping at apps that kept me informed. My obsessive social-media-and-news-outlet-checking persisted after the election. After the inauguration, I kept checking with renewed diligence, even flushing spare minutes at my day job down the Twitter wormhole.

While trying to check the *New York Times* on my phone and simultaneously walk my dogs, I'd tripped over a tree root, so in March of 2017, knowing my behavior was unhealthy, I resolved to keep at least my time outdoors screen free.

My compulsive checking had reached a level that felt familiar. I

---

[5] "Rape and Abuse Crisis Centers. Common Characteristics of Batterers." Accessed January 12, 2019. https://www.wbur.org/commonhealth/2017/03/10/psychologist-not-post-election-stress-disorder

was behaving the same way I had as a child in an abusive home and later as a teenager in an abusive intimate relationship. I walked on eggshells. I stayed alert to mood changes in the abusers. I exercised hypervigilance. Back then, I had hung onto the fantasy that if I could predict violence, I could prevent the next black eye, broken nose, split lip. Now, I was on alert for all the ways the government planned to abuse me and other women.

I published a short blog post, and later a poem, about the parallels between intimate personal violence and the politically induced terror in my [non]writing life. Women responded to the two pieces (many more than I'd expected), saying something along the lines of, "Yes, me too."

One woman, a survivor of extreme violence, wrote that she "understood instantly that having an openly avowed abuser elected to the presidency would give license to the closeted abusers everywhere." Afraid to leave her house after the election, she relied on social media for support from women who were expressing similar fears, and as a safe place where she could monitor political developments. Today, she uses social media to stay connected with allies and to keep tabs on political bullies and their agendas. "I would not say that the terror has abated," she wrote to me in May of 2017, "but that I have come to live with it, as I did in childhood."

Psychologists started talking about "Post-Election Stress Disorder" (PESD) soon after the 2016 Republican victory. Some argued that "creating a diagnosis based on an opportunistic situation" didn't make sense.[6] Others argued that women and other marginalized groups were already more likely to be victims of trauma than white men, and so a "collective fight-or-flight response is a reflection of all that has in fact happened and reflects for many a legitimate fear of what might happen."[7] Debate ensued over whether PESD trivialized the high-fatality experiences of "combat veterans," but the term

---

[6] Carrie Goldberg. "Psychologist: No, It's Not Post-Election Stress 'Disorder.'" wbur.org. https://www.wbur.org/commonhealth/2017/03/10/psychologist -not-post-election-stress-disorder

[7] Jennifer Sweeton. "Post-Election Stress Disorder in Women." *Psychology Today*. Accessed January 12, 2019. https://www.psychologytoday.com/us/blog/workings -well-being/201611/post-election-stress-disorder-in-women

was possibly associated with at least one death. Jeff Gillenkirk, who wrote an AlterNet article titled "The New PTSD: Post-Trump Stress Disorder," suffered a fatal heart attack two days after his article was published.[8] In the AlterNet piece, he'd diagnosed himself with post-election anxiety.

Can postelection anxiety end for anyone when the president, an openly avowed abuser and white supremacist supporter, keeps the hits coming as fast as he has in his first years in power? When the policies he promotes attack the health and safety of citizens? When he continues to deny or minimize his own bad behavior, lose his temper explosively, and insist on control like so many abusive men?

Abusers and batterers can snap at any moment, which is perhaps the cause of hypervigilance among survivors. Karen Sheets, a social worker who teaches life skills in a Displaced Homemaker Program in Florida, calls it "crisis mode." Her program frequently serves women escaping violence and collaborates closely with the local domestic violence agency. Sheets, herself an IPV survivor, says that women can become addicted to crisis and continue to act in crisis mode long after the abusive situation is behind them.

Long-term changes in both neurochemistry and the structure of the brain are linked to changes in how individuals handle stress;[9] for IPV survivors, triggers often take the form of reminders of a batterer's violence, intimidation, and control. In fact, to better understand PTSD brain function, researchers expose IPV survivors to trauma-relevant negative words and images, and then track their brains' responses in functional MRI scans. Traumatic reminders can literally trigger a cascade of biochemical stressors, in addition to creating changes in the size of different areas of the brain, especially in the amygdala, where fear resides.

Living on high alert as a PTSD sufferer can be exhausting, but hypervigilance can also make survivors more alert and function as an adaptive strategy, helping people to better handle decision-making

[8] "AlterNet Writer, Novelist and Trump Critic Jeff Gillenkirk Dies of Heart Attack." *Alternet.* Accessed January 12, 2019. https://www.alternet.org/2016/11/alternet-writer-novelist-and-trump-critic-jeff-gillenkirk-dies-heart-attack

[9] Bremner J. D. "Traumatic stress: effects on the brain." *Dialogues in clinical neuroscience* 8, no. 4 (2006): 445-61.

under stress and avoid future abuse.[10] At least that's what I tell myself. While IPV is often unpredictably explosive, institutionalized violence against American women, like institutionalized violence against African-Americans,[11] is the result of policies and ideas that have evolved over years. I need to monitor any development, alteration, or affirmation of these policies and ideas by my government, so I can make decisions under stress and avoid abuse.

And no vehicle is better suited to survivors of violence who are in political hypervigilance mode than social media, the twenty-four/seven panopticon. In the role of watcher we can monitor threats, and, at a safe distance, we can do it obsessively. And sometimes, this heightened alertness can manifest as tangible action.

During the summer of 2017, for instance, the social media hypervigilance of millions of Americans played a key role in thwarting GOP efforts to repeal the Affordable Care Act. It's too soon to quantify social media's role in keeping citizens informed and in giving citizens platforms to exert pressure on officials. However, the proliferation and popularity of voter-action sites like "5 Calls" and "Indivisible" since the 2016 election demonstrates the existence of a demand for ways to use social media to both monitor danger and take action.

The Pew Research Center, in a study released in October 2016, found that the majority of respondents believed social media helped users get involved with issues that matter to them.[12] Meanwhile, the anecdotal evidence is on your social media feeds and mine. Social media allowed me to track the status of proposed anti-ACA legislation, it gave me access to inspiration through posts from ADAPT members, and it gave me more ways to contact elected officials and

[10] Lindsay Fulham, Angela S. Book, Julie Blais, Mary B. Ritchie, Nathalie Y. Gauthier, and Kimberly Costello. "The Effect of Hypervigilance on the Relationship Between Sexual Victimization and Gait." *Journal of Interpersonal Violence* (June 2017). doi:10.1177/0886260517713714.

[11] Ibram X. Kendi. "Racist Ideas Are Spread by the Powerful to Support Racist Policies." *Newsweek* (October 2017). Accessed January 12, 2019. https://www. newsweek.com/racist-ideas-spread-powerful-support-racist-policies-553330

[12] Anderson, Monica. "Social media causes some users to rethink their views on an issue." (November 7, 2016), Accessed January 12, 2019. http://www.pewresearch. org/fact-tank/2016/11/07/social-media-causes-some-users-to-rethink-their -views-on-an-issue

make my voice heard. It gave that to me and millions of others.

We're not social media addicts—we're hyper-vigilantes who aim to enforce the principles of democracy.

In my nightmares, and in my obsessive following of both progressive and conservative social media feeds, I'm re-living the terror and anxiety of my teenage years on a macro level. America has long been awash in racist and misogynist violence. The recent election has validated and normalized that violence. Our government seeks to put the health and safety of the majority of Americans at risk: women, immigrants, gay, lesbian, and trans people, people with disabilities, people living in poverty, and anyone who doesn't look white. It's much too much like the not-so-old days, when men were legally entitled to rape and beat their wives, when parents could abuse their children with impunity, when communities and governments sanctioned such behavior and excused it as "private family business."

In the face of all this, I have mixed feelings about whether to stop my relentless checking of Facebook, the *Washington Post*, the *New York Times*, or Charles M. Blow's Twitter feed. Walking on eggshells doesn't guarantee that the sleeping monster won't wake up. Checking the news twenty times a day won't, by itself, prevent the next police shooting of an unarmed black teenager, or violence against immigrants, or the abrogation of women's control over their own bodies. But don't all those stories need to be told and re-told and read and heard and analyzed? After all, if I hadn't been checking, I might have missed Paul Ryan's response to Kevin McCarthy's assertion that Putin pays Trump: "No leaks, all right? This is how we know we're a real family here," said Ryan. "What's said in the family stays in the family."[13]

That sounds a lot like the twentieth century rhetoric of abuse that enabled and excused paternalistic violence against women and

[13] Entous, Adam. "House majority leader to colleagues in 2016: 'I think Putin pays Trump.'" (May 17, 2017) Accessed January 12, 2019. https://www.washingtonpost.com/world/national-security/house-majority-leader-to-colleagues-in-2016-i-think-putin-pays-trump/2017/05/17/515f6f8a-3aff-11e7-8854-21f359183e8c_story.html?utm_term=.6dbe43122753

children. The victim in me wants to say those days are over. But the watcher in me says pay attention. To everything. Every single word.

❧

Michele Sharpe, a poet and essayist, is also a high school dropout, hepatitis C survivor, adoptee, and former trial attorney. Her essays appear in venues including *The Washington Post*, *Poets & Writers*, and *Guernica*. Recent poems can be found in *Poet Lore*, *North American Review*, *Stirring*, and *Baltimore Review*.

HOPE AFTER TRUMP

By Kerry Neville

Five years ago, I sat across from my outpatient psychiatrist, an impassive, impersonal diagnostic dictator. Between us, on his desk, sat a thick stack of my files—a monolithic, supposedly definitive summary of my case history: anorexic, alcoholic, self-injuring chronic patient with escalating bipolar disorder, hospitalized more than twenty times, with long stints in inpatient programs (meant to save me from myself). His finger tapped the keyboard and his eyes scanned the computer screen. "There's nothing more I can do for you. You're a hopeless case," he said.

This was not the first time I'd been told this. My frustrated therapist of ten years had frequently pronounced, "You are the most hopeless patient I have ever worked with." Hopeless, not as in *he* believed that I was hopeless and would eventually die by suicide (unethical then to take my cash), but that *I* believed myself to be hopeless and destined to die by suicide. He said this in kindness, with both concern and intimate knowledge; and he was right. Truly, I believed this: I'd attempted suicide several times over the years, sometimes half-heartedly (jumping into a frozen lake while drunk in the middle of campus; cutting my arms deeper and deeper, daring the passive slip of the razor) and sometimes with full intent (seventeen shots of vodka in fifteen minutes and waking in the ICU with a blood alcohol level of .39; overdosing on my meds and waking in the ICU in four-point restraints; and the slow, deliberate death by starvation). Always, I returned to the world with regret rather than gratitude.

Hopelessness, contrary to common understanding, is characterized not by passive inertia, but by agitated despair. You work toward your own annihilation, though it is based not in nihilism, but rather in the persistent agony of wanting to hope again but daring not. The novelist George Eliot once wrote, "What we call our despair is often only the eagerness of unfed hope." How does one live between expectation and decimation, over and over and over again? Despair convinces us not to dare anymore but to yield to bleak desperation; and, for me, it becomes easier, really, to cut myself and my ties with the world.

And so, I set out to wreck myself. Why hope when I had an unremitting, unrelenting mental illness, careening between mania and depression? Hopelessness cut into my arms again and again, scars upon scars: *This is your end*, they said to me each day as I stood in the shower looking at the cross-hatchings; as I hid them under long sleeves, concealing my hopelessness and suicidal determination like you might a secret, wildly passionate love affair. *My pain, my pain, my pain, my despair, my despair, my despair. Mine mine mine. Not yours to see.*

But that afternoon, sitting across from that psychiatrist—who was so sure that I was going to kill myself (maybe not that day or that week or that year), so sure that I was no longer worth believing in, no longer worth imagining a future for—I pushed back my sleeves, and for the first time looked with self-compassion at the scars on my arms. Examining the angry red weals, I understood that all of it—the starvation, the drinking, the cutting, the suicide attempts—was only my failed effort to deny hope's tenuous hold on me, and its wobbly promise: *Maybe, but only maybe. Can you live with that? Despair as the eagerness of unfed hope?*

Threaded through my bruised and battered and frayed heart was the hope that maybe wanting, desiring, moving, acting, speaking, writing, loving again was worth the battering. That despair did not mean I had to die, but in fact, the reverse: I had to keep living, hoping for moments of joy and purpose which, while ephemeral, offered ecstatic flight. Emily Dickinson instructs, "Hope is a thing with feathers." We are fragile but capable of aeronautical miracles. Hope is tied to Edmund Burke's understanding of a moral imagination: we must embrace the duties and ethical obligations of endurance because we are sacramentally connected to each other.

Hopelessness severs connection, forces us into retreat: I have no hope for the world or have no hope for us or have no hope for myself and therefore I can retreat, take my leave. To believe that I must stay alive and endure and continue to hope and act—yes, here is the crux, *to act* on these hopes again and again, despite dashed hopes—is to strengthen my holy connection to you by which I am obliged to secure my future to yours and yours to mine. Hope restores us to each other. Hope asks us to live in truth with each other. Hope asks us to entangle our lives, over and over, in joy and in pain, in promise and in disappointment, with each other. Hope is no superficial undertaking but demands absolute allegiance even in apocalyptic times; times like these, when so many of us feel hopeless, despairing of this unjust and intolerant regime marching across a country founded in the hope of who we can be together—a just, tolerant, and democratic We the People.

Hope demands allegiance even when the psychiatrist who has defined your future sits so smug in his surety that he well knows your end. This is when we must gather up the threads in our hearts regardless of any final, though always premature, diagnoses; because that psychiatrist didn't know shit about me and my heart. I looked down at my arms and then back at him. "Fuck you," I said, and walked out. I never cut into myself again, never hid my scars again, and never believed that I should die again (well, not for any sustained length of bleak time). My sleeves, pushed back now, say: *Look at me, world.* This record of scars, of my despair, is not my end but my beginning, reminding me to risk flight, reminding me of my social contract, my sacramental connection to you in this world. If I risk flight, you might, too. Gravity is a force that draws two objects together. My body and the earth. Me to you. Some birds fall into flight, leaping from branches and cliffs, to what must seem sure death, and yet: wings and feathers. As Burke wrote, the moral imagination, necessary for enduring the chaos of despair, is "what the heart owns and understanding ratifies." We cannot be parsimonious, miserly in our hope, but must risk lavish flight together.

Kerry Neville is the author of two books of fiction, *Remember to Forget Me* and *Necessary Lies*. She is an Assistant Professor in the Creative Writing Program at Georgia College and State University, and was recently a Fulbright Teaching Fellow at the University of Limerick, in Ireland.

Panic Drapes the Look of the World: Literary Treatment for Anxiety in an Uncertain Age

By Emily Sinclair

June, 2016

I was having a panic attack while I walked the dog after dinner. Children rode skateboards and scooters in that last yellowed hour before bedtime. I felt unreal to myself, and the Denver streets I'd known my whole adult life seemed false and imitative. I felt a numbing and a derealization that left me somewhat incapable of speaking to other people, as if I were vocally paralyzed, as if some essential fluid in my body had evaporated. It was hard to believe that people lived in the houses we passed; instead, the houses seemed part of an elaborate ruse of which I had not been informed. When we encountered other dogs, my dog—who, at eight pounds and ten years old, was somewhat arthritic and embittered—lunged and snarled at them. A mother and two small children riding scooters stopped. The mother said, "That's a terrier," and her voice was firm, but her smile betrayed an uncertainty. So I said, "Yes." Her son, who wore a helmet that made his head approximately as wide as he was tall, said, "A Western terrier."

A Western terrier. I liked that. Like a Plains Indian. As if, in frontier days, the hills of Colorado had been populated with wild terriers, and I, her owner, was by proxy Western. Here we were, the dog and I, Western, like cactus or paint horses or coyotes. I smiled broadly at her, and then, located, I whispered the word to myself as we turned north toward the park and then home. *Western. We are Western.*

This was the shape of my panic: I looked fine on the outside. I did not experience heart palpitations, shortness of breath, chest pain, sweating, or nausea. It was less an attack than a physics problem; the world had become suspect and false, a stage set meant to look like a neighborhood, even as I recognized the irrationality of that thought.

After the dog and I got home, I got on the Internet and clicked around aimlessly. Hillary, Bernie, Trump. Gun control, politics, filibustering. A new word specifically for Latino/a queers. Images of women being burned in cages. The Orlando night club shooting was the largest massacre in American history, if you don't count what happened to the Native Americans at Sand Creek. The problem did not seem to be with me; there seemed to be a problem with the world. Or perhaps the problem is that we do not agree on what counts and what does not.

As the summer and fall of 2016 wore on, the panic attacks continued. I began to wonder if they were medical and psychological—as I had always understood the causes of panic—or if they were a rational response to the radically altered world in which I found myself.

Often when I travel outside the United States, people don't think I'm American, even though this is the only country in which I've ever lived. Most of the time, I'm mistaken for being English, Dutch, or German, most likely because my hair and skin are light and my eyes blue. I sometimes find it embarrassing to be an American, as was the occasion in Mexico, watching my fellow countrymen and women treat Mexico and its citizens like nothing more than a playground for a cheap drunk and a source of racist jokes. Other times—for example, when I see French tourists, who seem to have a deep love affair with Western cowboy and girl mythology, driving huge RVs through my state, gawking at its natural beauty—I'm proud to bursting. This is my country, I think, this raw and difficult terrain and the people who have made lives here.

When I come home from traveling, I am grateful for an odd assortment of things that I usually take for granted: clean streets, the extraordinary free services of my local library, the safety of my food, working stoplights, the presumption of innocence, a free press. These things serve for me as evidence of American ideals, even though in practice, our ideals are imperfectly realized, which is unsurprising given our history. Thomas Jefferson, while publicly opposed to slavery, enslaved more than one hundred people, including

Sally Hemmings, with whom he would have unacknowledged children from her early adolescence onward. Jefferson, for me, stands as the perfect metaphor for this country's beliefs—while his beliefs sound ethical and just, his practice was not. I have always felt that our job, as citizens, was to move our laws and practices closer to our beliefs. Despite inevitable policy disagreements with my fellow citizens, I thought we all shared an understanding of the beliefs upon which this country was founded—in particular, the Jeffersonian notions that democracy is made of common folk, not aristocrats, that the Bill of Rights is sacrosanct, and that the rule of law and the freedom of speech and press mattered. To be an American meant we mostly agreed on the what, but perhaps not on the how. That was okay: our national conversation would be ongoing, I thought. And while I know the devil is in the details, I believed in the long arc toward justice. I have always held some cloudy belief that we as a country would move closer and closer to what our historic documents said we aspired to be.

Hold my beer, said 2016.

To understand the political present and what now seemed like childish optimism, I returned to a work that had formed some of my worldview as a young woman.

The Outsider by **Richard Wright**

The African-American writer Richard Wright's final novel, *The Outsider*, was published in 1953. Wright was born in 1908, near Natchez, Mississippi, and although he was a gifted student, Wright had to leave school and move to Memphis to earn a living for his family. After Memphis, Wright left the South for New York, then Chicago. He sought to not only escape the racism of the South, but to be among like-minded thinkers and activists, whom he'd hoped to find within the Communist Party. Yet his time in New York and Chicago, as well as his involvement in the Communist Party, left him with a profound sense of rejection when their ideals clashed. In his autobiography of his childhood, *Black Boy*, he wrote, "I had fled men who did not like the color of my skin, and now I was among men who did not like the tone of my thoughts."[1] Wright wrote *The Outsider* in Paris, where he moved in 1946 and become a French citizen.

The Outsider is the story of Cross Damon, a man confronted with the problem of free will—at its simplest, that individuals make choices—while living within oppressive systems that appear to arbitrarily grant and deny that same freedom. It's a long, difficult book—difficult because of its bleakness and its occasionally turgid sentences—but it is also a book remarkable in its descriptions of internal, physical experiences of external circumstances. What results is a perspective of a man who cannot trust what he knows to be true or believe what he sees:

> One walks along a street and strays unknowingly from one's path; one then looks up suddenly for those familiar landmarks of orientation, and, seeing none, feels lost. Panic drapes the look of the world in strangeness, and the more one stares blankly at that world, the stranger it looks, the more hideously frightening it seems. There is then born in one a wild, hot wish to project out upon that alien world the world that one is seeking. This wish is a hunger for power, to be in command of one's self.[2]

Damon is African-American (Wright uses the term *Negro*). He is married but estranged from his wife who refuses to give him a divorce. At the same time, he has a sexual relationship with a young woman; although he tried to confirm that she was of age, when she becomes pregnant, he learns that she is fifteen years old. In despair because his attempt to do right has failed, Damon starts a new life under an assumed name after a train wreck in which he is presumed dead. Yet his new life is characterized by the same problems: women, 'crooks', and his own violent responses. These problems, Damon begins to understand, are internal, not external.

Raised by a deeply religious mother who issued relentless prohibitions against sexual pleasure, Damon feels overwhelmed and helpless

---

[1] Wright, Richard. *Black Boy (American Hunger), The Outsider.* (New York: American Library, 1991), 352.

[2] Ibid., 526.

in the presence of women's bodies. For him, women are objects in an internal struggle ("Deepening need of desire for the desirable: woman as a body of a woman") but his insight doesn't leave him any more capable of resisting or managing those desires.[3] Desire is the root of Damon's frailty.

His adolescent fantasies had symbolically telescoped God into an awful face, shaped in the form of a huge and crushing NO; a terrifying face which had, for a reason he could never learn, created him, had given him a part of himself, and yet had threateningly demanded that he vigilantly deny another part of himself which God, too, had paradoxically given him.

Damon's existential crisis of free will is this: how do we live in a world in which God has given us desire and yet condemns us as sinners for acting on it? Put another way, Wright's subject is What happens when what we see in front of us and know to be true is denied? In this way, Wright's work became something of a north star for me in this time of existential panic.

From "Here are the images that show Obama's inauguration crowd was bigger than Trump's," in the *Washington Post*, March 7, 2017, by Lisa Rein:[4]

> The [Park Service] images are the official record of the federal government—and they contradict Trump's claim that more than 1.5 million supporters crowded onto the Mall to watch him take the oath of office. Photos taken by news outlets during the inauguration also showed a crowd size smaller than Obama's during his first inauguration in 2009—about two-thirds smaller, according to several estimates by experts.

The *Washington Post* and other news outlets sought the official images after Trump boasted of his inauguration crowd size and his press secretary Sean Spicer accused the media of doctoring photographs to show angles with small numbers of attendees. Spicer also called Trump's inauguration "the most viewed in history."

[3] Ibid., 393.
[4] Lisa Rein, "Here are the images that show Obama's inauguration crows was bigger than Trump's," *The Washington Post*, March 7, 2017.

The specific name for the kind of anxiety I experienced in 2016 is called *derealization*, often described as a sense that a person sees the world as being false, or as if through a window. Generally speaking, derealization is fairly common and not of great concern unless it begins interfering with one's life, unless, for example, I begin to act as if the world is not real. Derealization is distinct from depersonalization, in which a person feels that she herself is not real, a more concerning feeling, often associated with more serious psychiatric conditions, like schizophrenia. In my case, when I am in the middle of an episode, I know that the apparent fakeness of the houses on my street is in itself fake. And so I carry on, outwardly normal, but inwardly suspicious that the world I believe is real is not.

Wright's friend and contemporary was the French writer and philosopher Jean-Paul Sartre. In those post-war years, Sartre, Wright, and Simone de Beauvoir spent time together in Paris, talking about the state of the world, existentialism, and literature. For Sartre, the story from which we cannot escape is encapsulated in his ideas of bad faith, or *mauvaise foi*, a phrase which means one is acting in accordance with a predetermined role. That is to say, one inhabits the attitudes and expectations of one's role—a waiter, a housekeeper, and so on—so that one's choices are erased because, to put it in English-teacher-speak, the form has determined the content. If one is a waiter, one must feel and choose in the predictable ways of a waiter. There are no real choices, and our lives, which are meaningless, are based on our living out bad faith, on our acquiescing to expectations outside us, rather than the desires inside us. We do not become because we have been made, and we are complicit.

The year after Sartre's first novel *Nausea* was published (1938), Sartre was drafted into the French army as a meteorologist, and a year later, in 1940, the Germans marched into Paris. He was later imprisoned by the Germans and then released, owing to his health issues. In 1944, a translation of his short essay "Paris Alive: The Republic of Silence" appeared in the *Atlantic Monthly*, with this paradoxical view of freedom:

Never were we freer than under the German occupation. We had lost all our rights, and first of all our right to speak. They insulted us to our faces every day—and we had to hold our tongues. They deported us *en masse*—as workers, as Jews, as political prisoners. Everywhere—upon the walls, in the press, on the screen—we found that filthy and insipid image of ourselves which the oppressor wished to present to us. And because of all this, we were free. The more Nazi venom crept into our thoughts the more each precise thought became a conquest.[5]

In early 2017, I repeated these lines to myself again and again— "Never were we freer than under the German occupation"—in hopes of feeling this freedom, but it did not work, and the days of late winter and early spring were characterized by dread.

I first encountered Richard Wright my sophomore year in high school when our assigned reading of his autobiography, *Black Boy*, coincided with parent visiting day. During class, we read sections aloud, and beside me, I felt my mother tense like a leopard.

"Of what lit-er-ary value is this book to these girls?" she said to the teacher while my gut roiled and I whispered "Shut up" to her.

I was not surprised by her reaction. I had listened to her tell the women of color who worked in our home how stupid and lazy they were. I hid on the stairs, listening, frightened and sick. She'd snap off the TV when I watched *Laverne & Shirley*, saying, "That show just glorifies the working class." She felt the same way about *Happy Days*, so I didn't watch Fonzie either. From her, I learned that racism isn't only about race; instead, I came to see racism as one part of a worldview based on one's supposed superiority in all areas and that allows for cruelties both petty and grand in scale. However small a thing, I felt the injustice of not being able to watch shows like all the other kids, as well as the sting of her temper and rages, and I felt myself on the side of everyone she belittled. The result of her criticism of *Black Boy* was that I understood it to be true.

[5] Jean Paul Sartre. "Paris Alive: The Republic of Silence," *The Atlantic Monthly*, December, 1944, 39-40.

All these years later, what my mother feared has come to pass: that I would take the words of an African-American man over hers in constructing my worldview; that I would turn to his work to find language for how I feel now.

A few years ago, I was diagnosed with celiac sprue, an auto-immune disease. About six weeks after the diagnosis, when the intestinal villi (described in medical literature as *small finger-like projections*) ought to have begun healing, I stopped sleeping. I began to worry about the upcoming Christmas holiday, about whether I had enough presents for my children and step-children. Then I worried about whether we had enough towels for our house guests and I bought more towels, for which we did not have room. Then, I fretted about how overstuffed the closet was. The whole thing came to a head with the dog groomer, who asked, "Do you want the dog groomed on Wednesday afternoon or Thursday morning?" I felt that there were permutations and problems with any choice I made: I felt the inescapability of all my choices.

I went to a therapist and asked him for medication. I had taken one of my brother-in-law's tranquilizers which left me tired but still aware of the false nature of the world in which I lived. The therapist sat in a chair that looked to me to be excessively ergonomic. It appeared to have adjustments at the low- and mid-back as well as a footrest. He began to talk about what he called a major task of mid-life: the acceptance of one's eventual death. I wondered if the tilt of his pelvis indicated back pain, and if so, if he'd had surgery or if he was the sort of person to do yoga. He had watercolors of birds on the wall and books of poetry on his bookshelves. Once, I asked him if he was a birder. No, he explained, it's just that they're professionally dull with a low associational quotient. I did not ask about the poetry.

He said, "Your problem is not in your biochemistry. It's in your thinking. It's about the meaning of life and death. You have come to the land of never. You will never eat another baguette. You will also not have more children. You will never be twenty-five again, trying to live as an artist in New York. You have made choices that you cannot undo."

I stared at the therapist, who had a habit of laying one index finger across his top lip. The facts of my life were in conflict with the way I imagined life to be. Who cannot eat bread? What sort of a person cannot have shredded wheat for breakfast or pizza for dinner? But this panic was personal, not political.

Sometimes I still, all these years later, stand in the grocery store among the loaves and rolls, shocked. *Bread? Really?*

Wright's work explores the point of origin for Damon's sense of dislocation: is it simply a matter of circumstance? Can you change your life by changing where you live it? Wright seems to think not. When Damon escapes after the train wreck, he remains powerless.

He had reckoned that his getting rid of the claims of others would have automatically opened up to him what he wanted, but it had merely launched him to live in the empty possibility of action whose spell, by purging reality of its aliveness, had bound him more securely in foolish drifting than he had experienced in the past. The world became distant, opaque: he was not related to it and could find no way of becoming so. It was this static dreamworld that had elicited from him those acts of compulsion, those futile attempts to coerce reality to his emotional demands.[6]

Freedom is not, Wright suggests, simply a matter of escaping the expectations of others. Existential crisis is precipitated by the self when that self merely perpetuates 'empty possibilities' in the form of actions that don't matter. The result? The false dreamworld in which we try, again and again, to make reality what we want it to be. This strikes me as a particularly American, even Jeffersonian, problem to have.

In an unpublished journal, on September 8, 1947, Wright wrote:

> [Jean-Paul] Sartre is quite of my opinion regarding the possibility of human action today, that it is up to the individual to do what he can do to uphold the concept of what it means to be human.

[6] Wright, *The Outsider*, 525.

The great danger, I told him, in the world today is the very feeling and conception of what is a human might well be lost. He agreed. I feel very close to Sartre and Simone de Beauvoir.[7]

It seems impossible to lose the feeling of what is a human. Except, in May 2017, *Time Magazine* reported that the Twitter-bots of 2016— fake accounts designed to re-tweet fake news, spread disinformation, and to respond algorithmically to real people, all in an attempt to influence the presidential election—had become more sophisticated.[8] This new high-tech system, *Time Magazine* reported, used malware to infiltrate U.S. Defense Department Twitter users and link them to Russian-run servers that could send information from the hacked user's account, thereby potentially giving the Russians the ability to send messages from seemingly legitimate Pentagon accounts.

Half the Twitter followers of the president of the United States are reportedly bots. Our national conversation is driven by machines which (who?) are programmed to track certain words and phrases and respond in a quasi-syntactic way that mimics conversation.

Sarah Nyberg created a Twitter account called @Arguetron that released four or five tweets an hour. The Tweets were programmed to respond to the alt-right, Infowars crowd, and were assertions of typical left-wing beliefs, although not insulting or sarcastic. "More than two genders exist," read one. In one case, a Twitter user argued with the bot for ten hours, seemingly unaware of what was or was not human.

The therapist said, "Here is the best definition of anxiety and depression I ever heard: Depression is the feeling you have lost something and anxiety is the feeling you are about to lose something."

"So, anxiety is a good thing," I asked. "It means everything is going well?"

"Not exactly," he said.

---

[7] Fabre, Michel. *The World of Richard Wright.* (Jackson: University Press of Mississippi, 2007), 162.

[8] Massimo Calabresi, "Inside Russia's Social Media War on America," *Time Magazine*, May 29, 2017. 189-20.

In an interview, given seven years after *The Outsider*'s publication, and just a few years before his death, at fifty-two, Wright said:

I didn't want to write an existentialist novel (*The Outsider*). I believe in the beauty of life, in its infinite richness. One can experience dread and anguish and the idea of being nothing, but then one finds again the multiple potentialities offered by life.[9]

Let's say, for the purposes of argument, that from 2016 to the present time, anxiety is mostly a political, not psychological disorder: an inability to find the multiple potentialities offered by life, an experience of depersonalization, or dysregulation, in the face of falsehood, in the face of threat to one's self via circumstance.

I'm not alone in making this argument. *Psychology Today* has run numerous articles about "Trump Anxiety."[10] Some urge us to acknowledge our feelings, rather than repress them. Others suggest self-care to prevent stress overdrive. Even the political news site *The Hill* covered the phenomenon with "The Science of Stress in the Era of Trump."[11] It notes that "we are wired for greater affinity with similar ideologies and opposition to those different from our own" and suggests everything from self-care to connecting and listening to others over a cup of coffee to performing random good deeds.[12] These remedies are not suggested for policy disagreements among political divides. They suggest that something like what I have been feeling has swept the country: a profound anxiety caused by dissonance between self and world.

Perhaps this is because an entire alternate world has been created

---

[9] Annie Briérre, translated by Michel Fabre, R. *Wright: American is Not Conformist: It Renews Itself Endlessly*, France-U.S.A. September-October 1960, p. 2, in *Conversations with Richard Wright*, ed. Kinnamon, Keneth and Fabre, Michel. (Jackson: University Press of Mississippi, 1993), 209.

[10] Jeremy Clyman. "Coping with Trump Anxiety." *Psychology Today*. February 9, 2017. Steven Stosny, "How to Cope with Trump Anxiety." *Psychology Today*. April 22, 2017.

[11] Frieda K. Edgette. "The Science of Stress in the Era of Trump." *The Hill*. July 21, 2017.

[12] Ibid.

by disinformation, the intentional spreading of falsehood to achieve an aim.

Some disinformation comes from without: one town in Macedonia hosts at least 100 pro-Trump websites, filled with stories made up by entrepreneurial teenagers, designed to whip people into a frenzy. Samanth Subramanian, in *Wired Magazine* reports:

> These Macedonians on Facebook didn't care if Trump won or lost the White House. They only wanted pocket money to pay for things—a car, watches, better cell phones, more drinks at the bar. This is the arrhythmic, disturbing heart of the affair: that the internet made it so simple for these young men to finance their material whims and that their actions helped deliver such momentous consequences.[13]

And some disinformation comes from within. In Los Angeles, Jestin Coler is a forty-year-old husband and father who grosses somewhere between $10,000 and $30,000 a month as a publisher of multiple disinformation sites. A registered Democrat, Coler tells NPR that he started his websites in late 2012 to "infiltrate the echo chambers of the alt-right" in order to "denounce" them.[14] His made-up stories go viral: one published in the non-existent The *Denver Guardian* about an FBI agent who was killed under suspicious circumstances after leaking Clinton emails got more than 1.6 million page views in ten days.[15]

The simplicity of their collective motivation stuns me: in helping to elect a con man to the presidency, they have changed the world for "pocket money" for a new car.

What I am seeking is truth in an era of falsehood as a matter of life and death. Draw a line from the clamor and clap for the lies of the pussy-grabber former tie and steak salesman to the death of a

---

[13] Samanth Subramanian, "Veles: Inside the Macdedonian Fake-news Complex," *Wired Magazine*. February 15, 2017. https://www.wired.com/2017/02/veles-macedonia-fake-news

[14] National Public Radio, All Tech Considered, "We Tracked Down a fake-News Creator in the Suburbs. Here's What We Learned." Laura Sydell. November 23, 2016. https://www.npr.org/sections/alltechconsidered/2016/11/23/503146770/npr-finds-the-head-of-a-covert-fake-news-operation-in-the-suburbs

[15] Ibid.

young woman at the hands of a white nationalist as she counter-protested a white nationalist rally, just steps away from the university founded by Thomas Jefferson.

I know what we are, but I do not know where to go from here.

☙

Thirty-five years after my first reading of *Black Boy*, the ending stands as a personal manifesto for the present time:

> Yes, the whites were as miserable as their black victims, I thought. If this country can't find its way to a human path, if it can't inform conduct with a deep sense of life, then all of us, black as well as white, are going down the same drain....
>
> I picked up a pencil and held it over a sheet of white paper, but my feelings stood in the way of my words. Well, I would wait, day and night, until I knew what to say. Humbly now, with vaulting dream of achieving a vast unity, I wanted to try to build a bridge of words between me and that world outside, that world which was so distant and elusive that it seemed unreal.
>
> I would hurl words into this darkness and wait for an echo, and if an echo sounded, no matter how faintly, I would send other words to tell, to march, to fight, to create a sense of the hunger for life that gnaws in us all, to keep alive in our hearts a sense of the inexpressibly human.[16]

Pause for a moment—even read those lines aloud. They were written by African-American man who, as a child, had to borrow a white boy's library card because he wasn't permitted one, a man who has written again and again of the anxiety and despair caused by living in a country where what we say and how we live are wildly divergent.

☙

June 2017:

I am trying to build a bridge between me and the outside world.

I am walking the dog in a new place because we sold the house downtown and moved west. The houses in the new neighborhood were built in the 1950s and early 60s, when Richard Wright was

---

[16] Wright. *Black Boy (American Hunger)*. 365.

85

considering leaving Paris for England, because he believed that France had become inhospitable to expatriate black American writers. He was especially wounded by James Baldwin's critique of protest novels, which Wright felt was directed at his own work when Baldwin wrote: "Literature and sociology are not the same." In the end, Wright stayed in Paris.

While Wright was in the last years of his life, which ended with a heart attack, the tidy modern houses of my neighborhood sprung up. Nearby, newly widened interstates led residents to shopping malls, which are now empty, because we order online. This worshipful consumerism is part of how we got here—*here,* meaning that I am a citizen of a country that has elected a failed businessman and reality TV show star president. We believe in buying and selling; we do not care about the ultimate cost. Some days, my new neighborhood feels like a graveyard memorial to another time, which inspires oddly tender feelings in me. I thought it would be better, that we would be better.

The streets through which I now walk the dog are unfamiliar, but they do not seem unreal. In fact, it is the opposite: everything seems hyper-real. In the evenings, children clamor outside, dogs bark, chickens squawk, and men drag sprinklers and hoses into position on the lawns. I am trying to decode these streets and people. I am trying to look at my fellow citizens as they are. There are times I want to look away and retreat into the distant opaque world. How am I to understand a place where an elderly neighbor, upon hearing that our last names are different, brings over a Bible to re-direct us into being a proper, male-dominated family? And there are times when this neighborhood is what I would hope for: when others post on our community media page that they need Arabic lessons, or that the local addicts who beg for change are *our addicts,* in need of help. I am no longer panicking, for the most part, but I am no longer innocent and unquestioning, either, even as I try to hold onto Wright's idea to keep alive the inexpressibly human. I cannot tell if these people, my new neighbors, are friend or foe, if they have a hand in building the world I know or destroying it. I am, as never before, seeking bridges, trying to ignore the walls, and considering what it means when what

I believe and what I see seem irreconcilable. Perhaps this is what it means to be American, to live within the ideals and the contradictions of our history as we create the future.

Some days, only the outdoors make sense. Cold water runs through ditches, and the dog balances on the grassy bank to take a drink. Rabbits flatten themselves in the grass, leaving only their coal-colored eyes visible. These things are true; there is no disinformation.

West of the house, there is a path up one of the foothills and within half an hour, I can be on top of the mesa looking east and south toward Denver's sprawl, then north toward Boulder, or west toward the mountains. Here, rattlesnakes and deer coexist, as do bikers and runners and horsewomen and men. This land is your land, this land is my land; it is irreducible, and this is where I begin. What I like best about being high up is that everything else gets very small and far away. Even the sun is the size of a nickel. In this way, I go on.

ॐ

Emily Sinclair is an essayist and fiction writer whose work has appeared in numerous literary journals, including *The Missouri Review*, *The Normal School*, *Colorado Review*, and *River Teeth*. Her work has been recognized by Best American Essays. She teaches for Lighthouse Writers. She lives on an apple orchard west of Denver, Colorado, with her husband.

OUR FAMILIES

DOES FAMILY TRUMP POLITICS?

By Susan Shapiro

"Get over it already," Mom said, after I had reiterated my shock that she and my father had helped elect Donald Trump and I'd told them I strongly backed the recount in my home state.

"Move on," Dad added on the other line. "Just worry about your own business."

While I usually called every night, I'd been too upset after the election to phone. As a Manhattan journalism professor still consoling distressed students of all backgrounds, this *was* my business—especially after swastikas were found in a Jewish student's dormitory room at the college where I taught, and a black friend's daughter was texted "N***** Lynching" at her Pennsylvania university.

As weeks wore on, my folks' candidate kept Twitter-blasting *Saturday Night Live*, the media, and Democrats' desire to challenge the election results; but he could not tweet, "Stop the hate speech and hate crimes" to the Ku Klux Klan and so-called alt-right groups he continued to empower. I felt sick, unable to sleep or concentrate. Never before had I been ashamed of my country—or my relatives.

On a tight book deadline, I'd begged off from visiting for Thanksgiving. Hanukkah and Christmas fell on the same weekend in 2016, but the thought of fighting my family over politics made me panic. My mind flashed to the old Southside Johnny song lyrics: "Whatever happened to you and I/that I don't want to go home."

Growing up in Michigan, I was so proud of my mother and father: chic, funny, former New Yorkers who seemed smart and cool for parents. On the Festival of Lights, my favorite holiday, we'd light the menorah, eat potato latkes with applesauce, and open a present on each of the eight nights. Yet I never really fit into our suburb. Though my public elementary was filled with fellow Jews, I was awkward and friendless. Luckily, my parents let me attend the diverse, artistic private school I'd picked. When I brought home a black class-mate in sixth grade, my neighbor used a Yiddish derogatory term for blacks. "What's that mean?" I asked my parents, both from Lower East Side, Yiddish-speaking families.

"It means our neighbors are idiots," Mom said, insisting we never use that term.

"Ignore the racist assholes," Dad snapped, surprising me with profanity. "We had relatives murdered in the Holocaust because Hit-ler scapegoated Jews."

"We treat everyone equal. No slurs are ever allowed in our home," my mother told us.

I didn't understand how this lesson applied to us until, when I was eleven, I was traumatized by TV coverage of 1972's massacre of Israeli Olympic athletes in Munich, as well as news of wars against Israel that my cousins fought in. Yet, my mom, a beautiful redhead, patronized stores owned by local Lebanese and Iraqi families. She taught me to hate only the enemies who had vowed to annihilate Is-rael and never to stereotype. My dad was a physician. Working at his Detroit office one summer, I was proud to learn he secretly treated many poor minority patients who couldn't pay.

After Mom put Dad through medical school, she chose to be a housewife while raising four kids. Like many who become more conservative as they age, my dad veered right, pushing conventional politics and professions on me and my three brothers. In junior high, during my raging Sylvia Plath stage, I was talking to Dad in his den and he said, "Go get me a cup of coffee."

"You already have one subservient female in the family," I an-swered.

"Feminism is an abomination," my brother joked.

"You know I'm the one paying tuition, allowing you to learn that feminist crap," Dad responded. I reluctantly fetched him coffee, with sprinkled cookies Mom added to the saucer.

As an English major at the University of Michigan, which Dad dubbed "the People's Republic of Ann Arbor," and later at New York University, I was the lefty outcast. Dinners with my Republican relatives were acrimonious, especially when my oldest brother turned into a staid doctor, raising four kids in the Midwest like Dad.

Now in my fifties, with a liberal husband who gets his own coffee, I have analyzed how my blood relations could vote for someone I see as dangerously nationalistic as Hitler. Since I don't want to hate my own kin or half the country, I have desperately tried to see their side.

After my father suffered a near fatal heart attack at eighty, he retired. Having grown up as a poor street kid, he was now most proud that he'd put his four kids through college and grad school. Now, as he was making trusts to help his five grandchildren pay for higher education too, he became obsessed with the inheritance tax Trump promised to repeal.

"You'll inherit more money," Dad wrote in an email.

That was why he voted for Trump? "Nothing's worth having a president I don't respect," I replied.

"Poverty's worse," he returned.

Dad shared a story I'd never heard. When he first applied to medical school, he didn't get in because of Jewish quotas. He worked a fellowship for a year before he was admitted. "It only paid $300 a week," he wrote. "Your mother worked to support me. We lived paycheck to paycheck for five years, sleeping on a sofa bed. After working hard for sixty years, why should my money go to the government instead of my kids and grandkids?"

That I understood. They'd both worked so hard to be successful. As they aged, my parents worried about their finances and their legacy. So did I. Still, I couldn't fathom their inability to see how Trump went against everything they'd taught me. I loved my parents, but I couldn't get over my devastation. Depressed and sleep-deprived, I felt like I was sitting shiva. When a Jewish activist colleague whom my mom knew died, I called to tell her. Before we hung up, I asked, "Aren't you afraid of Trump's sexism and racism and the hate crimes he's inciting?"

I didn't know how my mom, who'd been happily married for more than sixty years, could pardon Trump's five children with three wives and "grabbing pussy" tape.

"Look, Trump's rhetoric is disgusting. But I find Hillary dishonest and condescending. I couldn't stand either candidate the whole election," she told me.

"Trump's not anti-Semitic. Ivanka converted, and he has Orthodox grandkids," Dad said. "The Right is better for Israel."

Was that true? As a proud Zionist myself (for a two-state solution), with close cousins in Jerusalem, I'd also been dismayed by what I saw as the left wing's anti-Zionism. I'd been sickened by the whole boycott, divestment, and sanctions or BDS movement against Israel, preferring instead the nickname "bald-faced lies, deception, and slander." When an idiot burned an Israeli flag at the Democratic Convention, I was stunned that Hillary Clinton didn't publicly denounce it. But even if Republicans were better for the Holy Land and the economy, I didn't think that should be enough to win my parents' votes. Then again, who was I to dictate what their main issues were?

Next, Dad emailed me a *Los Angeles Times* op-ed about how maligned Trump supporters feel being called "racist, redneck, and uneducated." I found it hilarious how thin-skinned supporters of the nastiest candidate in history suddenly were. I responded, "Not all Trump supporters are racist. But all Trump supporters decided racism isn't a deal breaker."

Dad shot back a *Conservative Free Press* link blaming rich liberals for the hate crime increase. Oy. I returned fire with a piece quoting Trump's decree that American Muslims had to "register," the way Nazis made Jews wear yellow stars. I paraphrased the adage Dad once told me: "All it takes for evil to flourish is for good people to do nothing." It seemed encouraging that my father kept attempting communication. Was it from guilt? For a month after the election, that was how we maintained contact.

"All identity politics is the mantra of ignorance," my father said.

"Wait! So you do denounce Trump's hate speech?" I asked.

"It's all bluster and bullshit," Dad answered. "But better than Bonnie and Clyde back in the White House."

I rolled my eyes at his nickname for Hillary and her husband, whom both my parents saw as crooked. I slowly conceded that

Hillary came with too much baggage named Bill, and citizens unhappy with Obama wanted change. Though, when I realized that more than ninety-five million Americans hadn't cast a ballot—my biggest disdain was for those forty-one percent of voters who stayed home and thus decided the election.

"So, all the kids are coming for the holidays. When are you visiting?" my father asked me.

"Not this year." I decided to mail my Hanukkah cards and presents instead. I remained despondent, wanting to hide inside my home this December with my Democratic husband, a good book, and no makeup, like Hillary.

Scrolling through my Facebook news feed, I took solace in the fact that my middle brother's seventeen-year-old daughter posted "Pence Confirms Trump will be an anti-LGBT president" with other anti-Trump screeds. My older brother's son, a twenty-year-old Michigan college student, kept sharing images of Hillary, the Statue of Liberty sobbing, and Batman slapping Trump. I responded with lots of hearts. My blonde niece, an NYU freshman living around the corner from me, sent videos of herself at ongoing protests, chanting "Not My President." At least my family's next generation would carry the torch for anti-discrimination and diversity.

Sensing my continued distress, my two younger brothers let me know they had voted for Hillary and couldn't stand the president-elect. I hadn't known! Then my oldest doctor-brother texted me an image of Popeye saying, "I Yam Digustipated." I thought he was making fun of my hurt. Until he texted, #imwithher.

He was? My eyes watered. When the Michigan election clerks began their re-tally, I calculated my family's recount. Fascinatingly, all my brothers, sisters-in-law, and their kids were with her, and with me, for the first time ever. While I lost my dream of a female president, this felt like a historic shift. I chose to take these votes as proof that my parents were still the good people I thought they were, having taught us the right values after all.

After more public slurs against immigrants by our divider-in-chief, my mother let slip that she would never vote for Trump again "because of his big ugly mouth." I was so relieved.

When my father was rushed to the hospital with heart failure in 2018, he joked that he couldn't die until Trump's inheritance tax went into effect. Alas, he passed away on December 11, which meant he wouldn't reap all the benefits he'd voted for. Deep in real grief during his funeral and actual shiva, I missed everything about my dad, especially arguing politics. After publishing a short piece about him in the *Wall Street Journal*, his favorite right-wing newspaper, I told my brother, "I wonder if he'd hate that it's so personal."

"He'd love that you're making money from the Republicans," my older brother said.

❧

Susan Shapiro, an award-winning writing professor, freelances for the *New York Times, NY Magazine, WSJ* and the *Washington Post*. She's the bestselling author/coauthor of twelve books her family hates including *Five Men Who Broke My Heart, Lighting Up, Unhooked, The Bosnia List* and *The Byline Bible*. She and her husband, a scriptwriter, live in Greenwich Village, where she teaches her popular "instant gratification takes too long" classes at The New School, NYU and in private workshops & seminars. Follow her on Twitter at @susanshapironet and Instagram at @Profsue123.

CHILDREN QUESTION THE BULLY'S RIGHT TO THE PRESIDENTIAL SEAT

By Cassandra Lane

I was in sixth grade, that era of awkward limbs and suffocating self-consciousness, when a strange man told me I could not see.

"Young lady," he said, "I don't see how you've been walking around here all this time without running into stuff."

The optometrist turned to my mother, who stood on the sidelines of the dim room, her heavy brown leather purse hanging from her right shoulder, her shoulder bending under its weight. "This girl needs glasses," the optometrist said. "Immediately. You know, she is what we declare as 'legally blind.'"

I could see shock and then shame descending on my mother.

She touched her fingers to her lips. "Sand, why haven't you told me?" She turned back to the optometrist, exasperated. "She doesn't talk. She doesn't say what's going on with her, so you just never know."

A divorcée stringing together a living on an entry-level government job salary, Mama spent her days and evenings working on a military base just outside our small Louisiana town. While her job provided health insurance, there really was no time in her schedule for routine check-ups. Health insurance, then, was for emergencies.

"I don't even see how she's participating in class," the optometrist said. "All joking aside: She really cannot see."

I had, in fact, missed a whole year of fifth-grade math concepts because the tiny chalk figures my stoic, disengaged teacher scribbled on the board might as well have been clusters of spider webs, my potential for learning caught within their snares. At the time, I didn't understand what was happening. I went from being an honors student to getting my first C. I feared my struggle with math that year had something to do with my intelligence. I cringed at the thought of disappointing family and former teachers who had lauded me for my academic achievements.

When my glasses came in, I put them on with trepidation. They were a mottled brown—plastic and hideous—though I had to admit that I could see a stark difference in the world around me. Everything—people's facial expressions, street signs, my own reflection—was stunningly clear. But my hesitation in wearing the glasses proved prophetic: taunts from peers did come, and so I slipped off the glasses and continued to squint my way through days.

My son Solomon, who is a fourth grader, inherited my nearsightedness. In his early years, during our annual physical check-ups, his vision tests were perfect, but after he turned eight, the myopic gene awakened from its slumber. Solomon's glasses are stylish, a glistening onyx piece of metropolitan cool. The lenses seem to enhance his doe eyes and enviable lashes, but no matter: like his mother, he shirks his second pair of eyes. "Everybody's going to laugh at me," he cried. "They're going to make fun of me."

And the taunts and jeers did come, one in the form of a kid threatening to crush his glasses at lunch time. "I told you so," Solomon said to his father and me, his eyes full of blame.

Because schools, in recent years, have been intentional about building awareness around bullying, Solomon and his peers have a language for it. They know what bullying sounds and feels like; they know how to name it. This doesn't eradicate subtle forms of bullying.

Solomon has long been a toe-walker. And he stutters. When he was in preschool, my husband and I detected early signs of disfluency and enrolled him in a speech therapy class, where his jumbled sounds receded like a tumultuous wave that had washed ashore and folded back into the ocean, replaced by a calm ebb and flow. But by third grade, the impediment had reinserted itself with tidal force.

As he gets hung up on words—"th...th...th...th...that"; "Mo...mo...Mommy"— I have wanted to blame someone, something, anything.

"In this country, if you don't speak well, it holds you back," I told my husband. "And in this country, black boys can't afford to get hung up on words. They have to excel... I don't want him to get teased and lose self-esteem and interest in school, and then, who knows what will happen."

"Don't worry so much about it. He'll grow out of it," Marcus said, turning away from my worry.

But he has not grown out of any of it, despite the fact that we have tried to "fix" all of these perceived weaknesses—with therapies and prosthetics and prayer. Though I hurt for him, I am proud that he is growing up to be a sensitive and empathetic child, maybe partly because he knows all too well what being ridiculed, dismissed, and shamed feels like.

When he is mocked at school, I always, *always* ask him: "How did you respond?"

"I didn't say anything," he says way too often.

"Why not?" I ask. "You have the words. You have the power to explain why you need glasses. Or why you stutter. We've watched the videos together. We've read the articles. Why do you stay silent?"

"Don't be afraid, Solomon," I tell him. "You have a responsibility to speak up for yourself. To teach others. And if they keep bothering you, use your power-voice to shut them down." I raise my voice to a bellow: "Let me hear your power-voice!"

During the presidential campaign, Solomon was transfixed by the man who takes bullying, including cyberbullying, to new heights. He watched, his mouth agape, as Trump made fun of a person with a disability, mocked Hillary Clinton's stumble when she had pneumonia, verbally assaulted and demeaned women, made disparaging remarks about blacks and so-called inner cities, incited the physical assaults taking place at his rallies, and celebrated a virulently racist America.

On election night, Solomon's homework assignment was to watch the results, but ultimately, his body gave way and he fell asleep, like millions of children across this country. Just before succumbing to his dream state, though, he saw the numbers, he saw that Trump was leading the Electoral College, and he tried his hardest to differentiate each state's popular vote numbers from the overall national ones.

He went to bed confident that Trump would not win, because in the stories, the bully always loses in the end. The next morning,

Marcus and I tried to normalize breakfast: oatmeal with cream and butter, toast, tea. Marcus turned on the TV, but placed it on mute. Solomon kept asking us: "How could someone like Trump get elected to be president?"

The bully. As president of the United States of America.

For generations, little boys and girls have considered this seat the ultimate dream job in our nation of dreamers and achievers. They revere it, they aspire to it, and so, for the life of him, Solomon cannot make sense of how someone who shows such blatant disdain for others could be his president.

Because Trump used his own version of a power-voice, I tell him. As crude and uncouth as he is, the guy knows something about the power of language, and he used it as a weapon to dredge up some of our countrymen's fears, resentments, hatred, and ancestral sense of entitlement. This kind of power, without purity of vision, is dangerous.

We may not be able to see well outwardly, but I try to teach Solomon to rely on his inner vision to guide him through the world. I urge him to see people, for better or worse, for who they are inside: their dreams and shortcomings, their character traits and untapped capabilities. Trump cannot clearly see that which is not him, that which is not his own reflection, his own family, his own money and friends and power.

Trump Towers. There—he has named it.

He has no foresight into the future beyond protecting his own kingdom, his own ego, and so he is free—he thinks he is free—to say and do anything to those who appear fuzzy to him; those he does not understand or care to understand; those who do not serve his purpose, his vision of all-mighty power: an insatiable black hole incapable of ever being filled.

As a private citizen, that was his prerogative. To some degree.

As the highest public servant in the land, his ineptitude at seeing and, therefore, respecting all of America should be deemed as serious as it is for me to drive without some form of corrective lenses: illegal.

❧

Cassandra Lane is Managing Editor of *L.A. Parent* magazine. She received an MFA in creative writing from Antioch University Los Angeles. Her stories have appeared in a variety of newspapers, magazines, anthologies and storytelling venues, including *The Times-Picayune, The Atlanta Journal Constitution, Writer's Resist, Expressing Motherhood* and the *New York Times'* "Conception" series. Her book-length project explores the impact of her great-grandfather's lynching and her "late" entry into motherhood. She recently served on an AWP panel entitled "Writing & Mothering: Black Women Writing Under a Quadruple 'Minority' in America." A Louisiana native, she lives with her family in Los Angeles.

How I'm Teaching My Jewish Daughters About Donald Trump

By Lea Grover

The sky was still dark when I woke up the children. I put them in layers in case the unseasonably warm January day turned cold, comfortable shoes for the miles ahead on foot, and the pussy hats a friend had knitted for them. We piled into the car and drove an hour into the city, where we marched for six hours. My two seven-year-olds and my four-year-old, all girls, were surrounded by a sea of hundreds of thousands of people.

"Everyone is so happy to see you," I told them, and they were. Every few steps another protester stopped to take a photograph of my three little girls, holding their handmade signs. My twins carried signs that said, "Girls Can Do Anything," and "Equal Rights," and "I'm In Charge of My Body." The four-year-old carried a sign she insisted should say, "Girls can be smart AND fabulous!" They believe those words with all their hearts.

They know a lot about Donald Trump and a lot about the people who support him. During the presidential primaries we had many talks about the differences between Donald Trump and Ted Cruz, and even more importantly, their differences with Hillary Clinton and Bernie Sanders. Like millions and millions of Americans, my daughters and I are not Christians. And like a few million Americans, we are Jewish. That meant whenever a candidate talked about how America is a "Christian nation," I explained to my children that our Constitution, and our Bill of Rights, says otherwise.

Also, like millions and millions of Americans, I am a survivor of sexual violence. When Donald Trump was heard on tape, not only confessing to sexual assault but planning to commit more acts of sexual violence, I talked to my daughters about it. I told them what I tell them most days, "You are in charge of your body. Nobody is allowed to touch it, or grab it, or make you do things with it. If anybody, ever, touches you and you do not want them to, it is not your fault."

Like 2.9 million Americans, that Saturday morning we took to the streets. We marched for hours, then returned to our lovely, quiet suburban home, exhausted. And in the morning we woke again to go to Hebrew School. Only it wasn't Hebrew School as usual. Over the previous weeks, dozens of Jewish community centers in the United States had been targeted with bomb threats. Hate crimes against Jewish people had risen, in some places by 110 percent, in the ten weeks since election night. So on Sunday, two days after the inauguration of a man who appointed known anti-Semites to his transition team and cabinet, our synagogue and Hebrew School had a lockdown drill.

I watched children cower behind couches in the corner of the school library, as silent as they could be, pretending somebody might be coming to kill them. One of the girls had left her book on a seat—she was reading *Letters from Rifka*, a childhood favorite of mine—a story about a girl fleeing religious persecution in Russia in the years leading up to the Holocaust. On the shelf behind that seat sat a copy of *The Diary of Anne Frank*.

I stared at the cover, imagining Anne Frank and her family hiding in their attic. Silently cowering as people with guns went through the house, searching for Jews to slaughter, either themselves or by the machine of death in which they were crucial cogs.

Thanks to Donald Trump's election, thanks to the year he spent courting Neo-Nazis under the name "alt-right," garnering endorsements from the KKK and the American Nazi Party, this is what my children are being taught to do.

I realized I had spent the weekend teaching my children the two things they have to know to survive a Trump presidency. The first, to stand up and be seen, to demand to be treated with dignity and respect; and the second, that they must learn to hide, to be safe when the white nationalist tide Trump attempted to ride comes flooding toward our doors.

As a woman and a mother, I felt so much less alone on Saturday than I had in the days after the election. Surrounded by hundreds of thousands of my new closest friends, I—we—were part of a movement that could neither be ignored nor denied. But as a Jew, I feel frighteningly and increasingly alone. During my childhood I spent many weekends at Hebrew school, first at my home in the Jewish neighborhood of Squirrel Hill in Pittsburgh; then in New Jersey, where Jewish families were so few and far between that our synagogue gathered families from hours away into a dilapidated farmhouse with inadequate heating; then in the robust Jewish community in Ann Arbor; and at last in Chicago, where as a Jewish adult I entered into the real work of acquiring a Jewish education, learning how to live a Jewish life—even a deeply secular one—in a country inherently hostile toward any lack of a Christian faith. I spent those years of Jewish education not only memorizing my aleph-bet, perfecting a recipe for hamentaschen and how to dance the hora, but doing what is most important for Jews around the world—learning my cultural history. The Holocaust was part of my personal and cultural identity before I was able to frame it in words. Well before I came of age as a bat mitzvah, I studied how the czar and the inquisitors and Hitler and Stalin and Mussolini rallied countries full of reasonable, rational people into exterminating minorities.

Now I watch press secretary after press secretary flat-out deny that what people see with their own eyes is true. I see political operatives throw phrases around like "alternative facts" and tell us we cannot trust our own senses. To call it Orwellian has become cliché, but it remains true nonetheless.

On a warm, sunny Saturday in January 2017, I took my daughters to be part of something massive. Something meaningful and important, something they will someday read about in history books and remember the part they played. Maybe they'll see the signs we donated to the Chicago History Museum at their request, along the thousands of other signs collected from the march. The following Sunday I took them to what was already a routine in their lives— something more defining, more meaningful. When we practiced hiding silently from somebody coming to kill us, they were also part of something huge. They were part of why it was so necessary that we marched at all.

The two years that have passed since the march were full of other conversations, other signs, other protests. The children and I marched for science. We marched for gun control. We marched to protest refugee children being torn from their parents and placed in cages along our southern border. I told the children the story from *Letters From Rifka*, of a girl whose family only had to get to Ellis Island to achieve freedom, but the journey was so dangerous, so arduous, that she became ill and was denied entry into the country. She had to watch her family sail away to Manhattan, leaving her behind until, hopefully, she got well. And while we marched in unprecedented numbers across the globe, acts of hate—growing in the incandescent light of Donald Trump's bigotry—grew accordingly. Protesters, mowed down by white supremacists; women, murdered by angry men; journalists, gunned down by right-wing conspiracy theorists; children, killed en masse in their schools, over and over again; and then, the Tree of Life Synagogue.

The Tree of Life, in Squirrel Hill—in my childhood neighborhood, in the neighborhood I had once shared with Mr. Rogers— riddled with bullets, eleven bodies bleeding out into the pews. My childhood neighbor's bodies. Bodies like those of my grandparents'. Bodies like those of the family they had left behind in the old country, like those of Anne Frank's family, full of bullet holes and as dead as any unwillingly tattooed relative I never had the privilege to meet.

Bodies like mine and bodies like my daughters.

Human beings reduced to a body count for no reason other than hatred, hatred for the non-white, hatred for the non-Christian, hatred for anyone unlike Donald Trump or Steve Bannon or Sarah Huckabee Sanders.

Donald Trump remains in power, his followers invigorated and encouraged, and so we must continue practicing the skills of being unseen and unheard. But women all over the country, women like me and my daughters, are continuing to make themselves visible by winning elections, dancing, swearing, gathering together to protect our country, our planet, our children. All children.

I tell my daughters that they have been born with the burden of making this world better. But they have also been born with the burden to protect themselves from it. Every neighborhood must march in defense of justice, I teach them, because no suburb is safe from the hatred that is stirred up by the man in the Oval Office.

"Speak and be seen," I say, pushing them forward with one hand. "You are the hope I've dreamt of my whole life. You are the change we need. You are the future, and you deserve to control your place in it." With the other hand I hold them back and whisper, "Hide and be silent, my loves, and pray that silence will keep you safe."

∂

Lea Grover writes for *The Washington Post, Brain, Child Magazine, Esquire, Good Housekeeeping, The Establishment, Cosmopolitan, Chicago Parent, Yahoo!, Scary Mommy, YourTango,* and the many corners of the internet. Her writing is featured in a dozen anthologies and textbooks, including *Listen To Your Mother: What She Said Then, What We're Saying Now.* She speaks about sex positivity parenting and on behalf of the RAINN Speakers Bureau.

Breaking Bad News

By Suzanne Clores

"Did she win, Mama?"

"No, honey."

A single tear rolled down my daughter's cheek. She was still in bed, facing the giant maple out her window, which was almost empty of flaming orange leaves.

"You mean that rude man is our president?"

I probably should have let her get out of bed first, let her dress, sit at the table with a bowl of cornflakes, pick at her blueberries judiciously. Let her feel power over her breakfast at least. If you're a fourth grade girl, with a class ratio of 14:4 (that is, fourteen boys to four girls), the way to hear bad news about the first female presidential candidate losing to a loud, rude man is not lying down, snuggled in bed, vulnerable—especially when she has a daily fight on her hands: a micro-world in which she is constantly talked over, shoved aside, and outnumbered by voluminous, space-claiming, jubilant boys. In other words, she goes into a classroom very much like the world women endure every day.

I wiped her tear as my husband came in, wringing his hands, exhausted from being up all night. It's just an election, and yet the task of telling our daughter that her country elected a bully who made fun of a disabled journalist instead of a woman who worked hard serving other people most of her life is infuriating and deeply nauseating. We tell her, instead, that although she lost the presidency, Hillary won the state of Illinois, where we live, and many other states. We tell her Hillary won the popular vote. Within a few minutes, she is up and looking for matching socks.

I am relieved but struggling for next steps. I have been actively using this election as a tool to prove things can change, that the gender-typical hazing my daughter fights against and endures every day from a class of rambunctious boys will not be the norm forever. That as she grows, it will go away. The election of the first female president would have been a truthful illustration of this claim. Now I have to find another example or admit that, in some ways, it isn't really true.

The nearly four-to-one ratio in her class is just dumb luck, but its consequences are anything but innocuous. Four voices are literally fewer and quieter than fourteen voices. Four bodies are literally less noticeable than fourteen bodies. I am very familiar with the consequences of this mathematical deficit. Any woman who works in a lopsided corporate environment knows this dynamic, how it puts the focus on you at the same time that it takes away your power. You are scrutinized more, rewarded less. My daughter is only nine, and yet I wonder if the exhaustion she sometimes feels upon coming home from school reflects this added labor, the labor of making herself heard.

By most accounts, the children get along in groups and perform the musical and theatrical productions in harmony. But I remind myself that alongside this harmony, my girl is forced to advocate for herself constantly: in gym class, on the playground, and in discussions every day. I remind myself that she has run for student council since second grade, and, every time, has lost.

Nevertheless, for the past three years she has painstakingly made signs to post around the school, listing her qualifications for her candidacy. Teachers encourage all children who want to serve their school to participate, not acknowledging the gender imbalance. When she loses, I explain that she has not lost because she was not qualified. "None of the girls ever win," she tells me. "Keep trying," I say in a supportive, upbeat refrain. Because I do want her to keep trying.

What I don't want is for her to know exactly the nature of who, and what, has won. We did not tell her of the president-elect's threats to minorities, assaults against women, or his bigoted and treasonous leanings. Nor have we told her that Hillary's barely winning the popular vote meant that many Americans voted for a dangerous man rather than a flawed woman. We hid well what to me epitomizes the waking nightmare of a parent: that your child, upon realizing her parents can't control the outside world, worries that she is not actually safe. But we could not and cannot keep everything from her. After watching the second debate, she noticed that Hillary's opponent behaved like the boys in her class. "He keeps interrupting her," she claimed. "I can't hear what she's saying."

I'm preparing my daughter for the inevitability that she'll be called shrill and bossy, even as she's already internalizing the consequences of that kind of dismissal. "I don't want to hurt anyone else's feelings," she says, when I ask why she doesn't tell other kids to share the basketball court or stop kicking her seat. This translates to: "I don't want to be punished for speaking out." I tell her I understand, but that speaking out is how others learn to respect you. I'm hoping this lost election will change her sense of possibility, shift her focus to the value of speaking up and trying.

The fact that she spent Friday nights in October at the *Hillary for President* campaign office, making buttons one at a time, her small hands on a giant steel contraption, for volunteers to take to Iowa canvassing the next day, made an impact on her heart, if not on the rest of the country. She put her hard work into something she wanted and found out firsthand what it's like to believe in something, to put your faith behind a cause.

When I picked her up from school on Wednesday, she skipped into the car, almost completely recovered from the news that I and much of the country were still struggling with.

"This year I was elected alternate on student council," she said as she munched her pretzels. "That means two boys voted for me."

Change, though slow, is on the horizon.

Suzanne Clores is the author of *Memoirs of a Spiritual Outsider* and producer of the podcast, The Extraordinary Project. Her work has appeared in *Salon, Elle, The Rumpus,* and *The Nervous Breakdown,* among other publications, and has aired on Chicago Public Radio (WBEZ) and the Radiotopia podcast *Strangers.* Her BA is from Columbia University in New York, and her MFA in fiction is from the University of Arizona in Tucson.

Can We Reassure Our Kids Monsters Don't Exist When We Know They Do?

By Jaimie Seaton

Author, activist, political pundit, and Dream Corps founder Van Jones brought many parents like me to tears on election night. Speaking on CNN about what we tell our children in the wake of Trump's election, he said:

> It's hard to be a parent tonight for a lot of us. You tell your kids, "Don't be a bully." You tell your kids, "Don't be a bigot." You tell your kids, "Do your homework and be prepared." And then you have this outcome, and you have people putting children to bed tonight, and they're afraid of breakfast. They're afraid of 'How do I explain this to my children?'

Just hours earlier, I had put my thirteen-year-old son to bed as he cried and told me he was afraid Trump would come to our house and hurt us. Trump was not yet the official president-elect, and he was already terrifying my child.

When he awoke at six a.m., my son anxiously asked me if Hillary had won. When I said "no," he began to cry again, an anxious, worried cry. This time he was not crying for himself, but for other children. My son is white, and for months he has repeatedly expressed anguish over Mexican children, Muslim children, gay children, women— everyone Trump has targeted throughout the campaign.

As parents, when our children are afraid, it is our instinct to calm them by saying, "Don't worry, it will be all right," but I couldn't say that to my children on the morning after the election because I was in shock and honestly didn't feel like it would be okay. Instead, I hugged my son and told him to take his shower. Then I went to my sixteen-year-old daughter, who was also crying, buried in her bed. Her immediate reaction to the news was concern about women's reproductive rights. She knows enough about Trump and his positions—if one can call them that—to realize her body is no longer hers alone. She didn't get out of bed for the entire day.

As I walked past the bathroom to the kitchen, I heard my son in the shower sobbing loudly. Morning in America.

When I was a child, I asked my Republican father to explain the difference between the two parties. He said that the GOP favored strict fiscal policies, while the Democrats tended to spend more on social programs. He didn't demonize the Democrats, nor did he eviscerate the character of Jimmy Carter. The parties possessed starkly differing views on political, economic, and social values and priorities; their philosophies diverged greatly, but it wasn't personal.

When I was a teenager, I remember disliking Reagan because everyone I knew disliked him, but I didn't follow politics enough to know why I disliked him. This stood in sharp contrast to my children's political astuteness during this past presidential election, and their fears. I never feared Reagan, and I certainly didn't worry that he would come to my house or to the house of an immigrant classmate.

On November 9, millions of children in America woke up in fear—fear for themselves, their parents, their friends. Pundits talk about a paradigm shift, and indeed, there has been a shift of gargantuan proportions. Where politics used to be a vague idea to children, that boring topic their parents discussed over dinner, politics is now the stuff of nightmares. Our president has become the boogeyman.

When my children were little, I could calm their fear of monsters by opening the closet or turning on the light. Their father and I assured them that we would protect them, that nothing would hurt them. What do we say now? What do parents of color say now? How can we assure them when we ourselves are afraid and uncertain of the future?

We do our best. We gloss over the severity of the situation; we seek out the slivers of light and hope. We lie.

The evening after the election, my son found Trump's post-victory tweet which read, "Such a beautiful and important evening! The forgotten man and woman will never be forgotten again. We will all come together as never before."

To a thirteen-year-old's eyes, the tweet felt hopeful and conciliatory. But I knew that Trump was talking about his constituents, the "forgotten" white men and women who had been left behind by progress, by inclusiveness, by a world where Barack Obama was our president. The tweet made me sick, but I put a smile on my face and shook my head in agreement with my son.

"Maybe it won't be so bad. Maybe he'll change," my son said as he bounded away.

The day after Trump's election, I read about a group of children at the Royal Oak Middle School in Detroit, who chanted "build that wall" as a group of Latino students cried. That was Day One of the new era, the era where cruel bullies feel empowered—validated—because the biggest bully of them all was not punished for his behavior; he was rewarded with the presidency.

The incident in Michigan was not the only one of its kind. Students in Minnesota came to school on Wednesday to find "Fuck All Porch Monkeys," "Whites Only," and Trump's name painted on the locker of a student of color. Students in York, Pennsylvania, chanted "white power" as they marched through their high school.

Our president has done nothing to dissuade this type of behavior. To the contrary, he has actively encouraged it at his rallies and on Twitter. Indeed, it can be argued that he won (the Electoral College, but not the popular vote) precisely because he gave voice to the worst of our society: the bigoted, racist, and misogynistic fanatics who have always walked among us, but whose numbers we naively assumed were dwindling. At the very least, we believed that they would be kept in check with a collective shaming and, yes, intolerance of such ideas.

As Jones said, most of us believed that we were making progress and that our children were growing up in a better America than the one we grew up in. Most of us talked to our children about the importance of acceptance, decency, and above all, empathy. Many of us watched our children surpass our own ability to empathize with individuals or groups we may not have understood or identified with, or even known personally. My children took for granted that they lived in a world where it was safe to love whomever they wished, where diversity was celebrated, and where being different in any way, shape, or form was accepted.

But the students who committed these heinous acts were not raised that way. They were fed a twisted set of values at home, and they ignored the lessons at school; they stewed in their own disdain for anyone who was not like them, anyone who challenged their deluded sense of superiority. And now they've been granted free reign by the man who occupies the highest position in our country to unleash the pent-up hate and ignorance that's been passed down like cancer.

Many parents have comforted their children after a nightmare. We say, "Monsters aren't real." The greatest challenge for parents in the new America is reassuring our children that monsters don't exist—when we know that they really do.

❧

Jaimie Seaton is the mother of two, and has lived and worked all over the world—reporting for many local and international publications. She reported for *Newsweek* from Johannesburg, and was later their Thailand correspondent. Her work has appeared in a variety of online and print publications, including *ESME, Pacific Standard, CNBC.com, CNN, Glamour, Good Housekeeping, New York Magazine* and *O, The Oprah Magazine*. She is also a frequent contributor to *The Washington Post*'s "On Parenting."

When Parenting and Activism Collide

By Shannon Brescher Shea

"This is all wrong. This whole day is wrong," I said, banging my phone down on my lap. It was the morning of the Families Belong Together March. Instead of chanting outside the White House about immigrant children being separated from their families, I was in my oh-so-stereotypical Prius in the Washington, D.C. suburbs with my husband and two kids.

I ran my hand through my hair and sighed.

The work/life balance is a familiar struggle for many parents. I'm lucky that when I leave my office, I leave my job behind. But my responsibilities as a privileged person aren't something I can walk away from. As I read the news about the latest shooting of an innocent black person or the wildfires exacerbated by climate change, my jaw tightens. Too often, I stop reading because I already know too well the unintentional contributions I'm making to systemic injustices. At the same time, I never stop being a mom who wants to spend as much quality time as possible with my kids. The see-saw is constantly teetering, the conflicting needs and expectations pushing and pulling.

This was just the latest variation on a familiar struggle that occurred whenever one of these events arose. *Do I bring the kids? Do I leave them behind and miss out on my time with them? Or do I stay with them and ignore the event?*

If I brought my family to this march, images of children in cages would haunt my five-year-old's dreams. He ran from the theater when the grandmother in the movie *Coco* yelled at the little boy. I knew I wouldn't have answers for his repeated questions: "Why are there kids in cages? Why are they away from their families? Why is our government doing this?" After all, they were the same questions constantly repeating in my own head.

Nor did I want to miss Saturday with my kids. I'm out of the house five days a week, heading out at eight o'clock in the morning and returning ten hours later. From the moment I walk in the door to when I tuck a fuzzy blanket around my older son, I have only two and a half hours with my kids each day. Far too much of my knowledge about my kids' weekdays is second-hand. Weekend hours are sacred.

At the same time, the stories and images of those separated families played out in my mind, a background newsreel haunting my life. How could I enjoy my family knowing others were going through such pain inflicted by our own government? Among all of the world's injustices, this situation planted itself in my mind, resisting all efforts to uproot it. I donated money, called my Congressional representatives, urged my loved ones to support the cause. But it didn't feel like enough.

I went back and forth, back and forth. Going, not going, going, not going. In the end, I decided not to go. The single deciding factor was the fact that we had made plans with another family before the march had been announced. I didn't want to disappoint both my kids and my friends. But during that phone call, I discovered I had written the plans down incorrectly. It turned out I had no commitment at all.

Dammit, I should be there, I thought.

But it was too late. The march had started hours before, twenty miles away. Guilt-ridden thoughts swirled. *Who are you not to go? You have so much and others have so little. Don't you owe it to them?* I squinted at the bright summer sun coming in through the windshield. There was nothing to see but car dealerships and traffic. Kicking papers on the floor aside, I contemplated that I was failing at both being an activist and keeping the car in a non-disgusting state.

Although our original plan failed, my friend suggested, "Why don't you come bowling with us?" So the seven of us immersed ourselves in the neon-lit dark of a local alley. As our kids slow-rolled balls that often didn't reach the pins, we chit-chatted about work and school. If we didn't have two astute kids standing a few feet away from us, I would have brought up my regret about not going to the march. I would have asked my friends, "How are you handling all of this?" A few different times, I almost did. But the presence of those little ears kept my mouth shut.

Instead, we headed over to the arcade, where I shot up Space Invader aliens with my five-year-old and distracted my two-year-old from the Skill Crane full of basketballs. It was both comforting and shallow. When I went to the bathroom, I looked in the mirror and thought: *Am I a good mom? Yes. Am I a good citizen of the world? Maybe.*

This is the back and forth many of us now face, a conflict which has become a familiar weight for those concerned with the world beyond our immediate families, friends, and small communities.

There's a saying that change starts at home, but these days that doesn't seem like enough. But how much do we sacrifice? What kind of parents are we if we leave our kids right now to go build a better future for them? Yet, what kind of parents are we if we don't? How can we love everyone without it becoming a zero-sum game?

I've wrestled with these questions both before and after this march. Some days, I feel like I know that I'm doing the right thing. Others, it seems like there is no right thing.

But perhaps it's not a zero-sum game. That useful adage "show, don't tell" is more relevant than ever when it comes to parenting. Perhaps in showing our children that we care about these issues, we're modeling the type of people we hope they'll grow up to be. We could lecture for hours about morality or we could demonstrate that commitment to justice with our own two feet.

I didn't go to the protest that day, but I know there will be more protests in the future. Next time I go to a march or protest, I'm going to tell my kids why I'm going and why it's so important. In some cases, I'll even bring them along with me.

Perhaps by just being myself—activist and all—I can be the parent I've wanted to be all along.

Shannon Brescher Shea is a mom of two kids who's just trying to make a difference. Living in the suburbs of Washington D.C., she writes about parenting in a challenging world at *We'll Eat You Up, We Love You So* and on Twitter @storiteller. She's also published in the *Washington Post, Romper, Ravishly*, and *Sierra Magazine*. In her day job, she is a senior science writer / editor for the federal government.

Feminist Role Model

By Krystal Sital

> It's hard to be a parent tonight for a lot of us. You tell your
> kids don't be a bully. You tell your kids don't be a bigot. You
> tell your kids do your homework and be prepared. And then
> you have this outcome and you have people putting children
> to bed tonight and they're afraid of breakfast, they're afraid of
> how do I explain this to my children?
>
> —Van Jones

Van Jones's words acted as a balm, a temporary relief to the physical
and emotional ache that clawed at my chest in the twilight hours of
the morning. It hadn't yet been made official, but we knew Trump
was going to win; I knew he was going to win, but I sat there crying
till the bitter end.

I am a woman.

I am brown.

I am an immigrant.

I am bisexual.

The polar opposite of him, I am everything Trump hates, everything he wants to eviscerate. I am also a mother to two little girls of
color.

In a few short hours, after listening to Van Jones's words that
night, I knew I must wake my girls and try to make sense of what
had happened, to build a foundation for our future in their language.
My girls were two and four, which made it difficult because for that
task I couldn't seem to separate my adult lens from the simple and
straightforward language I used with my daughters. Like so many
others who I have bonded with since the night of the presidential
election, I didn't sleep. With tears staining my cheeks, I prepared
breakfast and said nothing of the election, pretending that that
morning was the same as the others before it. My girls were so young

and innocent; did they really have to know? And if I did tell them of what had happened, I felt a responsibility to arm them with so much more than just the facts—the burden of being a woman.

As I caressed my older daughter's face, contemplating whether or not I should tell her this news, I thought of an alternate narrative in an alternate reality that could have been our history—my children could have grown up and flourished in a country where a woman president had succeeded a black president. I could have read them one of their favorite books, *Grace for President*, and said this was emulative of our real world. I could have felt some peace for the time being, knowing a woman was our leader; I could have saved the brutal history of silencing, degrading, and disrespecting women—which forms so much a part of my own personal history as well as that of the world—for another time, for when they were ready. But that arc hadn't happened, and as I stood before those sweet faces that morning, I chose to ignore the news, to shelter them, to keep them close, to pretend nothing had happened.

I took my older daughter to school that day. While I was able to navigate the world physically, something prevented me from fully interacting; it was as if a shawl, or some diaphanous veil, had wrapped around me, dulling everything and everyone. I wondered if my girls felt the difference and what that must look like to them. As I drove home after school, my older daughter said, "Donald Trump is our new president." A twisting in my gut rendered me speechless for a few moments as I parsed through thoughts of how this information was given to her, why, and what that must mean. "My teacher told me," she said. What I said in the wake of my daughter's comment has helped to shape me as a mother, a woman, and an advocate. It was a visceral reaction, one I couldn't tame or hone; one, in retrospect, I would never change.

"Donald Trump is not my president," I said.

"Donald Trump, not my president," she echoes.

"Donald Trump, not my president," my four-year-old teaches her two-year-old sister to chant.

There are many conversations necessary to unpack this to a four-year-old but it was a solid start, one that let her and her sister know that when one decides to denounce someone holding a coveted position like the presidency of the United States, a country both of her parents came to as immigrants, it is not a decision made lightly. Unprepared and ill-equipped to handle the important questions my girls asked, I was thrown into these discussions in the same way that other parents were, and I needed to understand the kind of parent I wanted to be and what that meant to my existence in this new world.

Later that same day, Amy, my mother's helper, a smart, quiet young woman in high school, came over for her designated two-hour shift so I could work. Everything was different and I'm not sure if that was because I was preoccupied with my own thoughts and unable to work, but I noticed she had not brought her bag of supplies or the bag of books her mother had saved from her childhood. When I asked her if something was troubling her, she told me, "A boy ran through the hallways today yelling, 'Grab 'em by the pussy! Grab 'em all by the pussy!'" I gazed into Amy's eyes, my body shaking, my two girls tugging at our arms, not as oblivious as I would have preferred them to be about what we were discussing. I asked myself: How can I shield and protect this young woman from the abuse that is to come? Tears filled Amy's eyes and she blinked them away. I later learned that I would always be processing and reacting to the presidential election and all that that meant, but at that very moment it felt as if another chasm had opened before me. Was it my place to speak to this young woman? Would her mother be upset if I did? Amy stood before me, needing something I didn't yet fully understand how to give. But even then, I knew how we chose to handle conversations was as important as the issues themselves.

We talked. Using the language of my children so they could be included in the conversation, we talked about Trump's comments regarding women's bodies and his history of disrespect and what that meant to Amy as a teenager, and what that would mean to my girls in the playground. We talked with my girls about what it meant to have a man like this as president of our country, how his actions and words were objectively wrong. We connected, reaffirming the bonds that exist among girls and women and tightening and strengthening those bonds through the generations.

Since Trump's election, I've gathered stories from women about that night and learned that we collectively mourned. It was a grief that was immediate and raw, one that bound us together in ways we had yet to comprehend. We could only cry. But crying and mourning were necessary before we could join forces to resist and fight. This was our way of preparing for the days and years ahead. For we strive to not only shield our women, to protect them, but also to arm them; we do this through constant open and honest communication. Let all women know that they are being heard, that their voices and opinions are important and equal, despite who currently holds the presidential office. In this Trump era, I am scrambling to learn, to teach, to advocate for myself and the young girls and women around me, who should never be made to feel silenced. There has been too much of that in history already.

❧

Krystal Sital was born in the Republic of Trinidad and Tobago, and moved to the United States in 1999. She is the author of the critically acclaimed memoir *Secrets We Kept: Three Women of Trinidad*. A PEN Award finalist and Hertog fellow, her work has appeared in *Elle, New York Times Magazine, Salon, New York Times Well Section, Today's Parent,* and the *Caribbean Writer,* and elsewhere. Krystal has taught creative writing; gender, sexuality, and culture; and peoples and cultures of the Caribbean at NJCU and FDU in New Jersey. She now teaches in the MFA program at Sierra Nevada College in Lake Tahoe.

Our People

America, The Beautiful

By Katherine Morgan

We stood there proudly, like little toy soldiers—our feet planted firmly together, our backs rigid and straight, our right hands placed directly over our hearts. This was how we had been taught to show our love for this great country of ours. I attended a public elementary school in Chicago, Illinois, so there was always a sea of diversity surrounding me, a so-called "rainbow of faces." We were a tiny United Nations in that social studies classroom—brown children who had lived there all their lives; pale children who had emigrated from war-torn countries; and children of every color in between. As I stood there, it hit me that diversity was all that I had ever known.

I used to fix my eyes on the colossal American flag hoisted behind my teacher's desk. I would make sure to count both the stars and the stripes, without skipping one. After the principal finished her morning announcements, a child's voice began to recite the pledge over the loudspeaker. It was a big deal to recite such an important declaration so very early in the morning and the student chosen for this task was invariably the teacher's favorite, their praises proudly sung over the speakers. I was never chosen for the honor, so my place was always in the classroom, by my desk, staring straight ahead.

Every Monday used to begin in the same way: we would stand, listen to the announcements, and then pledge allegiance to our country. No one in my class ever questioned why we did this, and I don't know if any of us ever thought about it. It was just something that we did; *we*, meaning Americans. No matter where you were, if that anthem played, we would stand, proudly and silently, with one hand over our hearts and the other holding a baseball cap and or ballpark hotdog. As children, we were taught to be proud of the ground upon which we stood, and yet, no one ever acknowledged *why* we should feel that way. Yes, our country was great, but how and why was it great?

I was born on January 13, 1994, in Gary, Indiana. I am an American citizen and always careful to check that box on all government forms, especially those that relate to my student financial aid. When I was younger, I wore my American citizenship proudly. My relationship toward my country was familial—I could say whatever I wanted about America, but if another was to judge her harshly, my claws would sharpen along with my tongue. Sure, America has its problems, as does my family, but I love them just the same.

My elementary education taught me that America is a country that was founded on pride. We, the people, seldom talk about America in an unflattering fashion. My teachers tended to skim over negative aspects of our history; instead, they would linger on what made our country so remarkable. Slavery, Harriet Tubman, and the Underground Railroad were brushed over in order to concentrate on the moon landing. The decimation of the Native Americans failed to appear in our textbooks, but we made turkey handprints and discussed our families' Thanksgiving meals. Internment camps were never mentioned, but Christopher Columbus was the modern-day hero of our great country. Why he was given credit for "discovering" a country that was already inhabited by Native Americans was never explained. In the end, it seemed, it was always our pride that got in the way of really understanding our history. Star-spangled glasses clouded our vision. Black history, *my* history, was confined to the month of February. Female history, also mine, was restricted to March. There just wasn't enough time in the school year for all of us.

I was eight years old and in Ms. Davis's second grade class when the planes hit the Twin Towers. We left school that day, not yet realizing that the United States of America was already a different country than it had been when we had arrived that morning. When, in subsequent years, September 11 fell on a school day, we would stand for the pledge, and then listen to a man singing about how he was proud to be an American, where at least he knew he was free. I always hummed along because I liked the song and secretly looked forward to hearing it over the loudspeakers every year. It was the true American national anthem.

Even though my schoolmates were from diverse ethnic backgrounds, racism was inevitably a part of our academic experience. I used to trade insults with a white boy—on whom I had a crush—during recess. I called him "a cracker," and he retaliated with the word "nigger." I had never heard that word before but knew by my friend's sharp intake of breath that it wasn't nice. We whispered our insults in the hallways, the classroom, and in the library—where, a few months later, that same boy would give me my first kiss behind a tall wooden bookshelf. When my teacher overheard us, she was horrified and sent us both to the principal's office. We got in trouble and that was the end of that. We had learnt our lesson.

A few years later, at a stoplight, a man on a motorcycle called the driver ahead of him a nigger. I was embarrassed and walked to school with my head down, suddenly ashamed of my city. On another occasion, a boy, with whom I was chatting online, asked me to send him a photo of myself. Nervously, I sent him one and he immediately wrote back in all caps: UGLY NIGGER and signed off. My heart breaking, I texted my best friend and asked her, *Am I ugly because I'm black?* She texted back that she never thought I was ugly to begin with. I could tell that she didn't really understand the question and, in all honesty, I was glad she didn't understand. Another afternoon, my best friend and I were waiting at a stoplight, on our way to the roller rink, when a Jeep sped by and two white redneck boys leaned out and shouted, "Nigger!" They laughed raucously, leaving us in a cloud of dust. My best friend turned to me, horrified, and asked if I was okay. I stared straight ahead, focusing on the lights, and told her that I was used to it.

When I was in the eighth grade, I came home one afternoon to find my mother staring at the television, tears streaming down her face. She was happy because a black man had just been elected president. She called my grandmother, and they both cried, never imagining that they would ever see this day. The television showed footage of the First Family, and I was struck by how beautiful they were. And struck, too, by the fact that they were black, just like my family and I started to cry too. I had never seen someone like me in such a position of power, and I was so proud. President Obama grew up with a single mother, just as I had. He was the embodiment of the American Dream, which meant that I could achieve my dreams too. I was a young black woman, living in a two-bedroom apartment with my single mother and sister. We would soon be forced to leave it as a result of unpaid rent, and eviction notices eventually covered the doors of the next few apartments that we lived in. My sister and I learned quickly not to get too comfortable; often, the walls were never decorated and sometimes clothes never made it out of the suitcases.

However, as I write this essay, I am enrolled in a four-year university, and while I worry about how I am going to pay for tuition, I smile when I think about how I got this far. People tell me that I, too, am the embodiment of the American Dream; or at least, that's what this country *wants* me to believe. Others believe that I am the embodiment of affirmative action. I am okay with both of those viewpoints, because if I am moving forward, nothing can touch me. I am invincible.

After President Obama is elected, I stop reading commentary on photographs of the president and his family. The word "nigger" is frequently thrown around and there are occasional mentions of nooses and of apes; some find it funny and some find it horrendous, but the one who initially posted it somehow "never meant for my comment to be considered racist." One of my white coworkers doesn't understand why blackface is offensive; another calls me "the whitest black girl he has ever met"—which I dislike intensely, because there's no such damn thing. My interests are my interests; they are not determined by color.

When white people declare that racism is over, we black people look at each other in public spaces and we roll our eyes. When we insist that racism is still very much a part of contemporary American life, white people tell us to be grateful because we had a black president and, frankly, isn't that enough? I continue to proudly proclaim that I am a feminist and that black lives matter. My white boyfriend's father calls him up, asking if I am "too much woman for him." We both get a kick of that. I've never been "too much woman" for someone. Perhaps my boyfriend's stepfather would prefer it if I was quiet and polite, and if my laughter didn't occupy so much space, like my body does.

During my first year at Portland State, I watched the presidential election of Donald Trump. I had voted for Hillary Clinton. I did my part. In fact, black women showed up for Hillary, even when we would have rather stayed home. We felt sure of her victory. She had experience, while he had a reality television show. She had poise, while he had a megaphone. I was at work when the results started to roll in, and for the first time in my adult life, I was scared that America was going to let me down. By the time the election was finally called, I was heartbroken, as were the women sitting beside me. Walking home, I didn't hide my tears. I thought about my best friend, whose moms I had witnessed getting married. Would their marriage now be considered invalid? Other friend's parents were un-documented immigrants who had lived in America for over twenty-five years. Her parents came in order to give their children a better life. When people chant "build that wall," I think of her family. They are good people, who deserve the American dream as much as I do. After all, that's the nice thing about the American dream—there is no limit on the number of people who can achieve it. I thought, too, of my trans friends, my gay friends, and my Muslim friends, and I cried even harder. Now, two years later, I know how right I was to cry. Trump and his administration have implemented anti-gay and anti-trans policies, clearly believing that my friends don't deserve enriching lives. These are people who are sweet and kind, who sim-ply want to be themselves.

Many voters who supported Trump were white. They liked that he spoke his mind, no matter how racist his views. They liked that he was a newcomer without government experience. Most importantly, they liked that he wasn't Hillary. I was appalled and hurt. I felt as though my country had stabbed me in the back—even though as a black person, I expected to be shot instead. I wept, thinking about the millions of people in America who had decided that I wasn't worth a damn. Hundreds of online posts by white people demanded that we "get over it" because they had "survived Obama" and now we can just "survive Trump." But democracy is supposed to be about more than just surviving. Friends who voted for Trump begged me not to change my opinion of them, but how can I not? I am a millennial, a black woman who can barely make ends meet sometimes. I attend a university that I can scarcely afford, and I use services provided at Planned Parenthood. I thought that *I* was the American Dream.

Years after Trump's election, I am surprised that people are still proudly wearing their "Make America Great Again" caps, even though Trump has done nothing to make our country better. His supporters still believe that he is going to build that border wall, even though Mexico won't pay for it. They still believe that he will drain the swamp, which, given that members of his administration continue to be indicted at a rapid clip, he is actually doing, however inadvertently. When I encounter someone wearing that stupid red cap, a part of me recognizes their eagerness and enthusiasm. I also want to ask them what the breaking point will be, because there will be a breaking point eventually. Trump will make sure of that.

So while my citizenship might get me far in Trump's America, my black skin sure won't. So when I now stand to pledge my allegiance to this country, as I have been doing since elementary school, with my hand over my heart and tears in my eyes, I feel ashamed, I feel hurt, I feel wronged. While I am an American, this is not my America.

Katherine D. Morgan is an essayist living in Portland, Oregon, with her cat Ramona. Her work has appeared or is forthcoming at *The Rumpus, Portland Mercury, HelloGiggles, Ravishly, Huffington Post, American Progress, JMWW,* and *The Establishment.* She spends her evenings working at Powell's Books and is an undergraduate student seeking a Bachelor of Science in English and writing at Portland State University. She has spent countless hours sitting on her couch watching *Frasier,* and yet, she still cries every time she watches the series finale.

THE FIRE IN THE DISTANCE

By Dina Elenbogen

On the last day of the old world, I sit in a chair, talking to my erstwhile professor in his office, where I once spent many hours as a young poet. He had introduced our class to Moshe the Beadle, the madman prophet who saw the fire in the distance and cried out even if no one listened, in Elie Wiesel's Holocaust memoir, *Night*. He introduced us to Primo Levi, who wrote: *In Auschwitz not only man died, but the idea of man*. Together we read Emanuel Ringelblum's *Warsaw Diary*, which documented the cruelty he witnessed in the ghetto in Poland.

Those writers and prophets described a barbarism beyond anything we'd ever known. We vowed to keep their memories alive. To never forget. My professor listened to and honored my poems, my melancholy, and my search for truth. He became my honors thesis advisor. Each week, I'd bring a new poem to his office and he would listen to it, change what got in the way of my own music. He heard my timid voice grow louder through the years—he preferred whispers to screams.

On the last day of the "old world," my daughter turns nineteen at the same university, which is why I return to the chair in the corner of my professor's office. My daughter arrived at the school with a rich, soulful voice that brought her to the sacred music Jewish Studies program. My husband, fifteen-year-old son, and I are in Bloomington on election day so we can canvass for voters in a non-swing state of endearment, be with our daughter on her birthday, and cheer on the election of the first woman president together.

Or so we believe as we stroll down a street of hope, one I'd never been down before, near East Second, surrounded by other, more rundown streets. On this newly developed avenue, each house is a different bright purple or green, with sprawling porches holding tricycles, piles of collected stones, summer shoes still drying out, solar heating, and signs everywhere that say: *Fire Pence, Clinton/Kaine 2016*. The trees still carry the deepest reds of autumn.

When we ring the final bell and a light rain begins to cover our materials, we return to the Democratic headquarters, hand back unused flyers, and look at the returns on TV and the newly concerned faces of the workers there. "How do things look?" I ask anxiously, having been away from media all day and not sensing a jubilant mood.

"Too early to tell, not enough votes counted to really tell anything yet," a worker responds. He thanks us for our day of walking through the blue streets of a red state.

I return to Ballantine Hall, where I spent my formative years camped out in the hallway, waiting for my professor, on the campus where the falling leaves of my first year there brought me to poems I'd written with abandonment, love, innocence, and a sense that anything was possible, a place where I felt there was a huge poem living in me; I wanted to learn how to release it.

In our literature classes, the truth of our existence could be found in the books we shared. My professor never spoke of his own life but of worlds where men weren't free, where anti-Semitism and, finally, death camps defined the life of a Jew. Some of the words that began to enter our conversations were *Resistance. Uprising. The Third Reich.*

Three decades later, the hallway seems so narrow I can barely pass those sitting and waiting. I lean into my professor's same office with the hesitancy of a nineteen-year-old, until he looks up with shock and welcome; he invites me to sit down in the chair in the corner.

I am not here to discuss my poems or to ask why no one believed Moshe the Beadle when he spoke of the horrors he had witnessed in the death camps. I am here to offer my condolences. My professor's wife died suddenly and unexpectedly on an ordinary September afternoon, hours before the Sabbath and days before the beginning of the Jewish New Year. I sit quietly and absorb his emotion the way I once absorbed his words. He tries to bring me back and release me from his cloud of sadness by asking after my life, my writing. Aware of the student waiting in the hallway, I prepare to leave as we share our concern about the election results. Even the slightest possibility of a Trump victory brings us to despair. Although my professor has traveled throughout the world these past decades and has spoken on different topics, he tells me that these days he speaks only about anti-Semitism because it is so prevalent. Out the window, the day darkens into late afternoon.

My daughter meets me, and we wait near a stairwell in Ballantine for my husband and son as a blond, chunky student in a red Trump shirt and hat passes us with what I see as a glaring look. I clear my throat and my daughter sternly whispers, "Don't say anything." On that day in November, Election Day, my daughter's nineteenth birthday, this Trump supporter in a college town in Indiana is still a shock. The sight of him and the aggressive sound of his boots hiking up steps sends a shiver through my body. At this moment I still think he is an aberration, not a foreshadowing.

We celebrate our daughter's birthday at our favorite Afghani restaurant. We get a corner table and look out the window at the continuous light drizzle and blackening sky. My husband had thought we would be celebrating a Clinton victory by now, that we would have been toasting to the first election our daughter voted in and to our first woman president. Instead, election numbers are inconclusive. We try to cast the shadow aside and enjoy the four of us together for our daughter's first birthday in college.

On the way home I drive, and my husband navigates through rain and fog and the radio, which calls election results; states we never expected to turn red were turning red. I ask my husband to turn off the radio because the sound is distorted and distracting, and this can't be true. Too many votes haven't been counted. This can't be true. As we get closer to Chicago, my phone buzzes with texts from my Evanston friends who are on their way back from Ohio, where they had helped with voter protection. Their messages say things like "Are you as sick as I am?" and "I'm going to throw up." My husband, son, and I are also concerned but we think the election is still inconclusive. This doesn't seem right. Can't be right.

A day or so later we understand that, on a dark road in Indiana, we saw the beginning of the country changing.

Even after Hillary's eloquent concession speech, even after Trump's victory has been declared and the first horrific cabinet members chosen, even after the people around me begin to accept this and discuss the things we'll have to fight for and be vigilant about over the next four years, I am still on that dark road in Indiana. I am still saying: *This. Cannot. Be.* I look for any way out. I wait for proof that Russia influenced the election through hacking. I support Jill Stein's recount efforts. All I can see is the fire in the distance. All I can look for is a way out.

From day one I talk about the electoral college and how its job is to make sure an unfit, dangerous demagogue does not become president. When I say things like this during the first postelection week, before this idea has gained momentum, men of good will, including my husband, look back at me in surprise and, dare I say, judgment. These men say: *That won't happen. That can't happen. There would be a revolution.* I say *yes. I can't remember a time when we were more in need of a revolution.* In gatherings at rallies, synagogues, and town squares, people are still speaking of the next four years. I am still saying *this can't happen.* I think about Moshe the Beadle. I can't forget the fire in the distance.

We gather in front of Trump Tower to protest Trump's choice of Bannon. My fifty-something friends and I are with mostly twenty-somethings from a far-left Jewish organization that I don't agree with on many things except that we must speak out against Bannon. They are carrying signs in Hebrew. They sing Hebrew songs, smile, and say things like *we are the Jewish resistance.* These words alienate me to the point of tears. I want to say no, the Jewish resistance was Abba Kovner who said to his people, especially the youth in the ghettos of Vilna in 1941, *we must fight with everything we have.* The Jewish resistance was Emanuel Ringelblum who smuggled his *Warsaw Diary* through milk bottles hidden underground, documenting the daily horrors. Yes, we are Jews gathered together on a cold December night in Chicago; yes, we need to fight the anti-Semitism we see spreading around our world, but I want to say to *these* youth that we are not yet fighting for our lives. Our president-elect is not Hitler. We are not Jews in ghettos. We need a new language.

Yet hate has been unleashed everywhere in this country. The president-elect has given permission to hate women, blacks, LGB-TQ's,

Muslims, Latinos, and Jews. As Jews we need to speak out against all forms of hatred. We need to stop it in its tracks.

The people around me continue to look at me with alarm when I insist that we wait for electors, or recounts, or evidence of Russian interference to turn this around. People tell me to stop dreaming of the impossible. They say *he is going to be president. There is nothing we can do. This is a Democracy. An "elect" has never betrayed his state.* I say we have never had a leader who is as dangerous as our president-elect. It is time to do what's never been done.

Even after a Republican elect from red Texas says he won't vote for Trump, even after proof of Russian hacking, even after re-counts show slimmer and slimmer margins of Trump's victory, friends tell me to wake up. That this is going to happen. I say it can't.

There are small circles of people who speak as I do. The long-time journalist Dan Rather warns that this is not a time to sit but to stand and fight. He is a voice of reason. Those in this small circle of people who see the fire and don't want to walk into it, those who see injustices breaking out like an epidemic ask why Obama and Clinton don't seem to be fighting hard enough for a re-count or a probe into Russian involvement. Why aren't they shouting their outrage? Dan Rather says we will one day have to explain what side we were on and what we did to fight.

Months ago, in the "old world," resistance was an academic exercise. More poetically than politically inclined, I began to collect poems of resistance. I gave a talk for an open house at the university where I teach, on the way different poets used their art to sometimes document and other times protest injustice. I have always been drawn to poets of witness and resistance.

I most love the poets who continued to sing or shout during dark times: Bertolt Brecht, Adrienne Rich, Carl Sandburg, Jamaal May, newly discovered women poets from Syria.

Last summer I planned a course called "Can Poetry Save us?" and when it came time to teach it on November 20, it no longer felt theoretical and distant. We read the Holocaust poets Paul Celan, Elie Wiesel, Primo Levi, and we got so lost in the way they crafted their anguish, fear, and hope that we never made it to the American poets,

Rukeyser or Rich. The only weapon I have ever been taught to use is language.

It was different for my grandfather. In early 1900, my father's father, Saul, was imprisoned in Russia for being part of the movement that resisted Communism. My father's Uncle Leo, newly arrived in America, went with the Abraham Lincoln Brigade to Spain to fight fascism. He fell in his first battle. My father flew a plane and dropped bombs on Germany during World War II.

On Pearl Harbor Day 2016, one month after Election Day, my father and I pack my car and return to the road to Indiana to help my daughter move to a new room. This is the road where I first saw the country change and over the past month grow even more profoundly polarized. In my mind everything has become good and evil, black and white. I read reports from a newly formed group, Pantsuit Nation, about the injustices that women and minorities are facing throughout the country. When someone cuts me off on the highway in a big black Jeep, I imagine he is a Trump supporter. I come from a progressive town where people say hello when passing and where many come to each other's aid. There are racial divisions, areas of poverty and crime, but many of us try to fight this together. When a Quran at the Evanston Public Library was defaced with swastikas, a group of Jews and Christians immediately replaced it. Early in the morning, running along the lake, I'm aware that almost everyone I pass takes a moment to smile, brighter than usual, in a way that says *we are all in this together.*

But I know the main roads in the rest of the country are different. I don't want to drive or stop at gas stations alone. On this long Indiana highway, I ask my father to tell me the story of Pearl Harbor, what he was doing on a day when he saw the unfathomable happen, a day he felt his country change. My father had been in the middle of an ordinary day of school and then work at his father's store in Humboldt Park.

My father listens to my fear of the fire in the distance, the grassroots efforts to resist that I read about online. He hasn't read about any of this in his paper copy of the *New York Times.* Many times this month he has said things like, *we will get through this.* This trip helps me to believe this for small moments of time. It becomes my respite. When have I last spent uninterrupted time like this with my father? When during this last month have I forgotten the state of my country for more than two minutes? On our first night in Bloomington, at my daughter's a capella concert, we hear her perform, among other things, a song of peace in Hebrew, Arabic, and English.

In the morning I bundle up against nineteen-degree winds and jog along the Jordan River that runs through campus, where decades ago my early poems fell into my lap as leaves untangled from my hair. A student whose face is covered in a winter mask runs toward me, and I panic before realizing he is just late to class. I do not visit my professor this time because I don't have much time and because suddenly it feels too painful. I still want to know why no one listened to Moshe the Beadle. I want to shout in my poems and conversations. My professor prefers whispers. I run faster and faster against these snowy paths, searching for an image that will help me describe where I am today, one month after the world has begun to change. All I can find is my three-word refrain: This. Can't. Be.

Dina Elenbogen, a widely published and award winning poet and prose writer, is author of the memoir, *Drawn from Water: an American Poet, an Ethiopian Family, an Israeli Story* (BkMKPress, University of Missouri) and the poetry collection, *Apples of the Earth* (Spuyten Duvil, New York). She has received fellowships from the Illinois Arts Council and the Ragdale Foundation and her work has appeared in anthologies including *Lost on the Map of the World* (Peter Lang, NY), *Where We Find Ourselves* (SUNY, NY), *Beyond Lament* (Northwestern University Press), *Rust Belt Chicago,* and magazines including *Lit Hub, Bellevue Literary Review, Prairie Schooner, Poet Lore, December, Woven Tale Press, Paterson Literary Review, New City Chicago, Tikkun, Tiferet, Times of Israel* and other venues. She has a poetry MFA from the Iowa Writer's Workshop and teaches creative writing at the University of Chicago Writer's Studio.

HOW I FOUND LOVE FROM MY HOMELESS
NEIGHBORS

By Mahin Ibrahim

I had been doing it for years. Walking past homeless people like they
were decor on a dirty street, occasionally donating a few dollars or
leftovers. *I've made sandwiches for the homeless before,* is how I'd rationalize
it. *What if they use the money for drugs?*

Los Angeles has the second highest homeless population in the
nation (53,000), and it was after I moved downtown, close to Skid
Row where 4,000 homeless people sleep every night that I realized I couldn't just ignore the homeless any longer. They were my
neighbors, and though I hadn't been great about getting to know my
neighbors in the past, I wanted to change that.

At the start of the Trump era, I signed up to volunteer for Homeless Care Days, a bi-weekly resource fair organized by the city held at
MacArthur Park, originally built as a drinking water reservoir in the
late 1800s. The fair was a place where the homeless get HIV tested,
apply for housing, and more.

"Just show up," the coordinator told me when I asked what I'd be
doing on my first day.

When I arrived that morning after a twenty-minute walk, the park
was mostly empty, and the fair was sparse. Jessica, one of the workers, let us know why: "The park rangers came and told the homeless
they had to clear out of here with their tents for an EDM concert."

"They can do that?" I asked.

She nodded.

The next time I volunteered, it was an overcast day, my favorite in
L.A. Though I had passed the park hundreds of times, this was my
second time actually visiting. The park had a huge lake in the middle with a tall spurting fountain and flocks of ducks. Moms walked
around the block with their babies in strollers. Spanish music blared

through a speaker across the street while vendors hawked their wares: sneakers laid on a plastic tarp, fresh mangoes and avocados, plastic toys that lit up and spun. That day, the park was filled with homeless people, reading and chatting with friends. Jessica put us to work.

We canvassed the park handing out fliers about the fair. Prior to this, we read a training manual, which told us to be cautious when speaking with our clients in case they were on drugs or seemed dangerous. This wasn't an exaggeration; Jessica said they'd shut down the fair for a few months after a violent incident.

I walked around the park with two regular volunteers. We approached the first group of people who were sitting on a bench and chatting. I greeted a man on the left, with silver-grey hair and a crew cut. He had a giant purple scar running down his neck that I tried not to look at.

Before I could tell him about the fair, he said, "Please forgive Americans and us. I am sorry for everything we've done."

As a Muslim hijabi, I knew exactly what he was saying. Please forgive us for the anti-Muslim incidents that rose by fifty-seven percent the year Trump took office, with hijabis being murdered on the streets. Please forgive us for having a president who called for a "complete shutdown of Muslims entering the United States" through the Muslim travel ban;a president who fueled Islamophobia with public statements to CNN such as, "I think Islam hates us"; and, who repealed Obama's removal of Muslim-targeted language in the White House National Security Strategy.

The man's words made me feel incredibly loved. I told him there were good people in America and he had no need to apologize.

I couldn't stop thinking about him while we walked. There I was, ready to make social niceties, while this man had cut straight to the truth. I wasn't used to people being so blunt. In our everyday life, we try to be so politically correct, we often say nothing at all. Yet this man was completely unfiltered, offering up love as if he were my best friend. As a homeless person, he was—less. Less guarded, less removed, less apathetic.

As we closed our loop around the park, I saw a homeless woman with a jagged pixie cut perched on the fence, half-filled water bottles at her feet. She had a nervous energy about her, as if she couldn't sit still.

"Are you Muslim?" she asked me.

"Yes," I replied.

"Good. I, too, am a woman of faith." She pointed a finger up at the sky. She then reached out to hug me, and I hesitated before hugging her back.

The volunteer admonished me, "You shouldn't have done that. She could have a disease."

"She reached out to me, so I reached out to her," I said.

How could I do anything else? Here was another instance where people I'd ignored were not only aware of me but had my back.

Recently at the library, a homeless man asked what I was reading. I showed him *The Road to Mecca*, a memoir by Muhammad Asad, a Jewish convert to Islam responsible for the greatest English translation of the Quran of all time.

"You're Muslim?" he asked.

I nodded.

"That's great!" he exclaimed, as if I had cured a terminal illness.

In America, you're welcomed and loved if you're rich, pretty or famous, not religious. While Trump's continued demonization of Muslims makes me unsure whether the forty-six percent of Americans who cast their vote for him actually want me here, my interactions with the homeless showed me otherwise. While walking home that day, I was humbled to realize that of all the communities I had encountered, it was the homeless, the most marginalized, who were the most welcoming of all.

Mahin Ibrahim is a writer whose work has appeared in *HuffPost* as a contributor, *Narratively,* and the anthology *Halal If You Hear Me*. Connect with her @mahinsays on Twitter.

It's Been There

By Elena Perez

When I was younger, my mom and I used to review the clothing catalogs she'd get in the mail, searching the pages for non-white models. *Nope. Nope. There's one! But she's in the back corner. Of course! Never in the center.* We'd point to the token black models, pick out the occasional guest appearances by Asian or Latina models, and laugh at the blatant inequality. One thing I learned growing up is sometimes you've gotta laugh, because the frustration, the sadness—it'll eat you up if you don't.

Fast forward twenty-some-odd years and the places I've worked look a lot like those clothing catalogs; there's hardly any diversity. The only difference is that it becomes a men's clothing catalog once you reach upper management. We may find diversity in administrative positions, but the planners, researchers, managers, and decision-makers who shape our communities and our nation are far from diverse. If you're white, chances are you haven't noticed. If you're not white, it's a reality you're accustomed to. The bigotry my parents, grandparents, and great grandparents experienced shaped the present day. So it's no surprise that mostly white, male-dominated institutions, government agencies, industries, and organizations continue to shape our tomorrow.

That was the case before Trump even arrived on the political scene. So when explicit racism bubbled to the surface after he was elected, I wasn't surprised.

I knew our history and didn't believe people were going to change just because laws made explicit racism illegal. In 1954, for example, the Supreme Court ruled "separate but equal" unconstitutional, but racism already dictated where people lived, which by that time had established a blueprint for deeply entrenched disparities between white communities and communities of color. My father was born and raised in a Latino *barrio* in Texas; in 1954, he was about to turn nine. Brown vs. Board of Education didn't magically bestow inheritances and a rich school district on my dad and his family. Even if they'd wanted to move to a "better" neighborhood, that wouldn't have been an option until my dad turned twenty-three and the government enacted the Fair Housing Act prohibiting housing discrimination. Despite new regulations, redlining persisted, disproportionately devaluing property in communities of color, and further skewing the distribution of wealth in our country.

So I can't blame Dad for laughing at the outrage expressed over the racism we read about in the news today. "Did you think it would just go away?" Without waiting for our reply he'd retort, "Hell no!" It just went underground.

So let's be honest for a change. Stop pointing, appalled, at the blatant sexism, heterosexism, racism, or bias of whatever form that has risen up alongside—even supported by—the Trump administration.

It's been there.

Maybe you haven't noticed it if you haven't experienced it, if you haven't recognized your own role in perpetuating it, intentionally or otherwise. But it's been there. It's what got Trump elected in the first place; it's why politicians treated our forty-fourth president with blatant disrespect; it's why Middle Easterners posed as Latinos soon after September 11. "You know it must be bad if they're claiming to be Latinos," my dad chortled.

That was nearly eighteen years ago.

Yes, the Trump administration makes me depressed, demoralized, and angry. But this is nothing new. Trump is the result of how disconnected we've become from the realities of our society: a system riddled with racism, sexism, and biases of all kinds. Trump has finally brought this blatant discrimination to the attention of those who assumed everything was good—because maybe for them, it was.

I get it. It's not easy to identify implicit racism if you've never experienced it yourself. I recently read about a transgender woman's struggle with identity as she transitioned from being a man in the armed forces to the woman she is today. She admitted she hadn't realized how much white male privilege she had until she lost it. She hadn't noticed the advantage she had while she was a white man. But that understated white male privilege—it's been there.

Unsurprisingly, Trump's fiats by executive orders only further exacerbate existing inequities, from unjust mandates directed at those without the means to afford adequate legal representation to environmental rollbacks in poor neighborhoods historically slated to endure industrial pollution. These communities often lack the resources, political representation, and capacity to push for protections—protections that safeguard their wealthier and often whiter counterparts. And while Trump relies on his racist, sexist, and hateful rhetoric to reinforce his support base, his policies don't actually benefit the majority of the individuals backing him. Instead, his agenda quietly serves the wealthiest one percent of the nation, stepping on the backs of the poor, the weak, and the marginalized to increase the profits and advance the self-interests of a limited few. The outright discrimination and scorn of Trump's policies merely shroud deeper disparities, including growing economic disparities, which weaken our nation, disparities that impact us all.

While I certainly don't approve of the Trump administration's work, its divisiveness has been a wakeup call, highlighting the need to address the pervasive racism, the sexism, the intolerance in our country; the need to address disproportionate representation; the need to be a voice for those who go unheard or who are too afraid to speak. Institutional racism, systematic discrimination, widespread sexism, and even the unconscious bias that exists within us all has become clear, thanks to the Trump administration—and with this newfound clarity, we can see the need to call out and throw out the public policies and practices that perpetuate inequities.

About a year and a half into the Trump administration, I found myself in Ecuador speaking to the director of the country's Fulbright Commission. At one point in the conversation, she reached for the newspaper on her desk and began turning its pages, showing me the photos printed on them. "There's a man," she pointed out. "All men. No women—at least not in the politics or business sections," she continued, highlighting the disparities in her own country, just as my mother had once highlighted the disparities in mine, and as Trump highlights the disparities today. The marginalized know what needs to change. We've always known. It's been there. Our nation's history, our parents' stories, their lessons, as well as our own experiences have shaped us, making us more aware, more persistent, more resilient. Now finally, because of Trump, everyone recognizes the need to rise up and fight for change.

We must band together and seize this moment. If we don't, in this age of globalization, our nation will be left behind. Now's our chance to learn from our past, our failures. It's our chance to change the deficiencies in our system, to eliminate differential treatment, to engage those in the shadows, and to include the overlooked.

Now that Trump has everyone's attention, let's push for initiatives that close existing achievement and opportunity gaps. Let's increase diverse representation within our nation's governments, institutions, and private industry. Let's make tomorrow a reflection of the lessons learned from yesterday and today. Let's change our nation's metaphorical clothing catalog, because diversity has been one of our major strengths and has constituted the fabric that enriches our nation. Let's strengthen our nation and promote resilient communities and equitable outcomes that benefit everyone. Let's pay attention to the rumblings of a revolution, harnessing that unyielding might of the people, because it's been there.

੭

Elena Perez works to advance environmental justice, address climate change, and engage marginalized populations to promote healthier and more resilient communities.

Fight Like Hell

By Sarah Mina Osman Mikesell

When I First Learned He Had Won

My fiancé cannot stop shaking. His eyes are glued to the screen. He keeps running his fingers through his hair. It would be two days before Paul would stop shaking. A flood of texts came in from friends all over the world, asking, *Are you okay? Do you want to come crash on our couch for a bit? Canada is far colder than Los Angeles, but it's nice to live here!*

They joked. *Maybe now would be a good time for an asteroid to hit.*

They wondered. *I'm DACA. Does this mean I'm going to be deported?*

They reacted. *My dad just picked up an ancient Hawaiian dagger and hurled it into the wall. It's stuck. He's not going to take it out until Trump is impeached.*

I lay in bed, staring up at our popcorn ceiling. What would happen to me? Would I be sent to live in a camp because my father was a Muslim? Would I have to register? I wasn't even technically a Muslim but would that matter? Would my father's mosque be bombed? Would he be safe when he went to pray every Friday? He lives in Denver, which is a fairly liberal city, but still, one never knows where hate will strike.

And there were my students. My poor students. They could not control the fact that they were not white. They could not control that their new president considered them to be "rapists and criminals." They could not control that their parents had brought them here for a better life. They could not control that some Americans had dismissed a man's hateful rhetoric as nonsense while others sincerely believed it. They were criminals; I was a terrorist. And we had all received a massive middle finger.

First Day

I decided to wear black to work the next day. I was not the only teacher to do so. Hardly anyone smiled that day. Administration gave us no guidance as to how to handle the situation. I knew that as an English teacher—one who specialized in the analysis of rhetoric—much of this duty would fall on me.

I walked into class, not sure if I would have to lead a full therapy session or if we would continue analyzing a letter from Abigail Adams. One of my students wandered over to the board and wrote in huge letters: *Deportation Day*. We all chuckled at his joke as I erased it.

"I don't see this as deportation day, or as a day in which we should fall into despair," I told my students, most of whom looked as though a close family member had just died. "Remember that great change comes in times of strife. If there is never any strife, then we would never grow as a society. Remember that the greatest revolutionaries rose up because they had to. Revolution does not just happen because; it happens because there are rights being damaged, and one has to stand up for those rights. So I see this day as"—I scribbled on the board—*Revolution Day*. "It's our time to rise up. If we just sit back, then nothing will change, and we will have reason to despair. But if we fight, if we stand up, then justice will prevail."

My students nodded, relieved by my attempt at a *Dead Poets Society* moment. The rest of the day I let them write out their feelings. I listened as they confessed their fears for their families, for themselves, and for other minorities. Would their moms be taken away? How could those who voted for him be so stupid? Could they not see his rhetoric was damaging? Had they not studied history and seen this happen before?

As they spoke, a few asked if I would leave, as I had joked I would if Trump got elected. I had seriously considered it and had spent some time the night before studying what it would take for me to move back to Australia, where I had lived for a brief period, or to go to Canada (only to find that the website had crashed). I had even asked Paul if he would be willing to go abroad. But if I were to leave, I would be running away, and. I could not do that.

One student finally reminded us. "America has dealt with crap before and came back stronger than ever, so I have faith we will face this and continue to kick ass."

My Baba

I knew I needed to talk to my dad. My *baba*. Would he want to leave? Would this be the final straw? Was this the concrete proof he needed that Americans were idiots?

"How are you doing, Baba?" I asked, stuck in anxious L.A. traffic.

"I'm okay. Disappointed, but okay." His voice cackled over the phone. "I'm glad I campaigned for Hillary. I feel like I could have done more. But she was also a flawed candidate, if we had had Bernie, this might not have happened…"

I shook my head. Baba never missed a moment to fly his Bernie bro flag. "Are we going to be sent to the camps now? Are we going to have to register?"

Baba laughed. "Trump is as evil as Hitler, but he's not as smart or as charismatic. I'm not worried about that."

"Are you going to leave?" I continued, concerned. "Do you want to move back to Egypt?"

"No," he answered frankly. "This is my country too. I deserve to be here just as much as anyone else. I know a lot of your students are immigrants or have parents who are immigrants, so tell them that too. We have every right to be here. We're American too."

"So you're not going to leave?"

"No. I'm going to stay here." He yawned loudly. "Besides, Egypt has been through far worse, so this isn't as bad as that. Be proud of who you are. Don't start trying to hide your heritage because of these idiots."

"What are you going to do?"

"I'm going to fight like hell. And I suggest you and your students do the same."

Fight Like Hell

Over the course of the next few days, my students and I did attempt to fight, each in our own way. My students attempted a walkout, as they saw many other students across Los Angeles do. When they were blocked at the school gate, I helped them to write posters with messages of love, unity, and a few "dump Trump" ones for good measure. We consulted on whether or not another attempted walkout would be ideal, but a lesson in how to contact their reps was better.

I decided to declare my own pride, my own way of showing my students that they deserved to be here too. I wore a hijab for the rest of the week. I had never worn a hijab in America, nor had I ever attempted to tie one on my own. After multiple YouTube tutorials, I was able to adequately tie a hijab, and I began to wear the ones my cousins in Egypt had given me. It was my middle finger to Trump. You may want to register us all, but damn it, you can't silence us.

There were no Muslim students at school, so my hijab became a point of interest. The students who understood it as a protest loved it, and I suddenly began to receive comments such as, *You go, miss* and *You're the most kickass teacher*. Some asked what exactly it symbolized, and why Muslim women wore them. Others asked why I had started to wear it now and had never bothered to before. Some students walked by with a quizzical look on their faces, but a rude or ugly comment never passed their lips.

I had asked Baba about wearing the hijab. I explained the purpose and was assured that it would not be sacrilegious, because it was worn in support. This even convinced my sister to wear a hijab for a day or two at the Upright Citizens Brigade, much to the surprise of her comedian friends.

I only had one negative reaction to my hijab, and that came from my fiancé's mom. I had always thought of her as being liberal—she lived in the suburbs of Chicago and went to a church that flew a gigantic rainbow flag outside—so I was surprised when she was taken aback by my hijab.

"Why are you wearing that?" she asked as we sat down for dinner. "I don't get it. Are you Muslim now?"

"It's to show support for other Muslim women, because they have been getting harassed. It's also to show my students to stand up and be proud."

"But it's not even tied quite right, is it? I just don't—"

"That's enough, Mom." My fiancé cut her off. "We all have to fight, every way that we can."

Later that night Paul joined the fight. He became a member of the ACLU and Southern Poverty Law Center. He began to research different marches, different causes. He was no longer paralyzed.

Visiting Baba

Two weeks into the new normal, I went to visit Baba in Denver. While I was still disturbed, he was functioning as normal. I decided that my friends, my students, and I could use a bit of advice on how to carry on, so I interviewed Baba on the subject of how to survive Trump.

He expressed his shock, but he did not despair. He confirmed that he would call his members of Congress to oppose any proposed unjust laws. He voiced his support for peaceful protests, and how they are a reminder of the principles our democracy was founded upon.

He reminded me that, despite the madness, he had received more kindness than hate. The Friday after the election, he recalled that a group of white Christians, including a pastor, came to the mosque bearing food and signs of love. They reminded my father that he was supported, and that he would continue to be supported. He belonged here, in America, just as much as anyone else.

Constant Worry

Although life has calmed down a little since those first few weeks in November 2016, and we are no longer in a constant state of panic, it still does not feel safe. It's not so much Trump, the man, who is to fear but what he represents. We elected a man with no regard for humanity. Even if he accomplishes nothing, so many were willing to go along with his beliefs, were willing to dismiss his words.

I worry still that Baba will be targeted. I worry still about my students, about what this administration could do for their future. I still receive jokes, invitations, and reactions via text. I sometimes still stay awake at night, staring up at the popcorn ceiling, wondering if Baba's mosque will be targeted next. But then I remember Baba's advice. We cannot just stay silent. We cannot just run away. Now is the time to fight like hell.

࿊

Sarah Mina Osman's work can be found in *Argot Magazine, HelloGiggles,* and *Vocally*.

Viva La Raza!

By Jennifer Silva Redmond

Here's the deal. I was always an optimist, the Pollyanna in any group, always a glass half full kind of gal. That all ended on November 9, 2016. As a Mexican-American whose grandmother came here from Mexico as a child, I was appalled that my country, my American compatriots, could have elected such an obvious bigot, such a basher of our neighbor to the south, and a man so disrespectful of all people of color.

A bit of background. My mom was born in the part of Mexico known as East L.A. to a family of typical immigrants who worked hard to assimilate. But when my mom turned seventeen and married a white boy from Pasadena, she pretty much went her own way. My parents became hippies and in 1968 we moved to Venice, California, where no one cared who your grandparents were, as long as you were a *freak* and not a *square*.

My brothers and I loved my nana, though we didn't know that her father—a philosopher and poet—had been a revolutionary in his native Mexico and had come north with his family in search of greater artistic as well as political freedom. We just knew that she sometimes sung us songs in Spanish, called us *pobrecito* when we skinned a knee, and taught us how to make quesadillas before they were a staple of every Mexican restaurant.

Fast-forward to when I moved from Los Angeles to New York City in 1981 to pursue my acting career. Suddenly I was living in a city where everyone was known by their ethnicity, where my new friends referred to each other as spics and micks. I told my Puerto Rican friend that my grandmother was Mexican, and after that I was "the Mexican girl from California." I was also exposed to prejudice for the first time in my life, when I lost out on a few commercials and jobs for looking "too ethnic" (not blonde and blue-eyed).

All that changed when I got married and traveled to Baja California with my husband Russel, an artist and sailor with the soul of a Mexican. In Baja, I immediately sensed a connection to the land and the people that might have been genetic. Or maybe everyone who travels to Mexico for the first time falls in love with it—we certainly did, and we spent much of the first decade of our married life traveling there. Along the way, I began writing and editing under my pen name, Jennifer Silva Redmond, adding my nana's last name to mine to proudly proclaim my Mexican-American heritage. Back in San Diego, I took a position with a publisher that specialized in the history and cultural heritage of Mexico and Baja California.

So you can imagine how I felt when the man who had called Mexicans "rapists and murderers" suddenly became president of the United States. (Remember, I lived in New York City in the 1980s, so I knew exactly what kind of a con man Trump was, and is, and kept expecting the American people to catch on and get wise to him.) When, as president, Trump instituted a travel ban on Muslims, I thought he'd gone too far. I thought so again when he disparaged a highly respected Mexican-American judge. And then came Charlottesville, with Trump buddying up to the alt-right and distancing himself from the peaceful protestors who bravely stood up to American Nazis. Watching all this unfold on the news, I was devastated, as were my black, Jewish, and Latino friends. But since I believe in all Americans' civil liberties—even Nazis—I could do nothing but watch and hope that the rest of the electorate was as appalled as we were.

They were not. In fact, much of Trump's loyal and loud base continued to scream for "the wall" that was supposed to—*somehow*, unlike every previous border wall—keep out "illegals," these much-talked-about killer, drug-dealing Mexicans that Trump both feared and was fascinated by. He clearly knew that the idea was red meat to a large part of his fan base.

Now I get that a lot of Americans are casually racist, in a mostly invisible and unacknowledged way. I've been told with a smile, "You don't look Mexican, so why bring it up?" I even had one dear friend say to me, sincerely, that I wasn't "*really* Mexican" so I couldn't understand what *real* Mexicans are like. (To top that off, he told me, "California never belonged to Mexico." I mean, *Jesus Cristo*, seriously?)

But nothing I'd experienced in my half-century-plus prepared me for the Trump administration criminalizing asylum seekers crossing the border by instituting their "zero tolerance" ruling, thereby causing hundreds of already desperate parents to be separated from their young children. Of course, I marched and donated to politicians and agencies fighting the family separations. And I fixated on the midterm elections in late 2018, thinking, again, that this time Trump had gone too far, had revealed his racism to the world, all in order to fulfill an agenda that seemed a lot like white nationalism.

Then, Trump actually called himself a nationalist, in a not-very-veiled signal to every bigot and hater in the land that his administration was going to look the other way at acts of racism and hatred toward those who are *other*. That statement was quickly followed by horrific anti-Semitic violence, which was condemned by Trump in such mealy mouthed terms that no one could miss his pandering to the white nationalists and the alt-right.

As the midterms approached, Trump referred to a "caravan of illegal immigrants" coming north from Central America. Suddenly, this motley group of parents and children—much like those who come each year, attempting to outrun violence, torture, and rape—were full of "gang members" and "terrorists" who were "infiltrating" our country. Now, even zero tolerance was too tolerant—we needed soldiers to fight off these deadly hordes. The Donald dispatched thousands of soldiers to the border, right before the elections, spending millions of dollars for a perfectly timed publicity stunt that I'm sure every American saw through—even those who applauded it. Trump even instructed soldiers to fire back at anyone throwing stones, not that the soldiers listened to him, thank goodness. The soldiers rolled out barbed wire, enforced the already well-enforced border, and were sent home.

I was relieved to see the midterms heralding a return to national sanity, and my beloved home state leading the way in "flipping the House." But a few states and counties saw the election of politicians who'd clearly ridden the Trump administration's xenophobic coattails all the way to the polls. Fear and hatred of the migrant caravan, still hundreds of miles south of our border, had done its job. I gritted my teeth as Trump supporters were interviewed on the news, stating how glad they were that our laws were "finally" being enforced. I growled at the television, knowing our already tough immigration laws were being warped, even subverted, all to suit Trump's canny sense of self-promotion.

I followed along online as thousands of footsore men, women, and children reached Tijuana and watched in horror when tear gas canisters were flung over the border, and women and children got gassed in what was called *collateral damage*. Appalled, I listened as TV pundits smugly stated that the migrants had "been warned" as to what they'd get if they tried to enter illegally—not the succor that the United Nations Human Rights Declaration promises to those crossing our borders in search of asylum but hatred and fear and toxic gas.

Oddly, a friend at the border corroborated reports that the migrants had been promised that the border gates would open to them that very morning; would anyone intentionally spread such a dangerous lie simply to cause a panic and instigate violence? No one knows, though the rumor mills worked overtime, blaming journalists and agitators on both sides.

I can't see what was achieved by all these machinations—by vilifying, attacking, and arresting these "huddled masses yearning to breathe free" who had come, "tempest-tossed," to our shores. Of course, the highest-placed elected official in the land got to cater to the racists in his base, but that could hardly be worth losing our place upon the world stage as promoters of liberty and freedom. My friends across the country—where those who identify as Hispanic and Latino comprise the second-largest ethnic group—were outraged at seeing this humanitarian crisis play out on our southern border for such measly political gains.

As for myself, I hadn't thought of myself as a patriot for most of my life, but now that my country seems to be at risk of becoming something unrepresentative of American values, I find myself fiercely and fervently patriotic. And, yeah, I'm furious. And though some of my anger is directed at Trump, everyone knows that he's not the root of the problem we all face today. He's just a very ugly, painful symptom of a congenital, metastatic systemic disease. As long as we Americans hold onto our outmoded *us* and *them* mentality about race, we will continue to lose out as a country in every way.

Luckily, there are many of us who believe in social justice and equality, and when we band together we are very powerful. I like being part of that resistance, raising my voice among those who protest this administration's injustice, and being a peaceful soldier in that fight. I think my great-grandfather would be proud of me. I know my nana would.

❧

Jennifer Silva Redmond is a freelance editor and writing instructor. Formerly editor-in-chief at Sunbelt Publications, she is on the staff of the Southern California Writers Conference, teaches at San Diego Writers, Ink, and was prose editor for *A Year in Ink,* Vol 3. Her essays, articles, and fiction have been published in anthologies and national magazines, including *Latinos in Lotusland, Books & Buzz, Sail, Cruising World, Science of Mind,* and *A Year in Ink,* Vol 11.

Love in the Time of Trump (A Letter to My Beloved)

By Simran Sethi

"…soft or hard, love was an act of heroism."

- Ta-Nehisi Coates, *Between the World and Me*

In the fading daylight, we canvassed hand in hand. You made me feel safe in an unfamiliar neighborhood. I, in garbled Spanish, made our passage comfortable once the porch lights were illuminated and the doors opened. It was November 8, 2016, an hour before the polls closed. We asked those who opened their doors if they had voted and offered to give rides to those who hadn't. As the dusk deepened into night, we dropped off our campaign clipboards and headed home.

Early on, you tried to assuage me. "It's early. She'll pull ahead." Later, you tried to console me. I rejected both and pushed you away. "You did this," I hissed, as my anxiety swelled and my heart sank. I wanted you to acknowledge the overbearing weight of your power, to understand how deeply personal the political had just become. You shook your head and quietly reminded me that you were not to blame—while also processing the ways in which white men like you most certainly were.

Recognizing privilege can be hard. It was new for you—insidious, burrowed so deeply in your individual (and our collective) DNA that it felt normal, and for the working-class members of the community in which you were raised, likely imperceptible. But it's there, sweetheart: in standards of beauty, in suppositions about worth, in boardrooms, and in classrooms. Privilege is woven into policies and institutions that are supposed to offer equal protection, access, and opportunity.

Power looks like you.

It is revealed in the traffic violation that landed you in jail, not prison, and affirmed by the size of your paycheck and the weight of your words. You dwell in optimism. You move through the world with less trepidation. The space you occupy is wide and full; the world rises up to meet you.

The default for someone like you, explains author Nanea Hoffman, "is to assume everyone starts at the same place." We do not. I was raised to succeed—the primary directive from parents who knew that, in order to even be considered, I would have to be twice as good as my peers. "You're an immigrant," my father would admonish me. "You have to give more." I was six.

For decades after, I strived and fought. I struggled—as a brown, bookish girl—to find reflections of myself in the world around me. I strained to bear the oppressive weight of the American Dream and make it manifest, no matter the cost. And I succeeded. Yet, despite accolades, I was—and still am—reduced to a quota, a check in the "diversity" box.

"I don't see color," you say.

I, in frustrated resignation, respond: "There isn't a moment I don't."

You pull, I push. This is our life under Trump.

How did you become the man I love? You bake; I write. You're gregarious; I'm reticent. You're North; I'm South. You're local; I'm global. But we meet in vulnerability. You soften my edges. You are honest and kind.

After the death of my father, and the dissolution of a romance that never should have existed, you extended sweetness. You sang to me in bed and waltzed me around your kitchen. You baked me pie and brought me coffee. You took me to the mountains and showed me beauty. Your relentless tenderness helped mend what was torn.

Three hours after the president-elect's victory speech, you drove me to the airport for a speaking engagement in Vancouver. You leaned over to kiss me goodbye, but I remained still—stiff with fear, anxious of the world outside your unkempt Subaru. When we finally got out of the car, you squeezed me again, imploring me to come back to you. I offered no response, silently wondering if I could.

I wanted to skip the return flight and stay in Canada, trying to avoid the pain of living amid people who wanted to build walls around people who looked like me. But, of course, they are everywhere. Their desires to subjugate and eradicate are historic. I was awakening to a new depth of the ancestral terror people have suffered: unjust imprisonment, cruel indifference, trails of tears. The hot shame of my delayed, deepened cognition commingled with dread about the days and years to come.

Over the next few days, we exchanged several tense calls, each one punctuated with my pointed questions about what you were doing to take responsibility for the privileges of your skin and gender. In our final long-distance exchange, I heard you slowly exhale. From 1,400 miles away, my jaw clenched, and I doubled down. "What. Are. You. Doing?"

You struggled to respond, muttering the question felt like an accusation. I sighed in response. It was both.

I appreciated that you were trying to wrestle with the question but knew what you wanted, deep down, was for me to stop thinking about the election and for everything to return to the nest of naïve complacency in which we had so comfortably rested. Honestly, I wanted the same. But that choice existed only for you. For me, the architecture of systemic oppression stood in stark relief. I ached with a pain I had never fully comprehended and burned with accountability I had not fully owned.

After I hung up the phone, I peered into the tiny mirror in the hotel bathroom and asked myself the same question I had posed to you. *What are you doing to make things better?*

Our relationship was, at the time, relatively new. One that could end without much collateral damage: limited interactions with parents, a small handful of shared events we called our own. Questions continued to surface: *How do I take care of myself? How do I show solidarity? Is partnering with a white man a betrayal to my brown community?*

I did not know the answer. I only knew that I was—I *am*—tired of living in spaces where only part of my existence is reflected back at me. I swim in a pool of whiteness. I navigate dominant culture and history: I celebrate your holidays; I eat your food; I know your God. What do you know of mine?

At the end of the week, I returned home. I had tried to convince myself that Trump's election wasn't necessarily a reflection of racism. But I knew, even in those early days, that the so-called "repudiation of the establishment" was driven by anger, and that anger was stoked by hatred.

As I lumbered toward the exit where we had agreed to meet, I cast my eyes toward the tile floor, avoiding the gaze of the white men— and white women—who may have voted for the president-elect. I couldn't discern who among them hated people like me so much. I kept myself safe by assuming they all did.

Then, I heard you call my name. I lifted my head and saw you grinning widely as you walked briskly toward me. Unsmiling, I said loudly, "You were supposed to meet me at the curb." You ignored me, grabbed the heavy bag off my shoulder and pulled me close. Despite my fearful anguish, I sank into your arms and exhaled, my thoughts spiraling. One stood out from the rest: *I feel less alone.*

It's been over two years since that embrace. In the early days, we were united—protesting at airports, cooking meals for refugees, signing petitions, making calls. At our most courageous, we returned withering looks of disdain with our own determined gaze—undivided, unrepentant, nearly unafraid. And when more vulnerable, we tended to our psychic wounds and those of our community with tentative, compassionate curiosity. *Who are you? What is your story? How can we forge a path through these imperfect consequences together?*

But impatience and grief slowly seeped into those hard and soft moments. I grew exasperated with heart clutchers who wanted us to move past the election and just get along, and impatient that you—a man who was trying to reconcile the depth of your power—did not understand how best to wield it. I wanted you to take away my fear, rather than admit your own.

Initially, in an attempt to take care of myself, I recoiled from those who overtly wished me harm. Then, I distanced myself from those who remained passive, watching fissures of institutionalized racism deepen into chasms, cleaving our democracy and humanity. In time, I also distanced myself from you.

"They got exactly what they wanted," you wrote to me months after we ended. "They built a wall between us."

It is true. Some days, the barrier is dense, nearly impenetrable, others, as flimsy as gossamer. But this wall implies connection: you beside me. It sustains a portal through which we reach for each other, time and again.

In this space—where we are friends and no longer lovers—I love you tenaciously but cautiously, unsure of what our intimacy has taught us. The questions that remain unanswered are a reflection, perhaps, of a nation that is also unresolved. But we move forward. Changed. Stronger for our brokenness. Enduring, dismantling, re-building—together.

❧

Simran Sethi is a journalist and author of *Bread, Wine, Chocolate: The Slow Loss of Foods We Love*, named one of Smithsonian's best food books of 2016. She is also the creator of *The Slow Melt*, awarded Best Food Podcast of 2017 by *Saveur*, and a fellow at the Institute for Food & Development Policy.

What My Immigrant Mother Would Say About President Trump

By *Marianne Leone*

I hate bullies. But bullies and their jeering wingmen are becoming an everyday part of the American landscape. Whenever I go on social media or turn on my television, I feel as if I were the bespectacled little kid from *A Christmas Story*, being taunted by a yellow-toothed bully in a raccoon hat.

Bullies have always been admired and elevated in a fascist state. In *The Bicycle Runner: A Memoir of Love, Loyalty, and the Italian Resistance*, G. Franco Romagnoli chronicles his life in 1930s Italy: "To conform to the official mold, a Fascist boy had to be strong, courageous, a smart aleck and a bully." In Romagnoli's world at that time, "many were under the thumb of a few. The few, unscrupulous, violent men who were in power ...[t]heir purpose, more than to convert, was to intimidate and humiliate."

My mother left Italy in the 1930s to escape fascism and an arranged marriage to an old man who offered a dowry of adjoining land to her father's farm. As a child, she marched for Il Duce in a Balilla uniform holding a baby doll, a symbol of the regime's restriction of women to the role of breeders for the fascist state. My mother never talked about what it was like growing up under a strutting dictator. Newsreels of Mussolini look cartoonish today, his oversize chin jutting like the prow of a destroyer as he parodies a "manly" posture, dressed in military folderol, betasseled as a showgirl, barking out his demands to "Believe! Obey! Fight!"

Within days of her arrival in the United States, and with only a few words of English, my mother was soon sewing alongside other immigrants in Boston's garment district, women who spoke a different language and who gave her a different name, one that made my mother's "otherness" feel irreversible.

But she was safe from an arranged marriage to an old man and the war that would devastate her homeland. My mother met and married my father and found love too. They had a family and she cooked for his working-class bar, Leone's Café, until my father's untimely death at fifty. She was left a widow at forty-three with three kids, no marketable skills outside of cooking, and a tenuous grasp of the English language.

Ma persevered in this country; it was her home, this place seven miles outside of Boston where her Italian-American neighbors had all emigrated from the same town in southern Italy. In her later years, she lived with my sister and her family in the same house, surrounded by her grandchildren, the bullies in her life a distant memory.

My first experience with bullies was with my teachers, nuns who were masters in the art of humiliation. First graders who talked in class were paraded from room to room wearing baby hats, to be ridiculed by their classmates. Our bruises were invisible in view of actual thuggery, but the fear was pervasive and kids routinely peed their pants, ramping up the humiliation into a hellscape that seemed as eternal as the one we were threatened with every day.

In my adult life, there was a special education director bully who decreed that my late quadriplegic son should be denied his basic civil rights to a free and inclusive public education. That guy's not the special education director any more, and my son Jesse became a straight-A student and a bully slayer by default.

This past November, I watched a video of a young man bullying cowed women on a plane, shouting the name of the winner of our recent presidential election as a threat to silence them. The women sat, heads bowed as if at a ritual shaming ceremony, and said nothing. I wondered if I would be silent, too, if I were on that plane. I remembered all the times I had sat like a stone in first grade, disappearing into my seat, feeling powerless yet complicit as I watched my classmates groveling, dissolving into tears of shame as they were paraded before us like Chinese dissenters during the Communist Revolution. I was glad I wasn't the one being punished but by doing nothing I felt as if I had somehow become the bullies' accomplice.

I don't want to live in a place where bullies are elevated to the status of gods. But that has already happened. I wonder if my mother, twelve years dead, would recognize her adopted country today.

Of one thing I am certain—my mother could recognize a bully. And she felt compassion for people new to this country, as she had once been herself. When our Italian-American neighbor of fifty years sold her house and three generations of a Muslim Pakistani family moved in, my mother was glad of a playmate the same age as her granddaughter and sympathetic to the little girl's older brother, who came to Ma with his problems.

"I know what it's like," Ma said, "to feel alone where you don't know nobody." She plied the kids next door with food and lied about her meatballs: "What pork? There's no pork in there." (Ma could be a bit of a bully herself when it came to food.)

What would Ma think of the bully-in-chief? A memory flood of her slushy dialect fills my ears. Most of the words are unprintable, but the loudest is *gavone*, the dialect version of *cafone*. The word has nothing at all to do with power, or strength, or humanity. Gavone describes a boor, a rude, lumbering beast who would knock over a small child or a grandmother to get to the food, then grunt inarticulately as he swallows everyone else's portion. And, in fact, our president did just that, for all the world to see, as he shoved aside the prime minister of Montenegro, Dusko Markovic, to get to the front for a photo op, a move that was the definition of gavone.

Ma may have struggled with the English language, but that didn't mean she wasn't smart. She knew how to parse her bullyboys, even in dialect, and she knew a gavone when she saw one.

ॐ

Marianne Leone is an actress, screenwriter and essayist. Her essays have appeared in the *Boston Globe, Post Road, Bark Magazine, Coastal Living, Solstice*, and WBUR's *Cognoscenti* blog. She is the author of two memoirs, *Jesse* (Simon & Schuster) and *Ma Speaks Up* (Beacon Press.) She had a recurring role on HBO's *The Sopranos* as Joanne Moltisanti, Christopher's mother.

OUR WORK

THE CHALLENGES OF BEING A
PSYCHOTHERAPIST IN THE AGE OF TRUMP

By Alissa Hirshfeld, MFT

The last two years have been a tumultuous time to be a psychotherapist. I've had to contend with the effect of President Trump and Trumpism not only when it came to the well-being of my clients, but also to my own mental health. As a Jewish woman, President Trump's misogyny and his dog whistles (hell, sometimes overt support) to anti-Semites and white supremacists feel deeply personal. As the parent of a mixed child, I am fearful for my daughter's future. I continually have to confront and manage my own anxiety and despair before I can be helpful to my clients.

I've counseled clients—as I've tried to do myself—to strike a balance between self-care and political activism. This is a good time to do more meditation and yoga and to take breaks from the news with comedy shows and escapist novels. Or, as Nina Gaby suggests in her essay, sometimes we may need to find non-harmful yet physical ways to express our rage. But we cannot deny the reality of what is happening to our country. For me, the balance has swung more toward activism in the last three years. I seem to be in a heightened state of fight as opposed to flight (although I'll admit that in November 2016, I did check to see that my family's passports were up to date, and I considered the practicality of moving to Canada, Europe, or Israel). My anxiety manifests as a strong desire to fight the system. In the past, I have tended to dip, in brief spurts, into activism around issues of reproductive freedom, apartheid in South Africa, and Jewish advocacy, but never before have I called and written my Congresspeople, signed petitions, written editorials, and marched with such regularity as I do now. I never fully understood on a neurological level the meaning of the phrase "the political is personal" until now. As Dr. Lorraine Camenzuli explains in her essay, "Trauma in the Age of Trump," early on in the campaign, my neuroception picked up on Trump's dangerousness.

In this changed cultural miasma, I've become increasingly aware that it is not enough to address the typical issues I usually address with clients: family of origin themes; internalized negative self-thoughts; maladaptive patterns of behaviors in relationships; or how to manage symptoms of depression, anxiety, or trauma. Taking a page from feminist psychologists, who focus as much on how the social system impacts clients as their family systems do, I am very curious about and sensitive to their experiences under the present administration. As one woman put it, "My inner world feels okay; but how do I deal with the outer world?"

The moniker "Trump Anxiety Disorder" began as somewhat of a joke among liberal therapists, but it was born out as an actual "thing" when the American Psychiatric Association published evidence that, since 2016, cases of anxiety and depression have been rising at alarming rates. A May 2018 APA survey found that thirty-nine percent of people reported that their anxiety level had risen over the year, and fifty-six percent were either "extremely anxious" or "some-what anxious" about "the impact of politics on daily life."[1] A 2017 study reported that two-thirds of Americans see the nation's future as a "very or somewhat significant source of stress."[2] Among those I've seen particularly affected in my office are those with narcissistic or sadistic parents or partners, who already suffer daily from the dysfunctional system they live in and now see similar behaviors in their president; survivors of sexual harassment and assault; members of minority ethnic and religious groups; women; and teens whose schools have received threats of gun violence. There is also a new psychological term, "eco-anxiety," which describes the symptoms of clients who feel despondent about the climate change crisis, despite the president's denial that it is happening. In 2017, the American Psychological Association published "Mental Health and our Chang-ing Climate," which explores the psychological impact of climate

---

[1] John F. Harris and Susan Zimmerman,"Trump May Not Be Crazy, But the Rest of Us Are Getting There Fast," *Politico Magazine*, October 12, 2018.
[2] Ibid.

change. Younger clients considering starting families, for example, wonder if it's fair to bring new life into what they see as a dying world.[3]

I've been exploring the boundaries between my training as a therapist and a newer voice compelling me to become an activist. As a therapist, I was trained to be a blank slate, who disclosed little-to-no personal information to clients, but I was also trained to be authentic. When it comes to politics, those two approaches to my work can conflict. When clients talk to me about their anger, fear, and frustration at the current state of politics, it feels wrong not to validate their experience sincerely, in a manner that I'm sure conveys that I agree with them. There is also an element of reality testing for me here. In an age of "alternative facts," I want to affirm that I see the same concerning elements in the actions of this president and his inner circle as they do.[4] I also believe that empowering clients to take action, by educating them about various local political groups and encouraging them to speak up, can be healing, not only giving them a sense of agency regarding current politics but more generally teaching them that their voice matters.

In terms of how the current political reality impacts my subjective experience in the room with clients, since the massacre at the Etz Chaim Synagogue in Pittsburgh by a neo-Nazi terrorist, I have become increasingly self-conscious of being Jewish. My clients have on rare occasions in the past made anti-Semitic remarks. One teenager thought Jews had horns. I chose to make that a teachable moment by disclosing my religion to him. Another referred to someone "jewing someone down" and then quickly apologized. In this national climate when anti-Semitic incidents were up by almost sixty percent in 2017 and continued to be at historic levels in 2018, according to the Anti-Defamation League, I brace myself when I need to address an issue of collecting fees or when a client opens a topic that feels like

---

[3] Lauren Dockett, "The Rise of Eco-Anxiety," *Psychotherapy Networker*, January/February 2019, 11.

[4] Of course when I see a client who is a Trump supporter, I am challenged to validate their experience without affirming their politics. In these (few) cases, I keep my politics to myself.

it could veer into an anti-Semitic trope.[5] My religion was always an aspect of my life in the background, rarely touched upon or relevant, except to my Jewish clients. But after the Pittsburgh tragedy, when clients acknowledged their awareness of how I might be affected, I again chose authenticity over being cagey or over the therapist's trick of turning their questions back on them. As an American citizen as well as their therapist, I validated their disbelief, shock, and rage at what is happening in our country. This holiday season, more clients than in seasons past have wished me a happy Chanukah. In the past year, more Jewish clients have specifically sought me out as a therapist who can validate their unique cultural experience, with whom they can feel safe expressing their fears and concerns.

I feel touched and also a bit vulnerable. Ironically, this situation has only deepened the authentic and human connection between my clients and myself, by making me more of a real person to them. At the same time, I cannot help but recall how Jewish doctors were forced to close their practices in Nazi Germany or how Sigmund Freud had to flee Austria. Part of me wants to wear my Star of David proudly in the streets. Another part actually considers my daughter's request that we hang our *mezuzah* inside rather than outside our doorpost, after our local Starbucks is graffitied with a swastika. I never would have thought this question would have crossed my mind in our progressive Northern California community.

I took another step toward integrating my life as a psychotherapist and as an activist by becoming involved in the Duty to Warn movement. This movement grew out of a petition signed by seventy thousand mental health professionals, who feel compelled to warn the public about the dangers to the public health and well-being that President Trump exhibits from a psychological perspective. The petition, started by Dr. John Gartner, calls for invoking the twenty-fifth amendment to remove the president from office due to mental incompetence. There is controversy, based on the Goldwater rule, about the ethics of mental health practitioners weighing in on

---

[5] https://www.adl.org/news/press-releases/anti-semitic-incidents-surged-nearly -60-in-2017-according-to-new-adl-report;https://www.adl.org/news/press -releases/anti-semitic-incidents-remained-at-near-historic-levels-in-2018-assaults.

Trump's pathology. The Goldwater rule states that it is unethical for psychiatrists to give a professional opinion about public figures whom they have not actually examined and from whom they've not received consent to discuss publicly. However, the arguments on the other side are compelling. With pundits throwing around words like *narcissism* and *sociopathy*, ought we not be hearing from those with actual training in these conditions? The Goldwater rule was written at a time when the art of diagnosis was far less precise than it is now, when it was not based on observable behaviors. Furthermore, one need not issue a formal diagnosis to observe the behaviors and attitudes of this president, readily visible to the entire country on the nightly news and on his Twitter account. Dr. Bandy Lee, a psychiatrist at Yale Medical School who leads the sister movement Duty to Protect and who specializes in domestic violence, explains that one need not assign a diagnosis in order to warn about a danger of violence from someone who routinely threatens, bullies, and intimidates—one who also happens to have access to the nuclear codes.

Aside from my more overtly political work with the Duty to Warn group, which included organizing a town hall and participating in the making of the group's upcoming film #UNFIT, I have realized that since psychotherapists are in the business of promoting communication and interpersonal relationships, within our private offices we have a crucial role to play in fixing our broken system. People on different sides of political issues have forgotten how to debate civilly or even how listen to one another, much less how to negotiate and compromise. I never imagined that empathy would become a political act, but—alas!—it has. People on opposite sides of the political divide, as well as people of different cultural backgrounds and faiths, seem unwilling and sometimes unable to empathize with different perspectives. But when we listen deeply to one another's stories— meaning we practice seeing things from another's perspective while silencing the voice inside us that wants to disagree or tell our own side—we learn that we all want the same basic things: a good life for ourselves and our families, good health, an adequate income to provide for our needs, a community to belong to, and a sense of meaning and purpose. When I teach clients to feel compassion for themselves and to empathize with their partners and family members, I hope that I am also providing them with the skills to empathize with their fellow human beings, whomever they may be. This may be the most important political action I can take in this period in the country's history.

၁

Alissa Hirshfeld balances a psychotherapy practice with parenting and writing. Her academic articles have appeared in *American Journal of Psychiatry, Creativity Research Journal,* and *The Therapist Magazine.* She is the author of a memoir, *This Whole Wide World is Just a Narrow Bridge,* and a novel, *Living Waters: From Harvard Halls to Sacred Falls.* Ms. Hirshfeld is active in the Duty to Warn movement, warning about the danger this president presents to the public mental health.

References:

Dockett, Lauren. "The Rise of Eco-Anxiety." *Psychotherapy Networker,* January/February 2019.

Harris, John S. and Susan Zimmerman. "Trump May Not Be Crazy, But the Rest of Us Are Getting There Fast." *Politico Magazine, October 12, 2018.*

TRAUMA IN THE AGE OF TRUMP

Lorraine Camenzuli, PhD

A thirty-year-old version of me stood before the physician's committee overseeing a hospital's rehabilitation department in the late 1970s. As director of speech pathology, I was presenting the case for the purchase of biofeedback equipment some time before its efficacy had been unquestionably established. I cited evidence, discussed the range of potential usefulness to rehab, and ended with a request for a $500 investment. The fiftyish male Chair of the committee, an orthopedic surgeon of some stature, stood up as I finished, turned toward the department Chair, and erupted with a blistering tirade about me and my frivolity in considering such a too-new and too-expensive device. In my recollection his performance was a startling overreaction, stunning everyone present and shaming me. Later I learned through department gossip that his young wife—of approximately my age—had just asked him for a divorce. He was spitting mad and apparently took it out on me. While he later apologized to my superior, he never made contact with me again, even as he begrudgingly approved the expenditure.

This was no big trauma. But the initial shock still went deep, stirring old self-doubts, triggering helplessness, and freezing my capacity to respond. As I later learned why he may have behaved so badly and that others in the room supported me, my frozen immobility thawed, and I felt myself able to move again. My frustration at how little I could do in the state he had put me in gradually morphed into anger, then fury, at him and at a system that gave him the power to diminish me. Thanks to the support and validation I received, I was eventually able to restore calm and recover my ability to think critically. But that fury fueled two decisions that shaped the rest of my professional life, and probably my personal one too. First, I determined to learn how people could behave so badly and get away with it, so I studied psychology. And, second, I resolved to get on an equal footing in a setting that was hierarchical and power-driven, so I got a PhD. Not the noblest of motivations, but I reasoned that if he had had to address me as "Doctor," it might have mitigated his entitled superiority. While an older me now sees the naiveté in such assumptions, the helplessness, rage, and eventual decisions launched me into another, more satisfying life, one that has brought me to this moment as I share with you some of what I have learned about trauma, rage, and the abuse of power.

In the last thirty years, neuroscience has advanced our understanding of stress reactions and trauma exponentially, shedding light on how our nervous systems work under various conditions of threat. Though immensely complex, our nervous systems activate responses at three major levels of processing, all to ensure our survival under each different threat scenario. You might say that these levels interact with each other as a kind of crisis intervention team, firing in sequential and hierarchical fashion. While the top level works to identify a potential threat, the second level works on mitigating it, and, if that fails, a third level activates to preserve energy and shuts down responding. More specifically, at level one the cerebral cortex, particularly the pre-frontal lobes, registers what we perceive and assesses its relative safety or danger. If safety is signaled, our conscious thought processes engage and guide our voluntary movements and decisions. On the other hand, a signal of "danger" activates level two. Sitting beneath the upper lobes of the cerebral cortex, the limbic lobe, and the site of the "emotional brain," enable the automatic but involuntary response we know as "fight or flight." That is, when survival is threatened, even in intangible ways, we mobilize into defensive action either to run from the danger or to fight it. Under circumstances of more extreme threat, a third level of response takes over, also automatic and also involuntary, that works to preserve our energy and makes us "freeze." It is the vagus nerve—the super highway of the nervous system, running from the upper brain down the spinal cord—that conveys all these signals, thereby converting our perceptions into action. You might say it is this vagus nerve that literally connects mind with body. The overall process works something like this:

When people, especially people who are new to us, first approach, the upper branch of the vagus determines whether the approaching person is "safe" or "dangerous." Features like body size, movements, gestures, eye contact, tone of voice, quality of voice, and loudness are quickly assessed. A soft, higher-pitched, well-regulated voice in a smiling, welcoming, and approachable person will signal "safety." So when two or more individuals approach each other in this non-threatening way, they spread and share a mutual sense of safety, openness, and cooperation, effectively *co-regulating* their nervous systems.

However, when someone approaches with a loud, lower-pitched, raspy voice or a tense, scowling face, it signals "danger." In the animal kingdom, this danger signal warns of a "predator." At that first sign of danger, the lower branch of the vagus nerve signals the emotional brain, at tier two of our model, to activate the sympathetic arousal of "fight or flight." Whether fighting or fleeing, a cascade of bodily changes instantly redirects precious energy in the form of muscle tension, hormonal release, and blood flow to the extremities to help us run or stand our ground. Recall that "fight or flight" is the juice that famously equips mothers with the Herculean strength to lift cars off their pinned children. It is the evolutionary survival mechanism we share with the entire animal kingdom.

However, for humans there is one important caveat to this super-power, one that I believe helps explain one very frightening aspect of the Donald Trump presidency. In the interest of speed, this second-tier survival response, "fight or flight," will bypass conscious thought because it's just too slow and energy consuming to consider alternatives, anticipate consequences, or even verify those initial perceptions. The pre-frontal cortex, our center for abstract and critical thinking, takes a back seat in a crisis, essentially rendering our life-saving actions less than conscious. Though the "fight or flight" response affords immediate action, it can also represent thoughtless or impulsive action, flying in the face of new information, feedback, or collaboration. To enhance speed it must sacrifice accuracy, tending to rely on perceptual shortcuts and filters like those we derive from long-standing biases and unchallenged assumptions and prejudices.

Threats

Our neuroscientific-based model suggests that when we successfully manage a particular threat, our nervous systems should return to calm and restore homeostasis. Now imagine what might happen if threats kept coming relentlessly—one tweet, one decision, one signing, one appointment, one firing, one treaty withdrawal, one trade war, and one more conservative judgeship at a time, to name but a few possible triggers. Presumably, we would keep getting thrown into a frenzy of wanting to run, wanting to hide, or wanting to hurt someone. We'd be stuck in a whirlwind of continual arousal, leaving little or no time for recovery. Chronic stress leads to chronic hyperarousal. And chronic hyperarousal results in a boatload of unfortunate consequences. We risk becoming exhausted, in mind and body, and vulnerable to physical and mental conditions, even diseases. Nor are we able to regulate our emotions over time or circumstance. Specifically, we would either stay "lit up" in "flight," and feel chronically tense, anxious, fearful, and out of control; or, we would stay stuck in "fight," experiencing chronic irritability, anger, impatience, explosiveness, or even become abusive; or, we would become emotionally labile, constantly flipping from fear to anger, from terror to rage, from love to hate, and back again. Without relief the likelihood of turning to outlets like alcohol, drugs, or other high-risk behaviors also multiplies, magnifying the risks to well-being. In all these cases our relationships suffer, eventually impairing daily functioning at home, work, and leisure. But worst of all, over time, as sub-cortical arousal dominates cortical self-regulation, our rational judgment will deteriorate, narrowing our thinking and rendering it less curious, less flexible, and less creative. The by-product is an intellectual rigidity where novel situations are handled in stereotyped and biased ways.

When "stress" becomes "trauma"

There is one more step downward in the nervous system's mechanisms for dealing with threats to survival. It's hard to imagine a situation worse than chronic stress that keeps us hypervigilant and exhausted. But consider the one where, despite our best efforts, there is no possibility of either fighting or running. Think of a child being repeatedly abused, a woman being raped at gunpoint, a soldier trapped in a tank hit by an IED, a couple watching their home disintegrate in a fire, a concert goer watching other attendees gunned down and not knowing where to hide, or even a voter watching while an election goes awry and political institutions they held sacred are dismantled before their eyes.

Possums play dead. Reptiles go still. Humans faint, shut down, dissociate, or even die. We collapse as fully functioning humans because we've essentially learned we are *helpless*. We cannot make the danger go away or restore safety. Even if an escape route appears later, we do not move. We cannot move because our nervous systems are in lockdown, just as mine was when I got blindsided.[1] Or better yet, recall the inexplicable behavior of an abused spouse who cannot leave her abuser. She is too "frozen" to help herself.

This collapse is the third tier's most devastating response: "freeze." Though it, too, is essentially meant to help us survive in the moment, recovery from this state is a major challenge. There is no easy return to homeostasis, rest, or self-regulation without a significant change in our environment. Thirty-year-old me had the support of colleagues and heard a story that explained in some measure why the rehab physician had unloaded on me. But without something like that supportive intervention, we cannot move back up the nervous system ladder to arousal and action on our own behalf. Worse, there is certainly far less hope for returning to rational thought and constructive problem-solving. We're stuck. While fight or flight can get us through when we *can* act, when we *cannot* act, helplessness can defeat us.

Enter Donald Trump

In New York Donald Trump was generally known as a charming playboy real estate developer who reportedly failed to pay vendors, discriminated against minorities, engaged in scandalous affairs, and often sued his opponents. Initially bankrolled by a wealthy father, he later failed to avoid bankruptcies and incurred huge business losses. Then in 1987 he "wrote" *The Art of the Deal* and his business acumen

[1] Steven Maier and Martin Seligman, "Learned Helplessness: Theory and Evidence," in *Journal of Experimental Psychology: General* 105, no. 1 (1976).

became legend. Except that in 2016 the real author, ghostwriter Tony Schwartz, went apoplectic when he saw Trump was running for President. Schwartz confessed to *New Yorker Magazine* that in fact it was he and not Donald Trump who had written the book, admitting that most of how he'd portrayed Donald Trump's business genius in *The Art of the Deal* was pure fiction. He deeply regretted painting Donald Trump in a sympathetic light, describing the real Donald as virtually incapable of focusing attention on this book or any other, as a man "obsessed" with publicity, who valued only power and money; a man who was emotionally reactive and a consummate liar, among many other excoriations. David Frum in 2019 cited Jonathan Braun, one of the producers of *The Apprentice*, admitting that the television show that made Donald Trump a reality TV star was also a "fake." Unfortunately, only New Yorkers must have been listening because Donald Trump's charm, and the false narrative about his business genius, carried the day.

Those of us who had been wary of him all along were in shock when he won, a shock not unlike the manner in which I had been ambushed in that meeting. According to our nervous system model, the reactions of many, if not most, voters in this country must have descended from the highest level of "reason" right down to the lowest level of "freeze." Not only did Donald Trump's victory defy logic, it rendered all of our fighting activism during the campaign ineffectual, even impotent. If we couldn't run away and we couldn't fight, what was left? Many felt helpless and trapped. Even when we'd heeded the danger signals in Donald Trump's nonverbal cues—his raspy, strained and monotone voice; his large, imposing body and staccato repetitive gestures; his frequently scowling face, and his predilection for smiling only at his supporters. Even when our automatic arousal systems drove us to fight against the "danger" by working furiously to get out the vote, we had failed to stop him. And even though the popular vote put Hillary Clinton out ahead by almost three million votes, it didn't change a thing. So, if in reading this you see yourself as one of those who collapsed, take heart. You were and are not alone.

Sadly, over the past few years since Donald Trump took office, we have not had a chance to recover from what has felt like a roller coaster of chronic hyperarousal, utter deflation, and massive efforts at recovery. His style of communication, impulsive reactivity, lack of curiosity, inflated sense of importance, and disdain for federal institutions have kept us off-balance and in a continual state of shock and exhaustion, vacillating between despair, rage, and an increasingly wobbly faith that our institutions will protect us from danger at home and abroad. (Our model captures the possible mechanism through which that extreme instability is maintained.) In thought, action, emotional expression, and moral direction, Donald Trump both displays and triggers in us a chronic state of arousal, arresting all of us in a cycle of "fight," "flight," and "freeze."

Besides being endlessly reactive, Donald Trump's observable feelings move within a narrow range. Supporters stimulate warmth and charm, but opponents are received with angry mistrust, defensiveness, belligerence, intimidation, and retaliation. Yet when his ideas, actions, or decisions are confronted or scrutinized, he sometimes fails to engage. He "runs away," dodges or avoids. Press conferences, for example, have been virtually eliminated. Also, subtler feelings like empathy, curiosity, doubt, sorrow, or tolerance are rarely on display; to wit, hurricane victims are offered paper towels in the context of underfunded disaster relief and asylum-seekers are separated from their families and put in cages rather than offered safety. His presentation seems geared toward a relentless show of strength laced with intimidation and deflection.

Furthermore, under the influence of chronic fight or flight, actions tend to be immediate, impulsive, life or death/win or lose propositions, reflecting little or no thoughtful consideration or awareness of nuance, subtleties, or gray areas. Judgments about people and situations lean toward all-black or all-white and appear to rely on little more than bias and prejudice to assess their relative danger or value. For example, Norwegian immigrants are welcome, but Mexican immigrants are not; to stem domestic terrorism, Muslims should be banned, but white nationalists should not; to stem school gun violence, teachers should be armed, but potential perpetrators, unrestricted. The solution to unwanted immigration is a wall and a threat that children will be taken from their parents. Similarly, authoritarian, sometimes barbaric dictators are welcomed, while complex but discerning leaders of democratic nations are ignored or shunned. Statecraft is thereby reduced to glad-handing, ignoring decades-old processes of international relations based on cooperation, planning, research, and witnessing of negotiations with vigilant follow-up. Finally, in an effort to please the base, Donald Trump, a life-long supporter of a woman's right to choose, does a one-eighty and acts to reverse *Roe v. Wade* by appointing relentlessly conservative judges to the Supreme Court. Actions such as these not only reflect more bias than critical thinking, but speak to a compromised moral integrity that is sustained by no unifying or overriding set of values. Rather these actions reflect an unapologetic expediency that is unconcerned with the human or societal impact of his words and deeds and is focused instead on enhancing himself and those he perceives to be like him.

Other examples of rigid, uncompromising, and inflexible cognition are reflected in his tendency to rely upon Executive Orders rather than working to get cooperation from Congress on long-reaching and complex issues such as immigration, nuclear containment, Middle East relations, and trade deficits; not to mention his attempts to single-handedly establish relationships and agreements with non-democratic countries like North Korea, and his permitting vague threats about a war with Iran to circulate. He fails to warn us, and perhaps even his staff, that he is even considering such sweeping decisions, fails to explore their possible repercussions, and then fails to justify his actions sufficiently to convince the rest of us. Also representative of his difficulty engaging abstract reasoning is his penchant for trying to manipulate what is and what is not "truth," ranging from his arguing against the video proof of his inauguration attendance to denying wrong-doing or even knowledge of wrong-doing in contexts of housing discrimination, sexual misconduct, campaign finance laws, and financial conflicts of interest, to name but a few.

Women and Trump

If Donald Trump has shown signs of a chronic hyperarousal, then it can also be said that he has kept the nation off-balance in a similar state of chronic hyperreactivity just trying to deal with his brand of leadership on a day-to-day basis. The stories contained in this *Fury* collection are full of personal and horrifying reactions at all levels of our nervous system model. While many are angry, worried, and distracted, the most dangerous reaction, and one which tends to plague women even more than men, is that lowest level of collapse into hopelessness, where despite everything we do or everything we have tried, we feel helpless to change things. We are traumatized. But these women are resilient. Though many have descended into those frozen depths, they have also found their way back up the nervous system, through mutual respect and support, and felt mobilized once again, not just by the frustration of not being heard or seen by this administration, not just by anger toward one leader, but by their collective fury against a system that sustains him. If despair is the malady, then fury may just be the remedy.

For this presidency we might even think of American women as the canaries in the coal mine, directly experiencing in our minds, hearts, and bodies, just how toxic such a presidency can be. But when we use our nervous system reactions to fuel our voices and our votes, we can bring about a new level of leadership that restores the moral stature of the U.S. as a just and caring leader of the free world. What distinguishes women in this effort may be our very capacity for reading those first non-verbal cues of danger—honed by millennia of tending to non-verbal infants. In effect we were primed by nature to perceive and react to the danger afoot in the leadership of this kind of man. While many of his verbal expressions seem less than logical, repeatedly reactive, and singularly unempathic, his non-verbal cues are terrifying. In word and deed to many of us, this man signals "predator."

While we can appreciate that automatic mechanisms like "fight, flight, and freeze," are critical to survival, then so is our capacity to learn from these responses. As we become more aware of our reactions, our biases, what we need to feel safe, and how to use the information from these bodily alerts, we will be less likely to succumb to provocateurs such as Donald Trump, and more likely to see through his manipulations early on.

Hopefully, this shorthand model of our physiological, cognitive, emotional, and moral responses to trauma can offer a kind of mental scaffolding for understanding our human predicament, for more effectively acting on behalf of the many, and for moving societal organization and leadership to the next evolutionary level, far beyond Donald Trump and those who enable him.

Dr. Lorraine Camenzuli is a clinical and neuropsychologist in private practice in La Jolla, CA. Since 1977 her career has focused on the complex interaction of neurological and emotional substrates of dysfunction through evaluation and multi-layered treatment. In addition to private practice her work has spanned a variety of settings including acute care hospitals, rehabilitation facilities and forensics, serving as an expert witness in civil and criminal proceedings. Most recently she has turned her treatment focus to trauma-based disorders, recognizing and employing recent neuroscientific research into brain behavior. She also currently serves as a consultant on a critical response team addressing workplace trauma. Her research interests have included cognitive and emotional deficits in mild traumatic brain injury, the effects of depression on problem-solving and, most recently, on factors that improve therapist effectiveness. She has served on a number of non-profit boards addressing underserved populations through community education and political action.

References:

Gilligan, Carol, and David A. J. Richards. *Darkness now Visible: Patriarchy's Resurgence and Feminist Resistance*. Cambridge: Cambridge University Press, 2018.

Lee, Bandy. *The Dangerous Case of Donald Trump: 27 Psychiatrists and Mental Health Workers Assess a President*. New York, N.Y.: St. Martin's Press, 2017.

Maier, Steven F., and Martin E. Seligman. "Learned Helplessness: Theory and Evidence." *Journal of Experimental Psychology: General* 105, no. 1 (1976): 3.

Mayer, Jane. 2016. "Donald Trump's Ghostwriter Tells All." *New Yorker,* July 18. Frum, David. 2019. "The Great Illusion of the Apprentice." *The Atlantic,* Jan 6.

Van der Kolk, Bessel. *The Body Keeps the Score: Brain, Mind, and Body in the Healing of Trauma*. New York, NY: Penguin Books, 2014.

The Cat and the Cardiologist

By Ann Klotz

Our black cat, Cesario, does not care that Mr. Trump has been elected President. He wants only to go outside, to get out of the house. He has always been an outdoor cat. He wants his old life back. But we learned yesterday that he has a heart condition that requires medicine three times a day; if we let him out, we will not be able to give him the medicine. His old life is over. This morning, in the quiet dark, he prowls the house, puzzled, angry. I stroke his glossy head. He glares at me. We both know he wants to go outside. Why am I not letting him? It's been a strange twenty-four hours—the nation, our cat, heart conditions. We have a little kitten, too, Phoebe. She is also an indoor cat—too young and small to take on the world—careless, we fear. So we are keeping her in until spring. She is delighted by Cesario's captivity, wants only to be his friend. She leaps and feints and pounces, trying to engage him. He hisses, baleful. He is so much bigger than she, yet his is afraid of her—uninterested in her joy, her innocence.

Standing in front of my girls on the stage yesterday, I read from my carefully prepared script that congratulated the winners and offered strategies to those whose hearts lay elsewhere in the election. I watched girls all day embracing, weeping, averting their eyes. I felt tired, pretending an optimism I knew I must model, but one that felt strained, as if I were acting the role of Head, rather than inhabiting it.

What's wrong with me? I wondered, feeling muted, drained, teary. Our college daughter phoned, sharing that her feminist theory professor has told her students that she has spent thirty-five years telling classes that women matter. "Ahh," I sighed in recognition. "Me, too." I am not a feminist theory professor. I am the head of a girls' school; I have spent my life in girls' schools, been shaped by them, by the fierce and formidable women that populated them, by the good and generous men who joined those women in building essay by essay, problem set by problem set; a structure that convinced me I belonged, I was good enough, I had a place at the table, and a job to do in advocating for those more vulnerable than I. I learned to lead with optimism, with my whole heart, with authenticity. I chose a life as an educator in independent schools, and, long ago, when I was a young teacher, I fretted to my department chair, Judy, that I had chosen too easy a path, that I should have stuck to my guns and returned to the New Haven public schools, where I had cut my baby teeth as a student teacher.

"Annie," she said, looking at me directly. "There are many paths. Here, you teach the girls that will have the access and the opportunity to make change. If you are not teaching them, if you are not sharing your ideals and your insistence that they make a difference, then who will?"

That was a balm. I have liked my life, felt purposeful, certain, in fact, that we, as a nation, were moving forward. Part of me knows I need time to breathe. I need some more rest—the World Series with the Indians, the hopeful but defeated team, coupled with election drama wreaked havoc with my sleep. I need to figure out how to offer to my girls and faculty the type of hope Judy offered me long ago—when I wore Laura Ashley dresses and white tights.

Cesario crouches, ready to spring. He is bewildered, cross. And I cannot explain this change in fortunes to him in a way he can understand. He is still who he was yesterday, but not. Me, too. Sometimes, change is thrust upon us, like it or not.

Mary Catherine Bateson, Margaret Mead's daughter, talks about composing a life. I like the idea that we get to choose, that it is not all just random; rather, we have agency. That is what I have taught the girls, always.

"You are not a tumbleweed," I exhort to a child in my office, who has made a mistake. "You always have a choice. It's not the mistake that matters; it's how you move forward from it that counts."

I have a choice about how to move forward. I had hoped for a different outcome, one that more clearly demonstrated to my girls, my brown and black girls, my gay girls, my Muslim and Jewish girls, my immigrant girls that this country was committed to them, that they would be okay. They will be okay, I hope. They are strong and capable, feisty and resilient, amazing. It is a privilege to spend my life among them. But many of them are reeling, angry, let down.

In acting, we say, "You must hold the whole experience—sorrow, joy, outrage, vulnerability." That piece of my repertoire has gotten quite a workout since the night before last—I am a moth, darting from one screen door to another, drawn to the light, unable to get past the tiny mesh barriers. I can see the light on the other side—not a flame that will burn me up but an illumination. I just can't find my way quite yet.

Cesario is heartsick. We can treat him, help him improve. Is it right, I wonder, to force him to stay in? If his heart had simply stopped one night as he prowled this Circle that he loves, would it have been the worst outcome? We want to hold onto what we love, protect and keep safe those who matter. But he meows piteously at the door, brushes my legs, makes a nuisance of himself. I am having trouble figuring out what right is—for him. For all of us. Having trouble imagining what his future will be like. And our own.

๛

Ann V. Klotz is a writer, teacher and mother in Shaker Heights, Ohio, where her house is overrun by piles of books--both read and unread--and rescue pets. See more of her writing at www.AnnVKlotz.com

The Biggest Hole Is Where the President's Empathy Should Be

By Melanie Brooks

Since Donald Trump took office, we've had unfettered access to the flaws at his core. Stream-of-consciousness tweets, boorish behavior caught on camera, ignorant and misinformed rhetoric on the world stage, stunning inaction or shockingly inappropriate responses in moments of national crisis, harsh policies to "protect" our borders, leaked conversations from behind closed doors—all have pointed to colossal deficits in his character and, again and again, a conspicuous disregard for people of color.

Aftershocks reverberated worldwide in the wake of his vulgar and hate-filled comments about Haitian and African immigrants on January 11, 2018, when he reportedly used the word "shithole" to describe their countries of origin. His striking lack of compassion in that moment was startling, but no words can describe the added cruelty of maligning Haiti one day before a painful anniversary when memories of trauma and unfathomable loss inevitably resurface.

Eight years ago on a Wednesday night in January—the first night of a new business writing class at Northeastern University—I began the standard getting-to-know-you banter with my students. A young man in the back row quietly introduced himself. "My name is Henry," he said. "I'm from Haiti." An uneasy silence descended on the room. Twenty-four hours earlier, a magnitude 7.1 earthquake had devastated this man's Caribbean nation. After sending my two young children off to school, I'd spent most of the day in front of the TV watching as CNN's Anderson Cooper—whose crew brought us the first images of the catastrophic quake's aftermath—wandered street after street of collapsed buildings, filming the desperate efforts by ordinary men and women to rescue their loved ones trapped beneath the rubble.

I looked into Henry's eyes and found my voice. "Is your family okay?" I asked.

"I haven't been able to get in touch with them—yet," he answered, and I felt the weight of his hope land on that final word.

My evening plan to discuss the value of good writing in the workplace seemed so unimportant in the face of this personal crisis. I wanted to stop class there. Cancel it for the night, send everybody home, and let Henry go do what he had to do. But Henry was here in this classroom, his notebook open on his desk, ready to learn. Stoic. Poised. His demeanor spoke to a kind of resilience that I'd rarely encountered. One that says, *Today, this is what I have to do.* A resilience I needed to honor.

"Our thoughts are with you all," I said despite how hollow the words sounded, and the rest of the students murmured similar sentiments. We finished introductions, and I passed out the course syllabus. "Let's get started."

Later that night I sent Henry an email offering to extend any upcoming deadlines so that he didn't have to worry about falling behind and urging him to take the time he needed. His response, sent the next day, brought the reality of the news reports so much closer:

Some of my family is okay, but they are still searching for one of my sisters. She is buried under the debris, but my other sister told me that they heard her voice and are trying to free her.

Over the next three days Henry sent me sporadic updates.

They are still digging, but there's no sound coming out.

They haven't found her yet. Last night they found her purse.

They are still digging. Now, I am preparing for any news.

And five days after our first night of class, this:

They found my sister's body.

The cold finality of Henry's message swept through me. I'd watched the ongoing footage of people being pulled alive from beneath the ruins of homes and businesses and schools, and I'd allowed myself to feel a spark of hope for Henry's sister, too. Now all that remained was my imagined scene of his grieving family. How their exhausted muscles ached beneath the layers of sweat and grime. How their vacant eyes sank deep into their faces. How their hands, torn and bleeding, nails jagged and lined with dirt, cradled his sister's broken body.

When I commemorate the yearly anniversary of the Haiti earthquake, I am still haunted by that unbearable image. By all of the unbearable images of similar losses we witnessed in the days and weeks afterward. More haunting, though, is one man's inability to comprehend that when he separates himself from others' stories, refuses to lean in and acknowledge their pain, and fails to mourn when they mourn, he is turning his back on the very thing that could make him human.

❧

Melanie Brooks is the author of *Writing Hard Stories: Celebrated Memoirists Who Shaped Art from Trauma* (Beacon Press, 2017). Her work has appeared in *Ms. Magazine*, *The Washington Post*, *The Huffington Post*, *Creative Nonfiction*, and other notable journals. She lives in NH and teaches writing at Northeastern University and Merrimack College in Massachusetts and Nashua Community College in New Hampshire. She is completing a memoir about living with the ten-year secret of her father's HIV disease before his death in 1995. Learn more about her work at melaniebrooks. com.

VIGIL OF HOPE

By Meg Weber

When I was a child, my mom taught me to play pickup sticks. *Dump multicolored sticks into a pile. Some sticks carry more value than others. Claim one at a time without disrupting any other stick. If you move a stick other than the one you're trying to move, lose a turn. Unless no one notices.* She was the mother of eight kids (born over thirteen years). The game must have felt like the ultimate metaphor of her life. My siblings and I never talked about the election in 2016. We were raised in a family in which it wasn't polite to discuss politics. The only time I remember it being discussed was when my mom said she was a registered Democrat so that her vote would always cancel out my father's Republican vote.

I didn't want to know if any of my siblings or my father voted for Trump, especially with my mother no longer alive to nullify his vote with a vote for Hillary. I was resigned that at least some of my family would vote for Trump or against Clinton. I thought I might find clues on social media about how my family members were leaning. But Facebook was a vortex of uncertainty. (Most political things I share are ignored by my family, while a picture of my daughter gets several likes from my siblings and cousins.) I shared plenty of pro-Hillary, anti-Trump posts. Most of them were about what that kind of presidency might do to my kid and her divorced queer parents, or what it might do to the trans and queer clients in my counseling practice. How would *my* people fare in a game of pickup sticks at the hands of Trump and his cronies?

On election night we came home and put the kid to bed. My partner, Sara, and I switched restlessly between episodes of *Gilmore Girls* and the election returns. As more states were called red, I felt increasingly despondent, scared, sick. When we finally went to bed, after the news that Hillary had lost, I cried myself to sleep. When the alarm went off the next day, I hoped somehow it had all been a

185

bad dream. But it hadn't been. My ten-year-old didn't ask who won the election, and I chose not to bring it up. Not because I won't talk politics with her, but because I was too broken open to hold her reaction too. As a therapist working with marginalized communities, it was going to be a hard day. How would I support my clients when I felt so devastated? If clients needed to talk about the election, I'd go there. If they didn't, I'd enjoy the reprieve and pretend I was okay.

The first client of the day casually mentioned the election in a voice that sounded overly cheerful. She seemed unaffected but noticed my reaction to her tone. "Are you upset about the election?" she asked.

I was stunned. "Yes, it's terrifying, for me and my family."

I felt I'd crossed a line, disclosed too much. But my filters were off, probably water damage from all the crying I'd done the night before. Some clients were as torn apart by the election results as I was. I started sessions the way I often do, with the question, "How are you?" That day it held more context than usual. *How are you with the news of this terrible tyrant somehow being elected as president? How are you, a queer-identified person, a person of color, someone who works for social and racial justice, on a day like today?*

Between sessions, in the quiet of my office, I felt a familiar isolation, an echo of all the ways I am invisible to my family. For the last several years I had been working to show up as myself with my siblings and parents. I wanted to be seen by them. So I challenged myself to give them what I wished they'd offer me. The Wednesday after the election, I texted one of my brothers, a high school teacher: *Hey, I know you worked really hard for measure ninety-seven, I'm sorry it didn't pass. I know it's important.* He replied immediately: *Thanks. I appreciate it. I know the presidential election result isn't what any of us hoped. I'm thinking of you, Sara, and Tasha, too.*

I felt visible and noticeably calmer.

Later that day an email arrived from a different brother, who told me he was thinking of me and asked if we needed anything. Maybe my brothers were horrified about the result, too! No, they aren't queer like me, they don't support vulnerable populations in a therapy practice, they aren't raising a biracial adopted daughter as part of a same-sex divorced couple. But maybe for their own reasons they also didn't want a dangerous misogynist to be our president.

I contemplated how to use my power and privilege to speak out against a man who is Not My President. The Women's March on Washington was tempting. I wanted to be there, to stand up against bigotry and hatred. And then fear showed up. What if I go and something happens and I can't get back to my kid? It was pickup sticks all over again—every stick in a tangled pile. If I chose activism and something went awry, what would happen to my daughter? If I stayed home to stay safe, how could I use my voice to promote justice and equality? How could I balance all of those interconnected aspects of my life? I'd always wondered why my mom's entire life revolved around her family. Now I know. She was trying to pare down the number of sticks she had to manage.

Just before Trump's inauguration I went to see Dar Williams perform. Of all the lyrics on her Mortal City album, the one she put on T-shirts for that tour was a line that had always found a home in my heart. The line was *I am the others*, and it spoke to the ways I felt peripheral, outside, different. The chorus of that song repeats a phrase: "I will not be afraid of women." I was in my twenties and a young dyke when Dar's album came out. I was dating women for the first time. I was a college kid beginning to confront my troubled history with my mother. That lyric resonated.

Two decades later I hear it differently. It makes me wonder about all the voters in this election who are afraid of women, whose votes for Trump are strong statements about not only their refusal to have any female president but also, specifically, their resistance to Hillary earning that position of power. I don't understand the fine points of their fear, but if Trump was their only viable choice to lead this country, I believe their fear has to exist. As residents of Portland's liberal oasis, many of us are scared of what these next years will hold. We fear for our safety and our rights. We fear for the welfare of our children's education. We fear for the state of our health care, our green spaces, our freedom.

It was not lost on me that hope was what I was missing when I thought of four years under a Trump presidency. *Hope*—the slogan representing eight years under the compassionate leadership of Barack and Michelle Obama. As the reality of the election set in, I wondered where I would find and create hope during the Trump years. I imagined I'd hear it in the sound of my ten-year-old composing songs on her electric keyboard, or I'd feel it in the deepening relationships with my siblings. I would find it in the vulnerable courage of my students and clients, in their reach to learn, to understand, and to bring their true voices to the world. I committed to nurturing that hope within my communities of artists, writers, creators, and visionaries. I vowed to lean into the hope of my own small family and the home we create together every day. My words, my strength, and my own vulnerability would become a vigil of hope for all of us.

Now we're years into the Trump presidency, and, unsurprisingly, his policies have eroded so much of the progress the Obama administration made on issues related to LGBTQ rights and quality of life. The hope I intended to keep alive in myself and those around me has wavered in the face of the conservative hate at the core of Trump's regime. I've lost count of how many times I've reframed the increased anxiety in a client's life by telling them it is not only about the particular microcosm of their own life; it is also a reflection of the state of perpetual fear of living in a nation where being other— queer, trans, immigrant, person of color—is increasingly dangerous.

When the talk of potential nuclear war was at its height in mid-2018, I heard myself say to client after client that yes, I could see they were struggling more than usual and that at least part of that was due to the increased threat of nuclear war due to the idiocy of our president. As Trump worked to roll back any protection or advances for LGBTQ Americans, my clients in these populations found it increasingly difficult to move through their days with any sense of safety or security. As a queer woman making my living as a mental health therapist in private practice, I couldn't argue with them.

Several client stories led me to an analogy: living as a gender or sexual minority in today's America is a bit like trying to eat while recovering from the flu. At first, there's a tentative taste of a saltine paired with the overactive worry that one's stomach isn't quite ready to manage food. The whole experience feels risky even if you can keep the cracker down. My marginalized clients continually express that their experiences of living with Trump as president leave them as cautious and queasy as getting over the flu.

And yet these clients, and the counseling students I teach, find ways to keep their own hope and resilience alive. They challenge the increasingly conservative status quo in ways that inspire me and help me continue with my own goals of increased authenticity and connection within my own circles. In the time that Trump has been president, I've had honest conversations with family members about the impact of this administration's actions on my work and my personal life. I am more willing to tell the truth about myself to my siblings and my dad, even when I'm afraid they might not understand or accept me.

The relationship I've been in for the last three years recently underwent a difficult transition. It may not survive. In talking about this with my family, it finally sank in that my relatives don't have to understand me or the choices I make in order to love me. It's a relief to feel that truth in my body, especially in a country that has become decidedly less accepting and more actively hostile to folks who are different.

Maybe I can maintain this vigil of hope after all.

Meg Weber writes memoir, crafting true stories from her days. Meg's writing gives voice to how her life unfolds outside the boundaries prescribed for her. She writes about transgression, about edges, and about finding her way back into connection with her family through tragedy.

SMOKE

By Jessica Handler

The first one comes in crying. Not merely crying, but weeping, red-eyed, shaken. Dramatic, yes, but this kid's nineteen years old, maybe eighteen, and if they're registered to vote, this is their first election. The next kid into my classroom slams his books on the table, an unusual act for this soft-spoken, contemplative student.

Clearly, we need to talk, and not about our classwork. We're reading *Crito,* Plato's depiction of Socrates' argument for, among other things, whether it's right to do "wrong" when one is wronged. Three mornings a week, all semester, my college freshmen and I have been trying to pry open our understanding of what's right and who, at least through the lens of classic literature, gets to say so.

On the first day of the semester, I tell them, "History is written by the winners." This statement rattled me when I was their age. It never fails to disturb smart college freshmen, which is, of course, the idea.

What's right and who gets to say so shudders before me in the face of the weeping girl, the silent, thoughtful boy, and the anxious kid who asks guardedly what I mean when I say we will put our class plan aside for a while today to talk about the election, "without hate speech, without rhetoric." I tell him I don't want to hear any bumper sticker slogans. He relaxes.

Forest fires have been burning for days here in Georgia. Overnight, the smoke has drifted southward. The stink permeates our campus. The metaphor does not escape me, but I am too tired—too burned out, I would say if I had the energy—to create a jokey metaphor for my students.

I'm operating on less than three hours of fitful sleep. I am wearing what I wore yesterday, first to a bar with friends to watch the returns, then in my living room, then discarded at my bedside, now worn again because I cannot think. This isn't happening, I said to my husband beside me in bed, watching the returns. Florida will turn it, I said unable to sleep, but Florida did not. Neither did Pennsylvania, where in 1948 my grandparents hosted the poet Langston Hughes in their home, where during a college summer in 1978 I waitressed in a resort in the Poconos serving meals to the retired rank and file—the laborers—of the International Ladies' Garment Workers Union.

I must have slept, because I woke to the radio announcer telling me that Vladimir Putin had sent a congratulatory telegram to President-Elect Trump. The snooze button was too far away, and I heard the whole terrible phrase. President-Elect Trump.

"This is not," I said again to my husband, "happening."

"But it is," he said, and held me close.

Not two weeks earlier, we had left a friend's house disbelieving the not-very veiled anti-Semitic remarks directed toward us by her boyfriend. She, long one of my dearest friends, he until that moment unremarkable. We are Jews, and we are afraid of what may happen under Trump, I had said over a glass of wine, referring to a neighbor's yard sign.

My friend handed me the glittery bangles she had brought as a gift from a trip to India.

Minorities, the boyfriend advised us, would do well to prove to those they believe would oppress them that they are well-meaning and present no harm.

"Do you know," my husband asked, "the story of the 'Good German'?" The boyfriend inquired if we wanted to be the ones responsible for civil war. Ill at ease, we tried to alight on other topics; a mutual friend's health, an upcoming art show, but our friendship crumbled at that table. Sickened by the boyfriend's attempt to shame us and my friend's apparent disinclination to intervene, I have chosen not to speak to her again. On this post-election morning I fear how her boyfriend voted. I fear that she chose not to vote at all.

In my classroom, I open my briefcase and extract what my students expect; my copy of *The Last Days of Socrates*, my markers, a pen, a pad. I pass around the sign-in sheet, a page torn from the pad on which I have written today's date across the top. November 9, 2016.

In one of my other classes, a student always writes a funny message for me beside her name. I wonder if she will today.

Maybe today is not so different than yesterday, I tell myself. I know that I am lying.

"We're going to talk this morning about how you feel," I said, wishing for more muscular words at my disposal than "talk" and "feel."

"How many of you are first-time voters?" I ask. Almost all the hands go up. Did the others not vote, I wonder. Are they under eighteen, or perhaps misunderstood my question? I don't press it. A student tells me about the "Harambe Factor," the idea that some voters chose to write on their ballots the name of the mountain gorilla shot to death when he apparently attempted to save a child who had fallen into his enclosure at the Cincinnati Zoo. One kid thinks it's funny, but the majority is repulsed.

"What does it say about our society that we think so little of ourselves that we'd waste a vote on a dead gorilla?" asks a reliably penetrating thinker in the front row.

That we don't believe we have a voice that can be heard. That voting is a bottomless hole into which we throw our beliefs because we do not think they will be acknowledged. That the winning candidate had it all worked out from the beginning, and we were taken for a ride.

"So just screw it and vote for a dead gorilla?" I ask, unnerved.

"That didn't really happen," a student interjects about the Harambe factor, "but it might as well have."

Twenty minutes of talk calms us before we turn, with some relief, to the devilment of why Socrates refused to escape his jail cell and his death sentence. We concentrate on theory, on why Socrates would rather argue than take real action, on the concept of argument as action.

By noon, there are protests on campus, but they are weak. My students don't yet know what to do or how to do it. Neither do I. Colorful posters are scrawled with slogans about love. Kids in the student center are handing out flowers. Our theater department has recently mounted a production of *Hair: The American Tribal Love-Rock Musical*, and the results are evident.

The smoke from burned acreage sticks to my hair, stings my throat. As I give a thumbs-up to the poster wavers in front of the student center, I think of myself at nineteen, singing Jimmy Cliff songs in what I remember as a surging crowd outside the Seabrook, New Hampshire nuclear plant. "You can get it if you really want/but you must try," we sang, really wanting, believing that we were trying.

"Mutants for Nukes," read the yellow smiley face Cyclops button on my jacket.

We did not stop the proliferation of nuclear power, and neither did the Chernobyl disaster or the Three Mile Island meltdown. We didn't abolish apartheid in South Africa, either, although there's a strong argument to be made that voices for boycotts led to corporate divestiture from South Africa and the release from prison of Nelson Mandela. Advances are clearer from the distance of half a century; the protests of my parents' generation brought the end of the war in Vietnam, although my next-door neighbor will tell you that as a GI coming home in 1966, he was shunned and misunderstood. From so many years on, I apologize to him. They were kids, I say. They didn't fully understand. Those were the same voices that engendered the signing of the Voting Rights Act, the passage of the Equal Rights Amendment, the Supreme Court's affirmation of *Roe v. Wade*.

At a table in the center of the university dining hall are about a dozen kids. Is it my imagination, or are they hunkered down, backs to the room, shoulders hunched? An unmistakable, pristine red trucker's cap perches on a boy's head. The hat is a raw "fuck you" to the troubled. If these kids look up from their lunch plates, their phones, each other's nervous faces, will they see the fear that they have perhaps unwittingly helped put into motion?

Not a one in the group, each white, each privileged, will meet my gaze, although I've taught two of them in prior semesters. Another is a current student, absent from class this morning. Seeing him among this group disorients me. He is polite and well-read, his comments in class considered and thoughtful. My heart breaks for these students as much as it does for the weeping girl, the book-slamming guy.

A few years ago, I heard Rachel Maddow give a talk in which she suggested that we identify ourselves by our "birth president."

Knowing who was in office the year of our birth engages us in histori-cal context and contributes to a sense of citizenship. On my birthday this year, when my students asked how old I was, I demurred, telling them that my birth president was Eisenhower. I could see in their faces that "Eisenhower" registered somewhere between "Lincoln" and "Obama." Children born in the four years after this January will have Donald Trump as their birth president. When they are adults, contemplating the year of their birth, what will have transpired?

As Trump takes office, every one of the advances and more of my parents' generation and of my own will be under fire; every right will be questioned, every effort made to take away what is hard won. On Inauguration Day, marches for social justice are planned all over the country. I have volunteered to help out on the route here in Atlanta, the first step of many.

As I write this, two and a half weeks have passed since Election Day. In my classroom, a student successfully compares Antigone's righteous action on behalf of her brother to that of Fred Hampton, the activist and Black Panther killed in 1969. I taught this kid about Antigone, but I'd said nothing about Hampton. Listening to him, I am startled by my optimism.

Since the election, I find myself in conversations with friends and colleagues about topics we'd perhaps thought about but never dis-cussed: Federal judgeships, Senate confirmation hearings, what we can do from here.

For the first time in nearly two months, it's raining here. The for-est fires are out, and the smell of smoke no longer permeates our clothes. I think of Rebecca Solnit's essay, "Looking into Darkness," in which she compares the forward motion of history—and activ-ism—to the steady power of water to wear away stone.

My students, most of them, smelled the smoke. I take comfort in my friends, my colleagues, my students, and those of us who recog-nize that our task now is to take action. We can be the water.

❧

Jessica Handler is the author of the novel *The Magnetic Girl*, the memoir *Invisible Sisters*, and the craft guide *Braving the Fire: A Guide to Writing About Grief and Loss*. Her writing has appeared on NPR, in *Tin House*, *Drunken Boat*, *The Bitter Southerner*, *Brevity*, *Creative Nonfiction*, *Newsweek*, *The Washington Post*, and *More Magazine*. A founding member of the board of the Decatur Writers Studio in Decatur, Georgia, she teaches creative writing and coordinates the Minor in Writing at Oglethorpe University and lectures internationally on writing.

OUR PERSEVERANCE

Bring Back the Batakas: The Long View

By Nina Gaby

"Depression is just anger turned inwards."
- Stuff we said, circa 1977

At what point did anger lose its PC cred? I don't seem to recall a specific moment in which mindfulness became a buzzword or every strip mall boasted a Lululemon and a hemp shop; or when the cool therapists started to study dialectical behavioral therapy to get us to manage our anger. Channel it. Control our reactivity. Can't we just get the insurance companies to cover sessions in a Rage Room the way it covers DBT? Because I just want to smash something.

In 1977 my therapist suggested I join one of her women's therapy groups. My individual sessions had become pretty tedious, and although I balked at joining a group, I complied. The therapist was all about convincing me that the pretty smile on my face was really a mask of anger and that without acknowledging that anger I wasn't going to make it. I just wanted to talk about boyfriends and girlfriends and feminism and maybe a tiny bit about how scary it was to be an artist. I also needed to talk about my drinking. Somehow it didn't tie all together yet. If I had a panic attack, I popped a Valium or took a shot of Jack. Who knew from the self-soothing act of just *breathing?*

In group, we were all feminists. Many of us had trained to run CR (Consciousness Raising) groups and I used to take my consciousness-seeking housewives (a.k.a. white suburban women) to the pre-internet adult bookstores in sketchy neighborhoods so we could hang out and make comments as the men in the shops read porn and dropped quarters for peep shows. These CR visits allowed the uninitiated among our gender to see close up what was being said about women's bodies and how that perpetuated violence toward all of us. I might add that in those pre-Eve's Garden days, adult bookstores were the only places a woman could buy a vibrator so there was the occasional bit of shopping as well. I would lead the group in catcalls: "Hey! You look like such a nice guy, where do your kids think you are right now?" Or "Ladies, note the clean raincoat!" And "Such a deal! The double-headed Deluxe Mixmaster twelve inch only nine dollars and ninety-nine cents! Twelve inches? Beat that, buddy!"

The shops were usually on main drags in the fringes of downtown. They provided a community of sorts for their patrons, who nowadays would be indulging in these behaviors alone in front of a laptop—an isolation which seems somehow sadder than when they were standing in the flesh in a brick and mortar. Then the physical presence of these men provided a viable target for our anger; today, these guys exist in a much darker virtual space where anything goes. The adult bookstore browsers kept their heads down, as I recall. Maybe they glanced at the door when we piled in, all studious and serious, but they quickly looked away. I'd lecture calmly about misogyny (before pushing out more dramatic commentary), lead a little tour around the store, picking up a magazine here and there and opening it randomly to a crotch shot or a cum stain. We would crowd our way into a booth, trying not to come in contact with the walls. Some of the bookstores catered to the gay male clientele—which was more difficult for a woman to object to—so I had to do some preliminary reconnaissance to stay on script.

Everyone else—the women on the tour, the men paying for their selections before they rushed out—were mostly polite. On some occasions, the shop proprietor would try to get us to leave. The female owners were the worst; they had no patience for our antics. I'd chastise them for making a living off other women's bodies. Were they familiar with rape culture? Of course not. Years later, working professionally with addicts, I'd help these same men (men who frequented adult bookshops) figure out how to stay away, how to devise new routes around town to avoid the restimulation and the euphoric recall of those stuffy shops. We made painful eye contact and I often felt badly as I remembered my earlier attempts at using their pathology to construct our new world paradigm. But was it pathology or was it just the way things were? Was it their fault? Who, exactly, was profiting and who was suffering? Some of my friends worked in the sex trade business and found it oddly liberating. It paid much better than waitressing, after all. Nonetheless, these folks, too, often joined our ranks. Some of us shoved mirrors between each other's legs, just to see where all the parts really were. A lot of us fell in love with each other. It was a heady time.

Our group also sought opportunities for "direct action," which was fun, new, and provocative. Well, not always fun—in 1980 a local hospital organized a conference on rape and refused to allow us any time to present the new feminist perspective. The conference audience consisted of cops and social workers, professionals who had yet to view rape as assault. Trauma was not yet ubiquitous in our general vocabulary. We crashed the event and while most of the audience dispersed, we held fast to the microphone. A few attendees stayed back and thanked us for presenting the concept of rape as a violent act and symbolic of what would soon be known as rape culture. "You're welcome," we replied and went off to our next skirmish, likely filling the locks of the local porn theater with Super Glue, then situating ourselves across the street the next morning to watch them try to pry open the doors. We weren't angry; we had just changed the world.

When I travelled alone, I learned how to insult the men who were harassing me by insulting them in their own language. "Kos Emmuk"—or "your mother's cunt" in Arabic—is still a favorite, despite how differently harassment manifests itself now that I am almost seventy. In today's gun culture, borne of newly unleashed male rage, I might not suggest that a young woman chase down her harassers by screaming obscenities at the top of her lungs, as I used to do.

After being in therapy for a number of years, I eventually got sober, hiding my vulnerabilities under my bad-ass separatist feminist persona. I occasionally pounded a pillow against the bed as my therapist had taught me, screaming the name of whomever had pissed me off, or to protest whatever government shenanigans were taking place. The therapist's original office had been in her bedroom—complete with a king-size water bed, one of those things we didn't question back in the seventies. Her new office was located in an old building, with the basement door right off the group therapy room. Crates of empty glass wine bottles sat next to the door, and we were instructed to throw them down the stairs. At first we took cautious turns hurling the bottles, then we converged on the top step like a pack of hyenas, keening and hooting. One of the group members had been sexually abused as a child, and her story had produced a vicarious rage in me that I found terrifying and exhilarating, as well as confusing.

Almost forty years later, now a therapist and psychiatric nurse practitioner myself, I recall that confusion with embarrassment. It was as if I had taken over the other woman's right to rage. Today, Kavanaugh, Trump, McConnell, Graham, Cruz—the sanctimonious faces of these demagogues line up in my mind's eye as I entertain an ongoing fantasy about a human Whack-a-Mole. It is as if I were trying to breathe with the air sucked out of me. While CNN was running their coverage of the Kavanaugh hearings, my husband left his dirty dish in the sink. From somewhere deep inside, that anger blew forth all over again. I had to restrain myself from bringing the plate crashing down on his head. This unbridled fury brought to mind the bataka bats of therapies past, a practice frowned upon by the traditional psychiatric circles in which I had later trained. Violence, it was thought, would only precipitate further violence. It was better, they taught, to use self-soothing techniques. Mindfulness. Talk therapy. Meds. Today we might call it "the high road." And my husband might consider himself lucky that a foam bat didn't come crashing down on his unsuspecting head, knocking the remote off his lap and sending pieces of it skittering along the floor; a move that would shut up the CNN pundits for at least as long as it would take to find the battery.

Current evidence suggests that chronically elevated cortisol levels—brought on by systemic stress, trauma, and anger—lead to a host of inflammatory disorders, ranging from diabetes to a variety of autoimmune illnesses. Sometimes we can reduce the likelihood of these disorders occurring or reduce their severity by practicing yoga, breathing deeply, and imagining ourselves in our safe place.

In recent years Rage Rooms have presented themselves as another solution to tackle stress and anger. These rooms—safe spaces where you can go to throw things, hack at things, smash things—have been popping up around the country. Sessions cost anywhere from one to three hundred dollars but are cheaper if you BYOB (bring your own breakables). Certainly this would not be a session covered under your insurance plan. Individuals who have participated in Rage Room sessions report feeling cleansed and less stressed.[1] An article in *Psychology Today* denounced this strategy but offered little in the way of anecdotal evidence, much less scientific data.[2] *Vox*, meanwhile, described the marketability of rage as a sort of wellness/anti-wellness tool.[3] Reading this, I am reminded of that stairwell and our younger selves, almost ecstatic in our purging.

I think it is time for rage to make a comeback, and for Rage Rooms to be covered by insurance policies as a viable prescription for what ails us. Certainly throwing some household goods around entails far less risk than booze, heroin, fentanyl, and all the other deadly self-medicating substances we think we need. As for me, I am getting tired of the progressive "high road." I want to get down and dirty. I want to crash conferences and Congressional hearings. The enemy is more diffuse, more ubiquitous, more powerful. A little rage might take us a lot farther.

Because this other shit sure hasn't worked very well.

Maybe I've lived in Vermont too long. There are no Rage Rooms here, and we play the civil—not warm—but civil card. So my upstate New York-Jewish-grew-up-with-Italians demeanor has been challenging for Vermont natives. People get more upset here when they see an angry person than they might, say, in New Jersey. But anger is gaining traction elsewhere. In an *Atlantic* interview with anger guru Rebecca Traister, she says, "We need to understand their [women's] fury as politically and socially catalytic."[4] Traister is everywhere—on

[1] Vittek, Shelby. "Bashing Breakables is All the Rage at The Rage Room." *New Jersey Monthly*, September 25, 2018.

[2] Bennet, Kevin. "Rage Rooms Not a Good Idea." *Psychology Today*, March 30, 2017.

[3] Haigney, Sophie. "Rage rooms are the latest self-care craze that won't make us feel any better." *Vox*, October 23, 2018.

[4] Kitchener, Caroline and McCormick, Brigid. "Women's Anger Still Isn't Taken Seriously," *The Atlantic*, October 31, 2018.

Bill Maher, Comedy Central, Steven Colbert, in the *New Yorker*—making anger hot again.[5]

We were traveling to our hometown in New York as I wrote this article. I Googled Rage Room and I found it immediately—"Smash Therapy." The woman on the phone was chirpy and sweet. Yes, they were open. Yes, we could book a group room. I texted my daughter, my nieces, and my best friend. *ABSOLUTELY,* they replied. I made an appointment for Sunday. Texting back and forth, we began to put together a playlist. My daughter nixed Sara Barielles for The Used. Texts flew back and forth and my mood brightened just thinking about it. I found myself wondering who cleaned up the mess after a session. What did they do with the broken shards? I want to open up a Rage Room in Vermont and call it Smash Palace, meds on the side.

We signed up for the 20/20/20 package—twenty breakables and twenty minutes for twenty dollars per person. We brought several large boxes of our own bottles from a friend's party the previous night for BYOB credit. While waiting for the last of our group to arrive, I chatted about rage and anger with the owner of Smash Therapy and his mom, the woman who answered the phone. The owner had read articles warning that Rage Rooms could lead to more violence, but he didn't believe it to be true. After a Rage Room session, people leave in much better moods, he said. After signing the waivers, we were shown a safety video and issued our personal protective equipment (PPE). From another room we heard breaking glass but no music, no yelling, no swearing.

There wasn't a bataka in sight. This was hardcore, complete with sledgehammers, crowbars, and baseball bats. I laughed and cheered on my cohorts, watching my now-grown daughter and niece slamming sledgehammers against a microwave. I went after an indestructible Hoover with a vengeance. I imagined those faces—Trump, Kavanaugh, McConnell, Graham, Cruz—decorating plates and wine jugs as I smashed them. I replaced my heavy sledgehammer with an aluminum baseball bat because my wrist hurts, and I threw several

[5] Traister, Rebecca. *Good and Mad, the Revolutionary Power of Women's Anger.* Simon and Schuster: New York. https://www.newyorker.com/podcast/political-scene/rebecca-traister-is-happy-to-be-mad

plates into the air and missed. I had never been a sports girl, and the sweat blurred my vision under the band of the Plexiglas hood, making my aim even worse. Later, in the video they provided for an extra five bucks, we all seemed to be moving more slowly than it had felt at the time.

I left feeling tough, tired, and refreshed, as if I had had a good workout. In the evening, still in post-bad-ass glow, I am cc'd on an email that my nephew, married to one of my ruthless Hoover mates, proposed to send to the local paper. He demanded that they update their original article on Smash Therapy. While I only gave peripheral consideration to the microwaves and the printers we enjoyed demolishing, those appliances were potentially laden with beryllium, mercury, lead, and radioactive particles. While the larger pieces of debris were recycled, the owner assured us, the toxic dust that was generated by our rage drifted into the air and into our lungs. My nephew had the rage now. And while he was probably right, I felt a little cheated, just as I had done when I got mad on behalf of that woman in my group so many years ago. *Rage appropriation.*

Like the owner of Smash Therapy, I don't agree with the articles that suggest Rage Rooms don't make us feel any better. I don't agree that violence only begets more violence. I am only cheated if I remain cheated. I am happy to trade a few moments with toxic particles to cleanse these otherwise years of toxic politics. My nephew did not send the letter to the paper in the end. Maybe it was the glow of his wife's face when she arrived home; maybe he researched his complaints more deeply. I say, bring on the batakas, the sledge hammers, and the votes! Let the Rage Room be our safe place. Fire it the fuck up and take it to the streets.

❧

Nina Gaby is a writer, visual artist, and advanced practice nurse who specializes in addiction and psychiatry. Her essays, fiction, prose poetry, and articles have been published in numerous anthologies, journals and magazines, and her artwork is held in various collections, including the Smithsonian, Arizona State University, and Rochester Institute of Technology. Her anthology, *Dumped: Stories of Women Unfriending Women* was published in 2015. She exhibits her mixed-media widely in New England, and maintains a clinical practice in psychiatry. In addition to a master's degree in psych-mental health nursing, Gaby holds bachelor's degrees in fine arts and nursing, offers trainings, workshops, and has taught at several universities. More information at www.ninagaby.com.

Duty To Warn

By Jenny Holland

This is a story about integration, action, and psychotherapy. Mostly, it is about love.

As a mental health professional, I am used to taking a role in the advancement and welfare of others on a daily basis through my capacity to educate, evaluate, empathize, and advocate. For the most part, a therapist's work is done on a smaller scale—one-on-one in the safety of a confidential, therapeutic setting. It is because we have aligned with our clients that they trust us and make good use of our attention. They trust us to say what we see in a way that allows them to take it in and make use of it for themselves. They trust us to act in their best interest. Our help comes in many forms. Sometimes it's providing support during transitional or challenging times. Other times, it is in the work of exploration and helping our clients know when to sit back and when to take action.

We all have a different threshold that tells us when we must act. I crossed that threshold for the first time shortly after my eighteenth birthday. It was August 1989 and after soliciting a citizen to perform unlawful acts against public property, I got myself arrested. It was the first meaningful thing I did as a legal adult.

A friend of mine had asked if I wanted to take a road trip to protest the lack of accessibility for people with disabilities in Sparks, Nevada. So we packed both of our wheelchairs and our seventy-five-pound service dogs into my thirteen-year-old Honda and hit the road.

When we arrived, we came upon a small group of about thirty activists. Seemingly standing in the middle of nowhere, they gathered on a street corner in protest. They held signs with large letters that read, "Disability Pride!" Others read, "We Exist!" Holding their signs—each with an exclamation mark—the group chanted together, "In-dee-pen-dence is our right!"

I wanted to be inspired by the scene, but I wasn't. I had yet to integrate being disabled into my identity and I felt deflated. I had spent my limited resources on gas and trashed my used car. I was exhausted from the miles and the energy spent removing and re-packing the wheelchairs every time we needed to stop. And for what? To stand with a small band of misfits in one hundred and thirteen degree heat in the middle of nowhere? My thoughts raced. Had I driven all this way in pain and discomfort for this?

My friend remained encouraging and enthusiastic, so we pulled out our wheelchairs and joined the others on the street. Tolerating the heat was one thing; tolerating being part of this group was an-other. We were ragged around the edges, unsightly, disorganized. This could not be *my* group. We had no power. We didn't even have a critical mass. Our efforts felt like a lost cause. Once on the street corner, I sat in my wheelchair judging and criticizing my own people. While they tried their best to make a difference in whatever way they could, I did nothing.

I was lost in these thoughts when a woman in a power wheelchair rolled up alongside me. Her legs were sticking straight out in front of her, due to spasticity, and she held a sledgehammer in her lap.

"What are you gonna do with that?" I yelled over to her.

"I'm gonna use it to make a curb cut here. Do you think I should do it?" she asked.

A curb cut may seem insignificant, but it's one thing that grants people with disabilities entry into the public sphere—one that gives us a chance to cross the street or even be in the street at all. I don't know if it was my admiration for the fortitude of this woman—the *chutzpah*, the energy of the crowd, or simply my desire to have some-thing big happen, but I heard myself yelling, "Do it! Do it!"

I knew it was unlikely the woman would be able to physically lift the sledgehammer, but she didn't need to. Her actions created a tool inside me that was more powerful than any object of demolition.

"Do it! Do it!" I yelled even louder.

I looked over just in time to see a policeman approaching the woman with the sledgehammer—his baton already in hand. I knew in an instant that the police had interpreted her spasticity, her disabil-ity, and her very body as an act of resisting arrest.

After our arrest, I sat in a jail cell and wondered what would happen. Regardless, I had been changed. See, it was never just about a curb cut. It was a fight for existence—to have our issues count. We wanted to be treated like human beings—to show people that every life deserves equal and fair treatment, because no life is unworthy of life itself.

Inside the jail, we couldn't use the bathrooms. They didn't want to deal with the mess and weren't particularly interested in troubleshooting the issue. Eventually, they had to let us go. When I was released, the charges were dropped. They were dropped against all of us. The irony of the reasoning—the fact that the jail was not handicap accessible—was not lost on us.

A few days after the protest in Sparks, I found myself sitting in my first college seminar—a political science class at Sonoma State University. It was only the first day, but we talked about the United States and its role in World War II. We were wide-eyed and young, sitting around a seminar table, horrified to learn that our government knew about the systematic slaughtering of Jews and other minorities in Eastern Europe. They failed to act. For so long, our country did nothing. I was stunned by this new awareness of our capacity to tolerate, perpetuate, and engage in such horrific actions. I was shocked by the knowledge that we were silent—complicit—in the face of evil.

Sensing my distress, outrage, and feelings of hopelessness, my professor looked at me wearily and said, "There must be a special place in hell for those who knew and did not say."

In 1990, less than one year later, one of the most comprehensive civil rights bills was signed into law: The Americans with Disabilities Act. I'd like to think our small protest had something to do with it. The reality is, people with disabilities had organized and mobilized. Their protests and refusal to be silent in the face of oppression and injustice finally resulted in legislation. *Americans with Disabilities.* We now had a name and laws to help protect us. Over time, the legal changes even made way for attitudinal change. Our actions made a difference.

Like the protest in Nevada and political science course I enrolled in afterward, I learned to never remain silent when I can take action. My position as a mental health professional continues to reaffirm this belief. Psychotherapy itself is an act—a radical political act that is capable of influencing great change. When we empower others to trust their feelings and perceptions, to act in their own best interests, and to understand themselves and their motivations on deeper levels, we are fostering strength and resilience. We are contributing to a system where thoughtful and empowered people flourish.

Clinicians are in a position to be powerful and effective agents of change, but that requires wrestling with the part of the psyche that pulls on us to do nothing. Operating from this place, we cannot move and become stuck in the psychological concrete that stands between us and action.

While I am not interested in being arrested again for soliciting citizens to destroy public property, I am interested in motivating others to cross the threshold to action. I am interested in taking my specialized knowledge, coupled with action, to be a sledgehammer against ignorance, intolerance, and injustice.

So where is my threshold for action in light of the harsh realities we are facing now? It was Trump's making fun of a disabled reporter to get a laugh. It was listening to client after client express their feelings of deep despair over Trump's position of power. I was pushed to act by the marked increase in depression, anxiety, traumatic response, suicidal ideation, and hopelessness in my clients since Trump was elected. As one client put it, "It's like being raped all over again with every action he takes, every hateful word he says."

Whatever your threshold for action is, now is the time to cross it and keep going.

Jenny Holland is a licensed psychologist practicing in Santa Rosa, CA, where she specializes in treating mood disorders. Dr. Holland is a public speaker, writer, and activist with a passion for pursuing access and equality for all marginalized groups.

Rachel Maddow Sings Me to Sleep

By *Susan Fekete*

I have a lot of early memories that center around sleep and bedtime rituals—particularly, my mother's hand stroking my hair, tucking small strands of it behind my ear. This habit must have started long before my cognitive memory because its comfort was unmatched. Well into my adolescence, when in need of some unnameable comfort, I would lie down and place my head in my mom's lap on the couch, saying, "Play with my hair" and inevitably drifting off to sleep as she did. When in Catholic school, I'd lie in bed at night with images of the sacred heart—a heart on fire—in my mind's eye as I said my nightly prayers, and the flickering flames would lull me to sleep. By high school, I'd found that focusing on a good book would silence the rest of my day and let my mind drift into slumber.

No matter my age, I have always found a way to quickly ease myself into the waves of sleep as they lapped at my consciousness. When I was a child and my parents were divorcing, I could fall asleep. Struggling with financial difficulties, I escaped them when sleeping. Relationship issues, college exams, job interviews never got in the way of me catching Zs. In 1995, I slept as Hurricane Opal took down centuries-old oaks in my Atlanta neighborhood and left a quarter-million people, including me, without electricity.

In my very late twenties, I became a massage therapist. That career was short-lived when I developed serious carpal tunnel syndrome—the first thing in life to really keep me up at night, my hands aching in a deep, intense way. I'd shake them, flapping them in the air like I was back on Romper Room and pretending to be a do-bee. I'd rub, massage, and even slap them to bring the circulation back, to end the ache. After a career change and few months of sleeping in wrist braces at night, the respite of my deep, uninterrupted sleep returned.

In my late thirties, my husband and I bought a restaurant and I returned to the world of personal extremity abuse as a cook and kitchen manager. Within a year, the pain in my hands was back with a vengeance. Every night I was pricked awake by pins-and-needles. I'd sit on the edge of our bed, and shake, rub, and massage myself until I could lie down again for another hour. Eventually, the waking incidents became so frequent that I gave up sleeping in our bed entirely and moved my nighttime routine to the couch. I couldn't see ruining my husband's sleep, even though he quietly protested. I returned to sleeping in wrist braces, which helped, but did not cure the issue.

It's important that I point out that my disrupted nights and somnolent days were due to pain—an intense, undeniable physical pain. It was not my mind keeping me up at night. Even in the most difficult days when the recession was bearing down on us and a lack of tourism was strangling our gasping business, my thoughts floated easily under the moonlight and would only be whisked again into their whirlpool as the sun rose.

To this day, I continue to sleep in wrist braces, but they do the job and I am very rarely awakened by my hands. This does not mean, however, that I sleep. On November 8, 2016, the privileged comfort of easy sleep escaped me and has yet to return.

It was far past ten p.m. as I sat on our couch in disbelief that night. Nothing had been declared yet, but every indication was that my fears, and the fears of the majority of the American people, were coming true. I glanced at the clock over and over, hoping for a miracle. I was tired, and growing more so by the minute as my energy drained away, contemplating the looming reality. A cold, dank fog rolled into my heart and disappointment dripped from my eyelids as they began to droop shut. We went to bed.

Turning on the television in the morning is not my habit. It is my husband's habit and I abide it. However, on the morning of November 9, 2016, I was the one who rolled over the minute I woke and reached for the remote.

"Trump Wins" screamed at me in bold letters across the bottom of the screen.

I walked my dog that morning and called a friend to commiserate. Instead of the blanket of understanding that I expected her to wrap around me, I was greeted by something I never expected—a Pollyanna. This thoughtful, educated female attorney was not upset. She had not voted for him but was taking a "wait and see" approach. She works for a government agency that serves families and children in California. When my lament for progress was greeted by her insistence that perhaps the newly elected POTUS would rectify some of the challenges our country faced—specifically immigration issues—I finally gave up the argument, and the phone call. I told her that I didn't feel good, that I was so sad that I couldn't even explain my sadness, and that I was not in the least bit optimistic, even though she insisted that optimism was mandatory. I told her we'd talk again soon, but that I was too depressed to raise my head and look for a light at the end of the tunnel.

I did not sit quietly by and mourn the loss of our society and the ills of the Electoral College. Depression has a long history in my bloodline. I know better than to willingly plunge into its depths, so I paddle like hell to stay afloat when I feel it rush in around me. I have not always been successful, but I have always battled to stay in the boat through rough currents.

By January, I was fighting mad. I put on my boots and went to the Women's March alone, because I was new in town and didn't know anyone. Ten days later I showed up, alone, to the first Indivisible meeting in my area where I met about 150 powerful, engaged, exciting people—and within two weeks I was performing multiple functions as co-founder of Indivisible Sonoma County. My energy, outside of my daily job, went full-throttle into activism. My husband—not a rabble rouser—quietly observed as I hustled about to town halls, protests, and meetings at the offices of my members of Congress. I was indefatigable, or so I thought and was often told.

By March, my husband had grown accustomed to going to bed alone. Late night hours were when I accomplished much of my activism. There were meeting agendas to consider, call scripts to write so that our friends and neighbors could pick up their phones and keep Washington D.C. on task. There were newsletters to compose, emails to respond to, and new members to welcome. It wasn't long until I wished that I could make a full-time job of it, while simultaneously wishing that the work wasn't necessary at all. I hoped it all would be brought to a sudden end by some act of Congress, or God. Many nights I managed to get five or six hours of sleep. It was sufficient, because the fire in my chest burned hot enough to fuel me.

Eventually, though, my head had to hit the pillow. But my eyes stayed open. Working on electronic devices, it's been proven, interferes with our sleep habits. We've been warned to put them down an hour before bed, unplug, unwind. I agree with the *idea* of that but was more committed to our efforts to save our democracy than to my rest and needed every moment I could have with my keyboard to push the movement forward. Everything mattered. I repeated to myself over and over: "If not me, who?" Each night, when my hands had grown too tired to type or my eyes too blurry to see, I'd slip on my wrist braces, recline on our couch, and turn to the other screen—the television.

The advent of falling asleep with the television on did not come early in my life. Growing up, we were not permitted televisions in our bedrooms. It wasn't until I lived with my first husband that I'd had a TV anywhere outside of the living room. Then again, I'd always fallen asleep when I lay in bed. But by 2017, that concept had vanished. Lying on our couch in the spring of 2017, I'd turn to my recorded programs and find MSNBC from earlier in the day. Hoping that I would be able to watch it in its entirety, I'd turn on *The Rachel Maddow Show* and begin to listen. More tired than I knew, gently tucking her words into my ears, the reassuring cadence of Rachel Maddow's voice would begin to sing me to sleep. Anything past the first segment I usually only heard subliminally.

After several weeks of this, I became mildly frustrated, wondering why one of the most engaging voices in the whole of modern political punditry was functioning as a sleep aid for me. I found her thoroughly engaging and wanted so badly to hear what she had to say, but I couldn't keep myself awake to hear it.

By June, my fury had exhausted me. I'd hit the wall of "burnout" that we'd all been warned about. Six months of fear and loathing of the government was beginning to wear on me, just as it was wearing on our national psyche. I began to feel the pull of projects I'd set by the wayside in the wake of the disastrous election and resulting attacks on our liberties. My own house needed tending to, as the White House continued to lurch forward, haphazardly trampling regulations and careers. I worked to redistribute my attention and am now feeling balanced again, or as balanced as possible in a country where our government is run daily like an obstacle course set in quicksand.

Most nights now, I go to bed with my husband and go to sleep. My mind rests, knowing that I have done what I can for the day — not only for society, but for myself as well. Most nights now I can lie in bed, listing my gratitudes and imagining sacred flames flickering in the hearts of Rachel Maddow, Chris Hayes, Joy Reid, all the writers, editors, the countless reporters, the…and drift away.

Still, there are nights when I search for sleep. There are nights after the worst of our bad news days when, lying awake in bed, I can think of nothing but how to save the world—or at least our democracy. Those nights, I take a pillow and sneak from our bed, returning to my familiar spot on the couch, remote in hand, *The Rachel Maddow Show* on the screen, hoping to slumber.

I finally know now why Rachel Maddow puts me to sleep, and I'm perfectly fine with it. I think she would be, too. It's not that I find her boring. It's not her look, her voice, her content, her graphics. It's not her guests or the timing of her segments. And, nowadays, it's not because I'm simply exhausted. Rachel Maddow sings me to sleep because I trust her, and that trust comforts me. Even though I know that the show I'm watching was taped hours earlier, and even though I know that she is likely at that moment fast asleep as I hope to be, when *The Rachel Maddow Show* is on my television, I feel like someone has my back. I feel like somewhere in this world, someone other than me is still concerned with truth. Knowing that she and her writers are on the job, bird-dogging the lunacy roosting in our capital, I do not have to save the world. Not alone, not all at once, and certainly not now. Not until I've gotten some sleep.

ॐ

Susan Fekete's memoir about hoarding, *Ten Boxes: A Story of Stuff,* was released in 2018. She's been published by *Longreads* and *The Influence*, and her newsletters as co-founder of Indivisble Sonoma County were some of her proudest writing moments. She lives happily in California with her husband and dog.

Going to Ground

By Sarah Einstein

Like a good citizen, I call my senators at least once a week, but their aides are brusque. They tell me that Alexander and Corker support the president's education agenda/healthcare reform/immigration order or whatever I'm outraged about on a given day. In the first few weeks, they'd thank me for my call. Now they simply say, "Your objection is noted," and hang up as quickly as they can. Once, as if caught off guard, one said, "Are you sure you live in Tennessee?"

I carry my passport with me everywhere these days.

I've begun to sort that which is precious from that which is not. I make a small pile of the things I'd pack in the night, a larger one of the stuff I would leave. Everyone is insisting we're just one Reichstag fire away from fascism. On the news, I watch a steady stream of black people murdered by the State for their blackness, and I think it's more likely that we've already had the Anschluss.

When I travel, I wear an inherited diamond I feel silly wearing at home. I remember being told when I was younger that a Jewish woman should always have enough jewelry on her body to bribe her way over a border. At the time, it seemed quaint. Now it seems key. For the moment, the diamond ring's still on my finger. I wonder if there will come a day when I'll need to sew it into the hem of my coat.

Over coffee, my friend Meredith talks about joining the resistance in a way that suggests we're headed for a war she thinks we can win. I talk about going to ground, about building false walls to hide people waiting for fake passports and safe transport. We scare ourselves and then laugh at ourselves, but after the laughing we are still scared.

Meredith wasn't always Meredith, and there is a passel of bills in our state legislature designed to make it impossible for her to be Meredith now. I tell her I will shelter her in my hidden rooms, if it comes to that. She says she won't be hidden, but she might move to Atlanta.

My coffee these days is chamomile tea. I'm jittery enough as it is.

If we flee, we will go to my husband's family in Austria. They assure us that we'll be safe there, should it come to that, and I believe them. They've clearly learned lessons that we have not. The irony of this is not lost on me; there are Nazis in the family albums. My husband has stopped talking about becoming an American citizen and started talking about being an anchor relative.

My friend Jessica is spending all her vacation time in Israel this year, establishing the Right of Return. I've stopped questioning the politics of this; refugees go where they can. This Hanukah, I will give my niece and nephews passports if they don't already have them. If they do, I will give them whatever they ask for. I've lifted my moratorium on war toys. Maybe they should know how to handle guns.

My closest disabled friends and I swap lists of medications and start to horde the things one or some of us need against the day we lose access to them. We read up on actual expiration versus labeled expiration dates. We refill prescriptions before we need to, just in case.

I have six boxes of Plan B in my closet, even though I'm long past childbearing years. On campus, I spread rumors about a shadowy network of old women who will help younger women with travel and money for abortions if they can't get the healthcare they need here. I call all my old woman friends and build the network. I keep their names and numbers in handwritten lists and hide them away.

I refuse to let my husband put a "Stop Trump" bumper sticker on our car. "That's just foolish," I say. I let him keep the Cthulhu fish. For now.

A young woman cries in my office, afraid that if she comes out to her parents, they will disown her; she's still financially dependent on them. I tell her that she doesn't have to tell them she's a lesbian now, or ever, if she doesn't feel safe doing so. She looks shocked. It breaks my heart to have been the first to suggest the safety of the closet to her. I wonder what she is coming out of, if it had never occurred to her to remain in.

I've stopped going to protests and started going to meetings for which there are no flyers or Facebook event notices. To find them, you have to know someone who already has. We talk there of things I won't write here. At first, we turned off our phones. Now, we leave them at home.

And yet, still, like a good citizen, I call my senators at least once a week. Their aides are brusque. In the first few weeks, they'd thank me for my call. Now, they hang up as quickly as they can. I haven't yet given up on the dream of America, but I'm making contingency plans.

Sarah Einstein is the author of *Mot: A Memoir* (University of Georgia Press, 2015) and *Remnants of Passion* (SheBooks, 2014). Her essays and short stories have appeared in the *Sun*, *Ninth Letter*, *PANK*, and other journals. She teaches creative writing at the University of Tennessee in Chatanooga.

A Red Diaper Baby Returns to Her Roots

By Erica Manfred

I come from a long line of proud lefties. My grandparents were socialists who escaped the ghettos of Russia to fight for the right to unionize in America. My parents were Communists who fought for social justice in the 1930s. As the third generation, I am a Red Diaper Baby who wanted to follow the family tradition.

Although to their deaths they never admitted it to me, my parents were both card-carrying Communists. How do I know? I can't tell you. I was brought up never to reveal such information. When friends visited my parents, instead of telling me to put out the cheese and crackers, I was instructed to hide *The National Guardian*, a genuinely mind-numbing lefty publication. In addition to being told never to get into a car with a stranger, I was instructed never to answer a stranger's questions—the questioner might be FBI.

As a sixties activist, I wasn't hiding. I joined an anarchist study group, a feminist consciousness raising group, marched against the war in Vietnam, and took as gospel beliefs that now seem quaint: human beings are basically good; if people, not capitalists, owned the means of production, poverty would disappear; economic equality could cure all social ills. Misguided and dangerous though Communism was, the passion for social justice and the compassion for working people that it represented was not.

In 1968, I went to Cuba and signed up for the Venceremos Brigade, American leftists who were invited to help with the sugar cane harvest. That experience was my reality check.

I'd spent my time on the ideological left in self-styled anarchist groups with utopian dreams of participatory democracy. I discovered that an actual Communist dictatorship bore no resemblance to my fantasy. While the Cubans mechanically spewed forth the party line and methodically eliminated freedom of the press and speech, the notorious Weathermen, who had joined the Brigade to recruit new members, used Maoist brainwashing techniques, like brutal all-night criticism and self-criticism sessions, to induce us to sign-up. I realized I'd rather be ruled by Richard Nixon than by the kids in the Weather tent. At least you could vote him out.

Disillusionment followed. The Weathermen were clearly delusional as well as dangerous. My parents had passionately believed that the Soviet Union was the Promised Land, another treacherous fantasy. I recognized that anarchism was a utopian crock. My generation of leftists had splintered into interest groups each defending its turf with more arrogant political correctness than my die-hard Stalinist parents, without any unifying vision of a just and compassionate society.

It seemed to me then that political passion, no matter how idealistic, inevitably led to fanaticism. I became a cynic, disbelieving any group's claims to a corner of the truth. My political life consisted of voting for the least objectionable candidate. I gave up my dreams of changing the world and became a wishy-washy liberal, avoiding the subject of politics whenever possible.

In the late seventies, my parents moved to a condo in Century Village in Deerfield Beach, Florida, which became the retirement haven of New York City civil servants like my mom, a former teacher. At the time, Century was a hotbed of old Commies. In fact, Gus Hall, the original head of the American Communist party retired there. My parents and their friends were no longer marching, although they loved to talk politics. I didn't even want to discuss politics, much less get involved in it. My mother was dismayed, wanting to know who was supposed to carry the torch of radicalism into the next century.

"What torch are you talking about, Mom?" I wanted to know. "All my generation cares about is defending their turf. Gays, blacks, women—gay black women, la de da. Gimme a break. They're all so smug and self-righteous they make me sick. I don't see you waving picket signs either."

"I'm too old. It's your turn."

"Well, I'm not joining up until there's a movement I believe in."

I hoped that the next generation would create my fantasy left-wing movement—where the interests of the poor and working classes were paramount—not just the groups who proclaimed they were the most oppressed. Leadership would be shared and, most important, dissent would not only be tolerated but encouraged.

As the years passed, I watched with dismay as blow after blow fell from the right, starting with Ronald Reagan and continuing with the insane rants of the Tea Party. I kept my head stuck in the sand because the left had no grand social vision to energize me. The extent of my political involvement was showing up at the polls to vote Democratic. I was encouraged by the Occupy Wall Street movement, but no way was I sleeping on the streets of New York. Anyway, I thought Obama's election was a sign that racism was on the way out and human rights were alive and well. The next president was going to be a woman after all. That was certainly progress wasn't it?

How could I have been so blind?

I was living in Florida when Trump got elected and my head finally emerged from the sand. I was so horrified, I decided I just had to get involved. When I got an email about a MoveOn meeting in my area, I was surprised by the address: Century Village in Deerfield Beach, my parents' old stomping grounds. When I got there, I discovered a new generation of old lefties—Red Diaper Babies like me who had inherited their parents' condos and their parents' politics. The Century Village resistance had been born.

At seventy-four, with my parents long gone, I actually moved to Century and joined up.

I've discovered advanced age is no hindrance to political activism. In fact, it's an asset. Retirees have plenty of time to devote to worthy causes. And we make a difference here in a swing state that has determined the outcome of more than one national election—a bigger difference than we could ever have made up North where most of us come from. Red Diaper Babies are keeping alive a weekly Deerfield forum featuring left-wing speakers that our parents' generation started but was in danger of dying out until Trump won. The specter of losing our own Medicare and Social Security, not to mention a clean environment, an end to racism, the right to abortion, and just about everything else we—and our parents—believed in for our entire lives has reinvigorated us.

I went to the women's march in Palm Beach with a bunch of other Red Diaper Babies. I worked for Andrew Gillum and Bill Nelson in the 2018 midterms, proud to have a black Democratic candidate to campaign for. I was devastated, along with the rest the local resistance when they lost by a hair.

I'm prepared to keep fighting for whomever is the Democratic candidate in 2020. I will make phone calls, show up at meetings, and get involved in working for the vision of America I had given up on. Will my vision ever come about? I have no idea, but I've gone back to the barricades and will hobble along fighting for what's right as long as I can. No need to wait for the next generation. We are that generation.

Erica Manfred is a Florida-based freelance journalist, humorous essayist and author. Her articles and essays have appeared in Atlantic.com, Salon.com, Seniorplanet.org, Healthline.com, *New York Times*, *Village Voice*, and many other off- and online publications. Erica is the author of *I'm Old So Why Aren't I Wise, Snarky Senior in the Sunshine State* and *He's History You're Not; Surviving Divorce After 40*, GPP Life, 2011. She has also co-authored a memoir, *Demon of Brownsville Road Berkley*, 2014 and published a humorous novel, *Interview with a Jewish Vampire*, 2009

Radioactive: Trump's Masculinity and How Women Must Rid the World of Nuclear Bombs

By Heidi Hutner

Panic. Donald Trump is elected and everything I love and hold dear are at grave risk—women's and LGBTQ+ rights, abortion rights, racial rights, religious rights, immigration rights, the rights of the disenfranchised and poor, environmental rights. We now face a world of racist, sexist, xenophobic, heterosexist, unrestrained white male hate—a world of unethical and immoral destruction in which the weakest are disproportionately and unfairly threatened and harmed.

There's more to this (cluster-fuck of a) nightmare:

The president's provocative, hostile, hypersexualized masculinist language and behavior, coupled with his unmediated access to the nuclear button, puts all life on earth at risk.[1]

This is the presidency of Dr. Strangelove.

We need women and a feminist antinuclear force to save the world.

Today, experts say, we are inching closer to nuclear catastrophe. *The Bulletin of the Atomic Scientists* defines how close we are to nuclear war with their metaphorical Doomsday Clock.[2] On January 25, 2018, the *Bulletin* moved the minute hand to two minutes to midnight. As Trump's presidency continues, things have grown worse. North Korea has a greater capacity than ever to harm other countries, including the U.S., as does Russia. North Korea has provoked international tensions. So has Russia. In South Asia, Pakistan and other nations

---

[1] In her essay "Vigil of Hope," therapist Meg Weber notes her patients' heightened fear of nuclear war under the Trump presidency, in *Fury: Women's Lived Experiences During the Trump Era*, edited by Amy Roost and Alissa Hirshfeld (Regal House Publishing, 2020).

[2] Janice Sinclaire, "Watch the 2018 Doomsday Clock Announcement," *Bulletin of the Atomic Scientists*, January 17, 2018.

are increasing their arsenals, tensions over the Iran nuclear deal are mounting, and weakened U.S. international diplomacy under President Trump has advanced nuclear dangers worldwide. Most recently, Trump pulled out of the nuclear weapons treaty between the U.S. and Russia, and he's modernizing nuclear weapons. Expert nuclear war planner Daniel Ellsberg, author of *The Pentagon Papers* and *The Doomsday Machine*, warns of the likelihood of "nuclear annihilation."[3]

During this dangerous time, women are leading the charge to eradicate weapons of mass destruction and forestall nuclear war. We saw this leadership most recently in the 2017 U.N. Treaty to Prohibit the Use of Nuclear Weapons. Approved with 122 states voting for and one against, it is the first legally binding global ban on nuclear weapons, with the intention of moving toward their complete elimination. The preamble to the treaty recognizes the maltreatment suffered by all beings as a result of nuclear weapons, including the disproportionate impact on women and girls and on indigenous peoples around the world. The treaty has been predominantly championed and promoted by women.

My interest in nuclear issues began over ten years ago when I first uncovered my mother's work as an antinuclear activist with a group called Women Strike for Peace.[4] Learning about my mother's work radically changed my perception of her. It also changed my life. I have been following women engaging in nuclear activism all over the world—writing about them, making a documentary film about them (*Accidents Can Happen: The Women of Three Mile Island*), protesting with them, teaching about them in my university classes—and I often bring my daughter with me. My mother's story is being passed down through an intergenerational maternal line, and with it, the activism that may help save the world, or at least help shift its view on disastrous weapons.

Between 1945 and 1963, more than two hundred atmospheric, underwater, and space nuclear-bomb tests were conducted by the U.S.,

[3] Lucy Feldman, "'Don't Wait Until the Bombs Are Falling.' Pentagon Papers Leaker Encourages More Like Him." *Time*, January 17, 2018, http://time.com/5106039/daniel-ellsberg-nuclear-war-north-korea

[4] Amy Swerdlow, *Women Strike for Peace: Traditional Motherhood and Radical Politics in the 1960s* (University of Chicago Press, 1993).

primarily in the Nevada desert and the Marshall Islands. Hundreds more took place around the world. In many instances, citizens were not informed of the tests, nor were they warned about their effects. The negative health impacts of the testing and the resultant exposure to ionizing radiation turned out to be vast: early death, cancer, heart disease, and a range of other illnesses, including neurological disabilities, weakened immune systems, infertility, and miscarriage. Ionizing radiation damages genes, so the health ramifications of exposures are passed down through the generations.[5]

In the 1950s, scientists concerned with the health impacts of bomb testing and the spread of ionizing radiation conducted the St. Louis Baby Tooth Survey.[6] The survey showed that radioactive fallout had traveled far and wide. Cow and breast milk contaminated with the isotope strontium 90 had entered children's teeth. Strontium 90 metabolizes as calcium and this isotope remains active in the body for many years. When Dagmar Wilson and Bella Abzug—who went on to become a Congresswoman and co-founder of the National Women's Political Caucus with Gloria Steinem and Betty Friedan—learned the results of the Baby Tooth Survey, they formed Women Strike for Peace. The group brought together concerned mothers from across the U.S. The women organized, first within their own communities, and then fifty thousand mothers protested across the country, and fifteen thousand more descended on Washington, D.C., for Women Strike for Peace Lobbying Day on November 1, 1961. My mother was one of those fifteen thousand protesters. The group's efforts brought considerable political attention to the dire

---

[5] Numerous scientists—including the father of physics, Karl Zimmerman, Rosalie Bertell, John Gofman, Steve Wing, Alice Stewart, Tim Mousseau (and many others)—agree that there is no 'safe' dose of radiation, and low levels of radiation may cause inheritable genetic mutations. On health and genetic impacts from radiation exposures, see, for example: National Research Council. Health Risks From Exposure to Low Levels of Ionizing Radiation, Health Risks From Exposure to Low Levels of Ionizing Radiation (BEIR VII Phase 2), (Washington, DC: The National Academies Press, 2006), https://doi.org/10.17226/11340; Keith Baverstock, "Some Important Questions Connected With Non-Targeted Effects" Mutation Research 687 (2010a): 84–88. https://doi.org/10.1016/j.mrfmmm.2010.01.002

[6] Bernard Becker Medical Library, Washington University School of Dental Medicine, "St. Louis Baby Tooth Survey, 1959-1970," accessed February 25, 2019, http://beckerexhibits.wustl.edu/dental/articles/babytooth.html

health consequences of radioactive fallout; in 1963, the signing of the Limited Nuclear Test Ban Treaty led to the banning of atmospheric bomb testing by the U.S., Great Britain, and the Soviet Union.

Women Strike for Peace reflects a cultural, nuclear, gender binary, with women constructed as peaceful antinuclear protectors of children and the nation, and men positioned as perpetrators of nuclear war—the designers, planners, and regulators of weapons of mass destruction.

Has the exclusion of women from nuclear decision-making led to our current crisis—a host of locations worldwide contaminated with radioactive waste and the great potential for nuclear war? Leading antinuclear activists seem to think so. Since the dawn of the nuclear age, men have dominated and controlled nuclear weapon design and policy. As Benjamin A. Valentino—associate professor of government and coordinator of the War and Peace Studies Program at the Dickey Center for International Understanding at Dartmouth College—says, it is only recently that women have had access to positions of power in the military sphere.[7] This is true in weapons sciences and engineering as well. While many women worked on the Manhattan Project, most held administrative roles as opposed to scientific and decision-making positions.[8]

Carol Cohn, founding director of the Consortium on Gender, Security, and Human Rights at the University of Massachusetts-Boston, suggests that nuclear weapons discourse is deeply rooted in hegemonic patriarchy. In nuclear technology language, metaphors of male sexual activity are used to describe nuclear violence. Nuclear language is sexualized; terms such as "missile envy," "deep penetration," "orgasmic whump," are commonly utilized among men in industry parlance. The violence of nuclear war is described in abstract and impersonal terms, such as "collateral damage." In her recent *New York Times* op-ed, Cohn finds it unsurprising that hypermasculine nuclear language has surfaced so blatantly today with Trump's tweets

---

[7] Benjamin A. Valentino, phone interview with author, February 12, 2018.

[8] Carol Cohn, "The Perils of Mixing Masculinity and Missiles," *The New York Times*, January 5, 2018. See also: Carol Cohn, "Sex and Death in the Rational World of Defense Intellectuals," *Signs: Journal of Women in Culture and Society*, 12, no. 4 (Summer 1987): 687-718, https://www.jstor.org/stable/3174209

about the size of his nuclear button and his overall muscular championing of expanding the nuclear weapons complex.

Following the Women Strike for Peace model, legions of antinuclear non-governmental organizations worldwide are predominantly led by women, including Women's Action for Nuclear Disarmament; Women's International League for Peace and Freedom; Reaching Critical Will; the German Green Party; Mothers for Peace; Just Moms (St. Louis); International Campaign to Abolish Nuclear Weapons (ICAN); Greenham Common Women's Peace Camp; Green Action Japan; the women of Koondakulam in India; the antinuclear nuns, Megan Rice, Ardeth Platte, Carol Gilbert, Alice Slater, Petra Kelly (cofounder of the Green Party in Germany); Leona Morgan of Dine Nonukes, and many more. The leading voice for the antinuclear movement from the last quarter of the twentieth century through the present is Dr. Helen Caldicott, an Australian physician.

At the UN conference to ban nuclear weapons in 2017, I asked civil society experts and Russian participants about the importance of women as leaders in the antinuclear movement, and about the hegemony of masculinity in the nuclear weapons complex. They stated that women understand why we must ban nuclear weapons and how women take the lead in actions to do so.

"Of course, many men support disarmament and have participated in the treaty and current antinuclear efforts in general, but women overwhelmingly spearhead the actions," said Tim Wright, of the Australian branch of ICAN.[9] ICAN won the 2017 Nobel Prize for its work on the Treaty to Prohibit the Use of Nuclear Weapons.

Ray Acheson, of Reaching Critical Will, said the proliferation of nuclear weapons is deeply embedded in "a misogynist and hegemonic culture of violence."[10] She stated that this culture is oppressive to women, LGBTQ+, the poor, and people of color, and that "we must smash patriarchy." Such is the feminist cry heard around the world, but in this case, it might actually save us.

Beatrice Fihn, director of ICAN, explained that men are raised to be violent, to think it's necessary to resolve differences through

---

[9] Tim Wright, interview with author, July 6, 2017.
[10] Ray Acheson, interview with author, July 6, 2017.

force, while "women, conversely, are socially trained to negotiate and compromise."[11] According to Fihn, the problem in a patriarchal world is that peaceful negotiations are viewed as weak. The U.S. Misogynist-in-Chief, Donald Trump, feels that we must drop nuclear bombs, expand our nuclear arsenal, and strong-arm competing nations such as North Korea and Russia. The very act of supporting disarmament efforts in a patriarchal framework places "you in a feminine category," Fihn stressed. "Those in favor of abolishing nuclear weapons, whether male or female, are characterized in negative, feminized terms. This characterization must be changed. It is not weak to abolish weapons of mass destruction. It is life-affirming."

Women most often function as caretakers of children and the elderly; they are aware of the human cost of war and radioactive disaster. When thinking about nuclear war, they wonder, "If war breaks out, how will we feed our children, how will we feed our sick? What will happen to our communities?" Fihn says she fears nuclear violence in respect to the safety of her own children. Fihn's concern for her children echoes the concerns of my mother and her antinuclear cohort in the 1950s and '60s. Like Fihn, they worked to save their children—all children—from radiation contamination and nuclear war. I hope I can carry on that legacy, and that my daughter chooses to pick up the cause as well.

For the 2017 U.N. Treaty to Prohibit the Use of Nuclear Weapons, women helped prepare key elements of the document and gave vital health testimony. Particularly poignant were tales from Australian indigenous, Marshallese, and Hibakusha (Hiroshima and Nagasaki survivors) women. I interviewed many of them. Abacca Anjain-Madison, a former senator of the Republic of the Marshall Islands, told me that between 1946 and 1958, the U.S. conducted sixty-seven nuclear bomb tests on the atoll islands.[12] Many babies born during the testing period resembled jellyfish and died quickly after birth. The Marshallese developed very high rates of cancer and other diseases as a result of ionizing radiation exposure. Now, with climate change, the radioactive dangers persist. Rising sea levels threaten the Runit

---

[11] Beatrice Fihn, interview with author, October 20, 2017.
[12] Abacca Anjain-Madison, interview with author, July 6, 2017.

Dome—a sealed space that contains large amounts of radioactive contamination. The dome has also begun to crack, and the U.S. has no plans to assist the Marshallese with this crisis. They finished the cleanup and sealed the dome in 1979. Abacca Anjain-Madison asserts that the clean-up was insufficient and that the dome was never intended to be permanent. The Marshallese do not have the means to protect themselves from the impending disaster.

Mary Olson, southeast director of the Nuclear Information and Resource Service, gave a presentation at the U.N. on the unequal health impacts of radiation exposures. Women's and children's greater vulnerability to radiation exposures is not taken into account in nuclear regulatory safety standards. Based on the data set from the BEIR VII report that both Olson and Dr. Arjun Makhijani, president of the Institute for Energy and Environmental Research, have studied, women are twice as likely to get cancer, and nearly twice as likely than men to die from cancer associated with ionizing radiation exposures.[13] Children are five to ten times more likely to develop cancer in their lifetimes from radiation exposures than adult males, and girls are the most vulnerable of all. Scientists do not yet understand why there is an age and gender disparity. The standard "reference man" by which radiation safety regulations are set is based on a white adult male. Olson and Makhijani argue that safety regulations must change to account for age and gender disparities.[14] Further studies are needed to assess how people of different races are impacted by radiation exposure. To date, no such completed studies exist.

At the closing of the conference and signing of the 2017 U.N. Treaty to Prohibit the Use of Nuclear Weapons, two speeches were made—one by Setsuko Thurlow, a Hiroshima survivor, Nobel Peace Prize winner, and leading campaigner for the prohibition of nuclear weapons; the other by Abacca Anjain-Madison of the Marshall

---

[13] National Research Council, Health Risks.

[14] Olson, interview with author, June 20, 2017; Arjun Makhijani, Brice Smith, and Michael C. Thorne, "Science for the Vulnerable: Setting Radiation and Multiple Exposure Environmental Health Standards" (Takoma Park, MD: Institute for Energy and Environmental Research, 2006), https://ieer.org/resource/depleted-uranium/science-vulnerable-setting-radiation

Islands.[15] Setsuko Thurlow told her story of beholding the bomb dropping on her city in 1945. She described how, as an eight-year-old child, she witnessed the death of her brother and the "unthinkable" violence that was thrust upon her people. For Thurlow, the signing of the U.N. Treaty to ban nuclear weapons was a miracle, but she believes we must rid the world of weapons entirely. She will not give up her efforts until that day comes. Neither will I.

❧

Heidi Hutner, PhD, teaches, speaks, and writes about ecofeminism and environmental justice at Stony Brook University, where she is a professor. Much of her writing, research, and activism focuses on gender, nuclear power, and weapons. Until recently, Heidi was the director of the Sustainability Studies Program and Associate Dean in the School of Marine and Atmospheric Sciences (for nearly six years). Heidi gave her first TEDx talk, "Eco-Grief and Ecofeminism," in November 2015. She gave a talk on 'water rights as a human right' on NBC News Think! in 2017. Hutner's writing has been featured at news outlets and magazines such as the *New York Times, Ms. Magazine, DAME, Tikkun, Spirituality and Health, Yes!, Common Dreams, Garnet News, AEON,* and *Proximity Magazine,* as well as in academic journals and books (Oxford University Press, University of Virginia Press, Palgrave, Rowman and Littlefield, and others). With her film partner, Martijn Hart, Heidi is directing, writing, and producing the documentary film, *ACCIDENTS CAN HAPPEN: Voices of Women from Three Mile Island.* She is at work on a companion book of the same name.

---

[15] Setsuko Thurlow, closing lecture presented at the U.N. Treaty to Prohibit the Use of Nuclear Weapons, New York, NY, July 7, 2017.

Chop Wood, Carry Water

By Allison K Williams

We woke up and everything was different. Maybe we woke in the middle of the night, tried not to check our phone, checked our phone anyway, and spent the hours before dawn in a bleak haze, waiting for a decent time to call someone. Maybe a call came—your mother has died. Or, it's time to let the cat go. Or, our country has elected a demagogue.

Maybe we woke to the memory of yesterday. The doctor saying, let's discuss your options. Our lover telling us they've found someone else—found her, in fact, months ago. All we want is to go back to sleep, back in time, to the moment before the disaster, the break-up, the crash, to the moment of sweet unknowing, when everything was still okay.

How can we write? How can we read? How can we possibly address the page with our life or our characters' lives, so petty and small in the face of tragedy? How does what we create matter in the wake of the unchangeable? We search online—who else feels this way? Is there a support group? Someone else we know this has happened to? We click angry-sad-angry-sad-angry-sad. Grief comes in waves—an old photograph, the smell of a cast-off sweater, a yard sign we looked at on the way to work and thought of our neighbors: "That's all you know," our superiority mingling with disgust.

We go through the motions. There is a place I am due every day at nine a.m. My child must be fed. I've already paid for that class. We watch faces—who else has lost their mother? Who is on the ex-lover's side and who is still on ours?

My ex-husband's mother dies suddenly. He flies across the country and gets her dog. In the piles of knickknacks and clothes, boxes of paperwork, lists of phone calls and appraisals, there is one constant: an animal that must be fed and walked and loved whether his capacity to love is intact or not. He drives a truck back home, full of furniture and a fawn-colored pitbull mix, a dog that has grown up in Las Vegas and never seen grass. He posts on social media as the dog. The dog sees snow for the first time. The dog discovers kittens. The bottom of his world has still dropped out, but the dog is a bucket in which he can carry water. The dog is an axe with which he can chop wood. He carries her up and down the stairs until she learns, and each time he touches her, he touches his old world, the world in which his mother is also alive and carrying the dog. The dog is a lifeline from a better past. The dog is the seed of a pearl.

We grieve, and we see others triumph. Our lover shows up to get his PlayStation, looking happy and well-fed. After a few days, the essay or the book or the poem we've put aside goes from horrifyingly irrelevant to merely unappetizing. We sit down again. We tinker. We find the rhythm, we find that yes, it matters to say something, anything, on the page. That we are not just artists but craftsmen, and craftsmen go to work. We have spent—or are spending—our lives sharpening our tools, and they are not just for fine days. Our tools—our words—matter not for how we use them when all is well, but how we use them to shore up the levee when the waters rise. The people whose stories need sharing, who are not craftsmen enough to write their own, who need to hear our story to know theirs is not singular, still need us. Our words connect them from a better past to a seed of hope, string them a lifeline to the future. Our words say, me too.

I call my equally devastated friend, who has also lost her mother or her cat or her country, and she tells me a parable:

The novice says to the master, "What does one do before enlightenment?"

"Chop wood. Carry water," replies the master.

The novice asks, "What, then, does one do after enlightenment?"

"Chop wood. Carry water."

Two years pass. You are outraged. You are hopeful. You are exhilarated. You are destroyed. Social media cradles you. Social media affronts you. Caring is a pinball game—which direction must you rage this week?

Chop wood.

Carry water.

You join a group. You write letters. You press redial on your senator's phone number. Each day a swing of the axe you long to put down. Each day another bucket of water sloshing your ankles.

We are awake in a new world, after the thing has come to pass. It is our quiet revolution, to show up to the page and insist our words still matter. That we have the right to make art in the face of fury. Our anger is not unfounded; our stories are not frivolous. They weave a slender thread of understanding and possibility, not only in reaction to tragedy, but in recognition of the stories still to tell and be told, the need for human connection that exists independent of our own grief. Stories are our valuable labor, reminding us we matter. The world matters. Our readers matter. They say, I too chop wood. I too carry water.

಄

Allison K Williams is the Social Media Editor of Brevity and the host of the Brevity Podcast. Her work has appeared in *Kenyon Review Online*, *Creative Nonfiction*, and the *New York Times*. She's told stories for NPR's *The Moth* and *Snap Judgment*, and CBC Canada's *Definitely Not the Opera* and *Love Me*. Find her at www.idowords.net and www.unkindeditor.com

ACKNOWLEDGEMENTS

Amy Roost

This work would not have been possible without the support of the members of Binders Full of Creative Non-Fiction and Binder Full of Memoirists, two all-female Facebook groups to which Alissa and I, as well as many of the contributors of this anthology, belong. Not only did these women encourage and support my putting together this collection, they also provided daily inspiration from their relentless publication of quality writing.

Jennifer Gates at Aevitas Creative was also instrumental in this book seeing the light of day. Thank you, Jen, for your patience, guidance, and good humor.

I am ever so grateful to Amy Westervelt for her help distributing and promoting the complementary Fury podcast on Creative Frequency Network. Thanks to Mary McNaughton-Cassil for her initial interest and involvement in this project and to Alissa for stepping in to co-edit when I was losing steam. Your calm kept me calm.

Thanks to my husband, Ain, for his constant, loving encouragement and constant, loving interruption, respectively. Nobody has had more faith in my pursuit of this project.

Alissa Hirshfeld

I would like to thank my colleagues Dr. John D. Gartner; Mary Hirsch, MFT; Dr. Jenny Holland-Brown; and Dr. Peter Dunlap, who provided encouragement to venture out of my professional comfort zone and validated the importance of mental health professionals adding our expertise to the political discourse. Thanks to my friends on Congregation Shomrei Torah's Social Action Committee, who have provided inspiration, friendship, hope, and laughs over the last two years of Trumpian trauma.

Thanks to Amy Roost for inviting me on board to be her co-editor for what has been a life-altering project. Her steadfast vision, trust, humility, and generosity have made this collaboration a pleasure.

I dedicate this book to my mother, who taught me to think critically and to question authority, and to my daughter, who represents the future generation of wise and powerful women.

ॐ

Amy and Alissa both thank all of our courageous contributors for their honesty in sharing their stories and raising their voices. A thank you doesn't suffice for our Pact Press editors Jaynie Royal, Pam Van Dyk, Elizabeth Lowenstein, and intern Caroline Taylor. This work could not have been done in time without their dedicated expertise and alacrity. We also thank Ruth Feiertag and interns Nora Shychuk and Caroline Kaptchen for early editing and insightful comments. All of these women made this book better and our writing stronger for having worked with them.

PERMISSIONS

We'd like to thank the following publications for allowing these essay to be reprinted:

Einstein, Sarah. "Going to Ground." *Full Grown People*, June 27, 2017.

Elenbogen, Dina. "The Fire in the Distance." *Literary Hub*, January 11, 2017.

Ford, Mary Catherine. "Woven: Catholic Bodies, Or Notes From the Kavanaugh Hearings." *Entropy Magazine*, December 19, 2018.

Grover, Lea. "How I'm Teaching My Jewish Daughters About Donald Trump." *Bustle*, January 23, 2017.

Handler, Jessica. "Smoke." RoarFeminist.org.

Ibrahim, Mahin. "How I Used My Hijab to Hide—and Why I Don't Anymore." *Narratively*, December 18, 2017.

Kirchner, Lisa L. "Love in the Age of Trump." *The Huffington Post*, April 6, 2018.

Lane, Cassandra. "Children Question The Bully's Right To The Presidential Seat." RaisingMothers.com.

Leone, Marianne. "Donald Trump the Bully." *Cognoscenti*, July 27, 2017.

Manfred, Erica. "A Red Diaper Baby Returns to Her Roots." *Senior Planet,* June 25, 2017.

Morgan, Katherine. "She Loves Me, She Loves Me Not." *Pathos*, Fall 2016.

Neville, Kerry. "Hope After Trump." *The Huffington Post*, November 20, 2016.

Seaton, Jaime. "Can We Reassure Our Kids Monsters Don't Exist When We Know They Do." *The Establishment*, November 14, 2016.

Sethi,Simran, "Lovein the Time of Trump (A Letter to My Beloved About His White Privilege." *Yes Magazine*, January 10, 2017.

Shapiro, Susan. "Does Family Trump Politics." *Salon*. https://www.salon.com/2016/12/09/my-personal-mich-igan-recount-the-official-vote-review-is-off-but-i-only-needed-answers-from-one-family-my-own

Sharpe, Michele. "The Parallels Between Social Media and PTSD in the Age of Trump." *The Establishment*, August 31, 2017.

Sinclair, Emily. "Panic Drapes the Look of the World: Literary Treatment for Anxiety in an Uncertain Age." Empty MirrorBooks. https://www.emptymirrorbooks.com/personal-essay/emily-sinclair-literary-treatment-anxiety-2

Zaman, Reema. "How Does One Heal the Reaping." *The Huffington Post*, November 9, 2016.